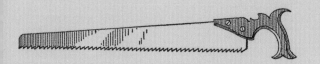

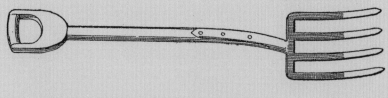

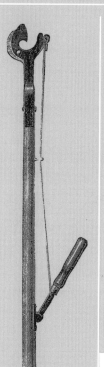
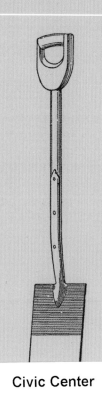

Civic Center

GROWING THE PAST, SAVING THE FUTURE

First published in the United States of America in 2016
by Ball Publishing
An imprint of Chicago Review Press Incorporated
814 North Franklin Street
Chicago, Illinois 60610

ISBN 978-1-61373-575-6

This book was conceived, designed, and produced by
Ivy Press
Publisher Susan Kelly
Creative Director Michael Whitehead
Editorial Director Tom Kitch
Art Director Wayne Blades
Commissioning Editor Sophie Collins
Editor Jamie Pumfrey
Designer Andrew Milne

Printed in China
5 4 3 2 1

HEIRLOOM PLANTS

A Complete Compendium of

VEGETABLES, FRUITS, HERBS & FLOWERS

THOMAS ETTY & LORRAINE HARRISON

 Ball Publishing

CONTENTS

A CAREFUL COLLATION OF ESCULENT, PHYSICAL, ECONOMIC, AND FLOWERING PLANTS

Mr. Etty begs (most respectfully) to bring to the notice of the Nobility, Gentry, Clergy, and Others, this his speciality seed catalog.

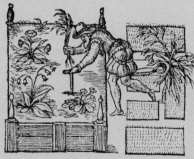

GROWING SAVING *THE* PAST *THE* FUTURE

I have yet to meet a gardening friend who does not relish the prospect of settling down on a winter's evening with a good seed catalog. Outside, a silvery moon may lighten the dark sky and the ground below may lie frozen and fallow, but the dreaming gardener, warm and snug indoors, has eyes only for the glorious seasons to come and a garden brimming with sunshine, flowers, fruit, and vegetables.

Lists are made and remade, order forms completed and dispatched, and then, at last, the seeds arrive. A rainy afternoon is filled happily arranging the little seed packets into chronological order: brussels sprouts to be sown indoors before the green beans, fava beans to go directly in the ground just before the corn, and so on. Next comes the anticipation of sowing: the cleaning of seed flats and small plant pots, the sorting of labels. And following on from sowing comes the thrill of germination, with the welcome sight of the first seedlings pushing up through the soil, so full of promise. The gardening year has begun.

So much of what gardeners do, and certainly what they dream of, is about the future. This may be as short term as sowing annual flower seeds that will germinate, grow, flower, and set seed in the brief time between spring and fall, or as far sighted as planting a sapling tree that will provide shelter and shade for generations unborn. Yet the past is important, too. All gardeners are aware of the cycle of life: how we all sit bracketed between the past and the future. Growing old varieties of seeds will keep us in touch with that past, and with all those who have gardened before us. Curled up in front of the fire turning the pages of our seed catalog or clicking through their virtual equivalents, we modern-day gardeners are lucky to have such a choice of old heirloom varieties of flowers, fruit, and vegetables. By growing these seeds and saving them for future generations, we in turn become part of their story.

However, beyond the simple pleasures of growing the same flowers as those sown by our great-great-grandparents, of tasting the best-ever dainty tomatoes, or of giving away little packets of favorite seeds to family and friends, lie some urgent and pragmatic reasons for keeping these old cultivars alive. Many sources estimate that as much as 90 percent of vegetable cultivars have been lost on both sides of the Atlantic since the beginning of the twentieth century—and that's just the vegetables, never mind the fruit or flowers. This has not only drastically reduced the choice of what gardeners can grow but has also raised alarming concerns among environmental and agricultural experts. They fear for the inevitable degradation of the gene pool and the effect this will have on the future feeding of an ever-expanding world population. The loss of biodiversity presents a threat to humans and wildlife alike.

This book, therefore, is intended to act as something of a clarion call to all home gardeners: do not allow any more rare and treasured varieties to be lost from cultivation. After all, it is we gardeners who are uniquely placed to rescue a bountiful cornucopia of flowers, fruit, vegetables, and herbs from the threat of extinction by the simple expedient of sowing some seeds. Trowel in hand, let our motto be "growing the past, saving the future."

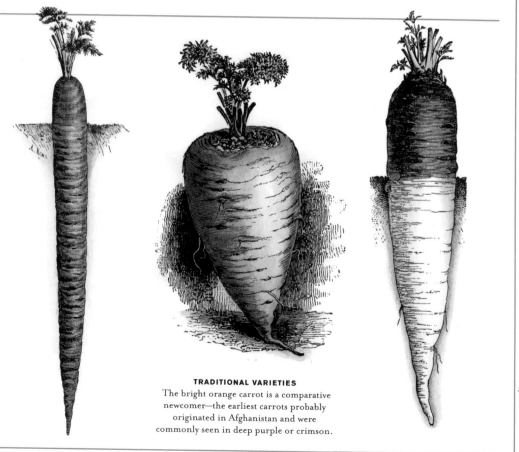

TRADITIONAL VARIETIES
The bright orange carrot is a comparative newcomer—the earliest carrots probably originated in Afghanistan and were commonly seen in deep purple or crimson.

KEEPING THE TRADITION ALIVE

Many of us would love to fill our borders and vegetable plots with the living ancestors of plants that have been passed down the generations of our family or friends. Today, unfortunately, few of us can lay claim to such a heritage. Yet with the invaluable help of seed savers, swappers, and sellers, we can still play our part in keeping these traditional plants alive.

Today's purveyors of heirloom seeds are many and varied. The sourcing, saving, and selling of these old varieties is a labor of love and something modern-day heritage seedsmen and women feel passionate about. An heirloom seed company may have a hundred employees or just one; some specialize only in tomatoes, say, while others offer well over a thousand different vegetable and herb cultivars. The common thread that connects all these companies is their eagerness to share and spread their expertise and enthusiasm for threatened and endangered varieties of plants.

The home gardener who wants to begin to grow old and interesting plants in their garden is well served by these dedicated champions of rare varieties. He or she can indulge in the tactile pleasure of perusing a printed catalog while simultaneously accessing everything that the world of the international seed catalog has to offer. It is perhaps somewhat ironic that the Internet, the great engine of globalization, is often the vehicle by which the enthusiastic vegetable grower can find a long-lost strain of cabbage ideally suited to raising in their own backyard. Heirloom seed merchants know firsthand the strengths and habits, the vagaries and the eccentricities, of all the seeds they sell, enabling them to offer in-depth advice about what may do best in their customers' gardens. Although you may not be lucky

Introduced into England in the sixteentth century, tomatoes were at first prized for their ornamental rather than culinary qualities.

enough to have inherited seeds of plants that have, over the years, become acclimatized to the particular conditions of your own plot, the chances are that a heritage seed supplier, whether local or virtual, may have just the thing.

Traditionally, all farmers and gardeners saved their own seeds; after all, without seeds there would be no farms or gardens. From the sixteenth century onward, seeds were traded like any other commodity, and scientific developments led to greater refinement in the selection and cultivation of plants. Alongside this trade, the seedsman's catalog emerged, and by the nineteenth century, they had often become things of great beauty. Fine line engravings and lovely botanical watercolors illustrated informative (and often idiosyncratic) text. It is such catalogs that have been the guiding spirit for seedsman Thomas Etty and writer Lorraine Harrison when producing this book. *Mr. Etty's Esteemed Seed Directories of Vegetables, Fruits, Herbs, and Flowers* form the basis of *Heirloom Plants*. Four sections entitled "Mr. Etty's Notes on the Cultivation of Esculent Vegetables" offer invaluable seasonal advice for the vegetable grower, based on tried and tested traditional advice and methods. Interspersed throughout are features on subjects such as horticultural tools and implements and the seed merchant activities of the Shakers, along with useful topics that include seed saving and companion planting. The "Garden Ghosts" features present potted biographies of influential figures from the past, while fascinating tales of endangered plants appear in the sections headed "Lost, Rare, or Simply Forgotten."

Among the many heirloom sunflower varieties are the aptly named "Mammoth" and "Skyscraper."

The seed company Thomas Etty Esq. is named after the founder's great-great-grandfather.

INTRODUCING MR. THOMAS ETTY ESQ., AN ENGLISH SEEDSMAN

The English heritage seedsman and bulb merchant Thomas Etty has striven to maintain the tradition of the seed catalog as a work of literary and visual art when presenting what he terms his "careful collation of esculent, physical, economic, and flowering plants." Founded in 1999 by Mr. Etty's alter ego Ray Warner, the seeds he sells mostly date from the seventeenth century to the end of World War II. Seeds are sourced from small-scale seed suppliers in the United Kingdom and Europe.

THOMAS JEFFERSON AT MONTICELLO

When America's third president, Thomas Jefferson (1743–1826), retired to his Virginian plantation at Monticello, he embarked on an extensive program of horticultural cultivation and experimentation. Between 1766 and 1824, Jefferson kept a garden diary, known as his *Garden Book*, and in the "Garden Kalendar" section he meticulously recorded details concerning the sowing, tending, and harvesting of the 330 varieties of vegetables and herbs and the 170 different types of fruits planted at Monticello. The garden has been painstakingly re-created, and today it grows many varieties of heirloom plants, the seeds of which are saved each year. In 1987, the Thomas Jefferson Center for Historic Plants was established, which "collects, preserves, and distributes historic plant varieties and strives to promote greater appreciation for the origins and evolution of garden plants."

A ripe strawberry.

WHAT IS A HERITAGE VARIETY?

Although there is lively debate among growers as to the time that an heirloom or a heritage plant must have been in cultivation before it can be classed as such, all agree that it must be open-pollinated.

Plums packed in straw.

LANDRACE

A landrace plant is a traditional variety that over time has become particularly suited to local growing conditions. Over many generations, growers of these plants will have selected the plants that perform the best, as well as discarded those that perform poorly; as a result, a landrace variety will be particularly suited to the environmental vagaries of a particular site and location—more so than a standard variety. Home gardeners can easily experiment with developing their own strains of landrace plants. Begin by planting a selection of varieties of (open-pollinated) seeds of a particular species, such as peas. Save the seeds of those plants that grow especially well and produce the best crops. Sow them the following year, and the resulting crop should be even better than the first time around, because you will have selected the seeds that are best-suited to the local conditions. In many cases, home-saved seeds from local seed swaps (see page 12) will also have a degree of adaptation to the locality, so it makes sense to compare your growing conditions with fellow swappers before choosing seeds.

A plant that is open-pollinated is one that is pollinated naturally, meaning that pollen from one plant is spread to another by insects or by the wind. Seeds saved from such a plant will breed true to type—they will be like the parent plant (exceptions to this rule are plants that tend to cross-pollinate with nearby neighbors; see page 92). Unfortunately, much of the seeds now available for sale are of F1 hybrid varieties. If you save the seeds from F1 hybrids, the resulting plants will be variable, meaning that they will not "come true." Indeed, they may not germinate at all, because many F1 hybrids produce sterile seeds. It almost goes without saying that all heirloom seeds are free from genetic modification.

In terms of age, some growers stipulate that a plant must be fifty years old before it can be called a heritage variety, while others say the magic number is one hundred. There is some logic to the position taken by those who claim that only pre-1945 varieties can be classed as heritage strains, because in the decades following World War II, industrial-scale agriculture became widespread and with it the greater use of F1 hybrid seeds. Some growers prefer to cite 1951 as the cutoff point for similar reasons. Certainly before the mid-twentieth century, most plants were bred to fulfill the needs of the home gardener. By contrast, F1 hybrids tend to be better suited to large-scale commercial production with certain considerations, such as uniformity, ability to withstand transportation, and the production of crops that ripen all at the same time, being prized most. Unfortunately, this is often at the expense of taste and variety.

WHY GROW HERITAGE PLANTS?

Most experts agree that the United States has lost 90 percent of its food plant biodiversity over the last hundred years, and the figure of 80 percent for Europe is only a little better. In the same period, it is thought that more than half of all food varieties have been lost worldwide. This matters because the need for food security can only increase as the world's population expands at an inexorable rate. Open-pollinated seeds are genetically variable and, thus, have adaptive traits—they can be developed in response to changing environmental conditions. To maintain a healthy collective gene pool, it is vital that as many different plant varieties as possible are grown. The sterling work done by gene banks across the globe is vital, but stored seeds are not a long-term substitute for growing crops in the field or garden, where they can interact with and adapt to the varying needs of site, climate, and human cultivation.

SEED SWAPS

The organized swapping of seeds between gardeners has grown in popularity and scale over the last decade. Gardeners come together and exchange their excess seeds in a variety of ways: online, by mail, or at local events. In the United States, the last Saturday in January every year has been designated National Seed Swap Day, and information on local swapping events can be found at www.seedswapday.com. Seedy Sunday is the UK's largest community seed swap and takes place in Brighton every year. As their website (www.seedysunday.org) explains, "The campaign to protect our seeds stretches around the world, but it has its roots in your garden. By growing open-pollinated varieties, then saving and swapping the seeds, the growers can keep alive 'outlawed' varieties, conserve biodiversity, and limit corporate control of the basis of life."

Traditional turnips.

Growing a limited number of hybrid varieties offers no protection against new diseases, pests, or drastic changes in climate conditions. One need only look at the Irish Potato Famine of 1845 to learn a sobering lesson from history (see page 103). Unless open-pollinated seed varieties are grown and their seeds saved, they will soon become extinct. The only choice then left for the home grower (and more worryingly for the farmer) will be the limited hybrid cultivars offered by major multinational seed companies. These corporations already control 50–75 percent of all seeds grown on the planet and have little interest in offering for sale an odd-shaped tomato or a cabbage that has been developed to thrive on a remote Scottish island or an island along New England's northern coast. The future of these varieties is literally in our hands; as gardeners we must all play our part in keeping as many plant varieties alive and thriving as possible. As the German plant-breeding trust Kultursaat has commented, "We consider breeding, seed saving, and varieties as a part of our cultural heritage and consider the maintenance of this heritage as a task of mankind."

A pod bursting with fava beans.

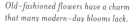

The future of these varieties is literally in our hands; as gardeners we must all play our part in keeping as many plant varieties alive and thriving as possible.

Old-fashioned flowers have a charm that many modern-day blooms lack.

HERITAGE PLANTS & THE LAW

The laws that apply to the providing of heirloom and heritage seed varieties are complex and seem to be under almost constant review. Variations exist in different trading areas; in North America laws can even differ from state to state. Commercial seed companies, no matter how small, need to be licensed. They, or the grower, are required to test seeds for quality and label them correctly, and each variety of seed must be registered. For seed-saving organizations and individual gardeners, the interpretation of these various laws can be confusing, and subtle differences exist between such nuanced terms as *exchanging*, *swapping*, and *giving*. Here, seedsman Ray Warner (a.k.a. Mr. Etty) gives his thoughts on this often vexed question.

SOME THOUGHTS ON REGULATION FROM A HERITAGE SEEDSMAN

A lesson can be learned from the European Union (EU), where there are rules and standards laid down as to which vegetable varieties may be sold. Some think these rules draconian, signaling the death of diversity in the range of vegetables that can be grown. Mr. Etty, however, while recognizing the value of diversity, takes a somewhat contrary view, seeing much merit in a system that makes sure that the seeds the gardener purchases will produce the vegetable crop that is hoped for.

Before the introduction of the rules, there was little or no guarantee of the purity and germination strength of any given variety, and many vegetable varieties were known by a gaggle of alternative names. Following the introduction of the rules, seeds are now tested to be sure that the resultant crop conforms to the variety "type," and that the number of seeds germinating comes within acceptable limits.

A few years ago, Mr. Etty questioned some of his seed suppliers in the United Kingdom and asked how many seed varieties they had deleted due to the EU rules. He was surprised to learn that none had been. It seems, therefore, that the prevailing reason why seed varieties are no longer offered is because people have stopped buying them. The farming of seeds is a business, not a leisure activity, and if unable to sell his or her crop, the grower will look to alternatives.

It should be noted that many of the vegetable varieties that seed guardian organizations and their supporters seek to save were never commercial crops, or they exist under another, EU-registered, name. Thus, they have never been "lost" at all.

I should not want you to think that Mr. Etty is opposed to these organizations; this is definitely not the case, because without landrace and noncommercial varieties, there would be a diminution of available breeding stock. However, he does think that the claims and counterclaims offered by all sides deserve to be weighed within the scales of both accuracy and fact. And that, sometimes, rules are there for a reason.

THE HERITAGE SEED LIBRARY

The UK's Heritage Seed Library (HSL) is run by the organization Garden Organic (formerly known as the Henry Doubleday Research Association). It is home to more than 800 varieties of primarily European open-pollinated types of vegetables and fruits. These include rare landrace (see page 11) strains, heirlooms that have been grown and handed down through generations of gardeners, as well as varieties that are no longer grown commercially. The seeds are raised at Garden Organic's Ryton Gardens in Warwickshire and also by their energetic band of volunteer growers, known as Seed Guardians. Each year members of HSL from the United Kingdom and EU receive a copy of the Heritage Seed Library Seed Catalogue; this lists about 150 varieties from which six packets can be selected for free. Find out more at www.gardenorganic.co.uk.

Heirloom pumpkins.

The Heritage Seed Library

garden organic
The national charity for organic growing

N   PEA
LATVIAN   LARGE
GREY   XMAS

Supported by members of
The Heritage Seed Library

NOT FOR SALE

Open Pollinated Seeds

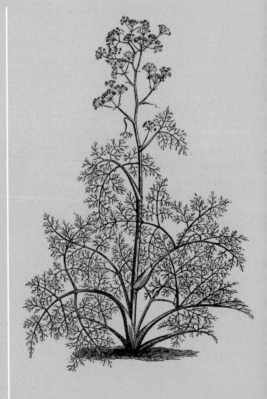

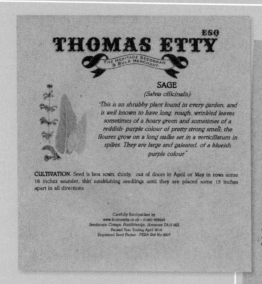

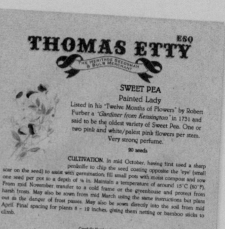

Angelica ... *Angelica archangelica*

Anise ... *Pimpinella anisum*

Aniseed ... *Pimpinella anisum*

Annual marjoram ... *Origanum majorana*

Antirrhinum ... *Antirrhinum majus*

Apple ... *Malus domestica*

Applemint ... *Mentha suaveolens*

Apricot ... *Prunus armeniaca*

Archangel ... *Angelica archangelica*

Arnica ... *Arnica montana*

Arugula ... *Eruca sativa*

Asparagus ... *Asparagus officinalis*

Asparagus pea ... *Lotus tetragonolobus*

Aubergine ... *Solanum melongena*

Aubretia ... *Aubrieta*

Auricula primrose ... *Primula auricula*

Bachelor's buttons ... *Centaurea cyanus*

Basil ... *Ocimum basilicum*

Batavia ... *Cichorium endivia*

Batavian endive ... *Cichorium endivia*

Bear's ears ... *Primula auricula*

Bee balm ... *Monarda didyma*

Beet ... *Beta vulgaris* ssp. *vulgaris*

Beetroot ... *Beta vulgaris* ssp. *vulgaris*

Belgian endive ... *Cichorium intybus*

Bell flower ... *Campanula medium*

Bell pepper ... *Capsicum annum*

Bergamot ... *Monarda didyma*

Black salsify ... *Scorzonera hispanica*

Blessed thistle ... *Cnicus benedictus*

Blue dandelion ... *Cichorium endivia*

Blue sailors ... *Centaurea cyanus*

Blueberry ... *Vaccinium corymbosum*

Bluebottle ... *Centaurea cyanus*

Borage ... *Borago officinalis*

Botany Bay spinach ... *Tetragonia tetragonoides*

Bouncingbet ... *Saponaria officinalis*

Break-your-spectacles ... *Centaurea cyanus*

Broad bean ... *Vicia faba*

Broccoli ... *Brassica oleracea* Italica group

Brussels sprout ... *Brassica oleracea* Gemmifera group

Bush bean ... *Phaseolus vulgaris*

Cabbage ... *Brassica oleracea* Capitata group

Calabrese ... *Brassica oleracea* Italica group

Candytuft ... *Iberis umbellata*

Canterbury bells ... *Campanula medium*

Caper ... *Capparis spinosa*

Caraway ... *Carum carvi*

Cardoon ... *Cynara cardunculus*

Card's thistle ... *Dipsacus sativus*

Carnation ... *Dianthus caryophyllus*

Carrot ... *Daucus carota*

Cathedral bells ... *Cobaea scandens*

Catmint ... *Nepeta cataria*

Catnep ... *Nepeta cataria*

Cauliflower ... *Brassica oleracea* Botrytis group

Celeriac ... *Apium graveolens* var. *rapaceum*

Celery ... *Apium graveolens*

Chard ... *Beta vulgaris* ssp. *cicla*

Cherry ... *Prunus avium, P. cerasus*

Chervil ... *Anthriscus cerefolium*

Chicory ... *Cichorium endivia*

Chilean beet ... *Beta vulgaris* ssp. *cicla*

Chili pepper ... *Capsicum annum, C. chinense*

Chive ... *Allium schoenoprasum*

Churchwort ... *Mentha pulegium*

Cilantro ... *Coriandrum sativum*

Columbine ... *Aquilegia*

Comfrey ... *Symphytum officinale*

Common thrift ... *Armeria maritima*

Cook's cabbage ... *Tetragonia tetragonoides*

Coriander ... *Coriandrum sativum*

Corn ... *Zea mays*

Corn on the cob ... *Zea mays*

Cornbottle ... *Centaurea cyanus*

Corncockle ... *Agrostemma githago*

Cornflower ... *Centaurea cyanus*

Courgette ... *Cucurbita pepo, C. moschata*

Cowslip ... *Primula veris*

Cuckoo flower ... *Cardamine pratensis*

Cucumber ... *Cucumis sativus*

Cumin ... *Cuminum cyminum*

Cup-and-saucer ... *Campanula medium*

Cup-and-saucer vine ... *Cobaea scandens*

Curly endive ... *Cichorium endivia*

COMMON & LATIN PLANT NAMES

Dead man's bells ... *Digitalis purpurea*

Devil-in-the-bush ... *Nigella damascena*

Dill ... *Anethum graveolens*

Douglas' meadowfoam ... *Limnanthes douglasii*

Dragon's mouth ... *Digitalis purpurea*

Dyer's broom ... *Genista tinctoria*

Dyer's chamomile ... *Anthemis tinctoria*

Dyer's greenweed ... *Genista tinctoria*

Dyer's rocket ... *Reseda luteola*

Dyer's weed ... *Reseda luteola*

Dyer's weld ... *Reseda luteola*

Earth chestnut ... *Conopodium majus*

Earth nut ... *Conopodium majus*

Echinacea ... *Echinacea pallida*

Eggplant ... *Solanum melongena*

Elecampane inula ... *Inula helenium*

English violet ... *Viola odorata*

Escarole ... *Cichorium endivia*

Evening primrose ... *Oenothera*

Fairy thimbles ... *Digitalis purpurea*

Fava bean ... *Vicia faba*

Fennel ... *Foeniculum vulgare*

Feverfew ... *Tanacetum parthenium*

Field bean ... *Phaseolus vulgaris*

Fig ... *Ficus carica*

Finocchio ... *Foeniculum vulgare* var. *dulce*

Flageolet bean ... *Phaseolus vulgaris*

Florence fennel ... *Foeniculum vulgare*

Fodder beet ... *Beta vulgaris* ssp. *cicla*

Forget-me-not ... *Mysotis arvensis*

Fox finger ... *Digitalis purpurea*

Foxglove ... *Digitalis purpurea*

French bean ... *Phaseolus vulgaris*

French endive ... *Cichorium endivia*

French marigold ... *Tagetes patula*

Frisee endive ... *Cichorium endivia*

Fuller's teasel ... *Dipsacus sativus*

Garden beet ... *Beta vulgaris* ssp. *vulgaris*

Gherkin ... *Cucumis sativus*

Gilliflower ... *Matthiola incana*

Globe artichoke ... *Cynara cardunculus* Scolymus group

Globe candytuft ... *Iberis umbellata*

Golden beet ... *Beta vulgaris* ssp. *vulgaris*

Golden chamomile ... *Anthemis tinctoria*

Golden melissa ... *Monarda didyma*

Grandpa's specs ... *Lunaria annua*

Green bean ... *Phaseolus vulgaris*

Grape ... *Vitus labrusca, V. vinfera*

Great cowslip ... *Primula elatoir*

Hamburg parsley ... *Petroselinum crispum* var. *tuberosum*

Haricot bean ... *Phaseolus vulgaris*

Healbite ... *Lobularia maritima*

Hollyhock ... *Alcea rosea*

Holy thistle ... *Cnicus benedictus*

Honesty ... *Lunaria annua*

Horehound ... *Marrubium vulgare*

Hyssop ... *Hyssopus officinalis*

Indian nettle ... *Monarda didyma*

Indian teasel ... *Dipsacus sativus*

Indian thistle ... *Dipsacus sativus*

Jacob's ladder ... *Polemonium caeruleum*

Kale ... *Brassica oleracea* Acephala group

Kidney bean ... *Phaseolus vulgaris*

Knob celery ... *Apium graveolens* var. *rapaceum*

Kohlrabi ... *Brassica oleracea* Gongylodes group

Lady's bedstraw ... *Galium verum*

Lady's mantle ... *Alchemilla mollis*

Lady's smock ... *Cardamine pratensis*

Larkspur ... *Consolida ajacis*

Lavender ... *Lavandula angustifolia*

Lawn chamomile ... *Chamaemelum nobile*

Leaf beet ... *Beta vulgaris* ssp. *cicla*

Leek ... *Allium porrum*

Lemon balm ... *Melissa officinalis*

Lettuce ... *Lactuca sativa*

Licorice ... *Glycyrrhiza glabra*

Lovage ... *Levisticum officinale*

Love apple ... *Phaseolus vulgaris*

Love-in-a-mist ... *Nigella damascena*

Lupine ... *Lupinus*

Madwort ... *Lobularia maritima*

Maize ... *Zea mays*

Mangel ... *Beta vulgaris* ssp. *cicla*

Mangelwurtzel ... *Beta vulgaris* var. *rapa*

Mangold ... *Beta vulgaris* var. *rapa*

March violet ... *Viola odorata*

Marrow ... *Cucurbita pepo, C. moschata*

Marshmallow ... *Althea officinalis*

Masterwort ... *Peucedanum ostruthium*

Meadow cranesbill ... *Geranium pratense*

Meadow geranium ... *Geranium pratense*

Meadowfoam ... *Limnanthes douglasii*

Meadowsweet ... *Filipendula ulmaria*

Medlar ... *Mespilus germanica*

Melon ... *Cucumis melo*

Mexican ivy ... *Cobaea scandens*

Mexican marigold ... *Tagetes lucida*

Mexican tarragon ... *Tagetes lucida*

Mint ... *Mentha*

Monastery bells ... *Cobaea scandens*

Money flower ... *Lunaria annua*

Moon flower ... *Lunaria annua*

Morning glory ... *Ipomea purpurea*

Mountain arnica ... *Arnica montana*

Multiflora bean ... *Phaseolus vulgaris*

Myrrh ... *Myrrhis odorata*

Nasturtium ... *Tropaeolum majus*

Navy bean ... *Phaseolus vulgaris*

Nectarine ... *Prunus persica* var. *nectarina*

Neep ... *Brassica napus* Naprobrassica group

New Zealand spinach ... *Tetragonia tetragonoides*

Onion ... *Allium cepa*

Oregano ... *Origanum vulgare*

Oregon bean ... *Phaseolus vulgaris*

Oxlip ... *Primula elatior*

Parsley ... *Petroselinum crispum*

Parsley root ... *Petroselinum crispum* var. *tuberosum*

Parsnip ... *Pastinaca sativa*

Pea ... *Pisum sativum*

Peach ... *Prunus persica*

Pear ... *Pyrus communis*

Pennyroyal ... *Mentha pulegium*

Pepper ... *Capsicum annum*

Peppermint ... *Mentha × piperita*

Perennial marjoram ... *Origanum vulgare*

Pignut ... *Conopodium majus*

Pink ... *Dianthus caryophyllus*

Plum ... *Prunus domestica, P. saliciana*

Poached egg plant ... *Limnanthes douglasii*

Pole bean ... *Phaseolus vulgaris*

Poppy ... *Papaver nudicaule, P. rhoeas, P. somniferum*

Pot marigold ... *Calendula officinalis*

Pot marjoram ... *Origanum vulgare*

Potato ... *Solanum tuberosum*

Pumpkin ... *Cucurbita argyrosperma, C. maxima, C. moschata, C. pepo*

Quince ... *Cydonia oblonga*

Radish ... *Raphanus sativus*

Ragged robin ... *Centaurea cyanus*

Ragged sailor ... *Centaurea cyanus*

Ramsons ... *Allium ursinum*

Red beet ... *Beta vulgaris* ssp. *vulgaris*

Rhubarb ... *Rheum × hybridum*

Rock cress ... *Aubrieta*

Rocket ... *Eruca sativa*

Roman chamomile ... *Chamaemelum nobile*

Roquette ... *Eruca sativa*

Rosemary ... *Rosmarinus officinalis*

Round-leaved mint ... *Mentha suaveolens*

Rucola ... *Eruca sativa*

Ruddles ... *Calendula officinalis*

COMMON & LATIN PLANT NAMES

Rue … *Ruta graveolens*

Rugola … *Eruca sativa*

Runner bean … *Phaseolus vulgaris*

Rutabaga … *Brassica napus* Naprobrassica group

Sage … *Salvia officinalis*

Salsify … *Tragopogon porrifolius*

Scotch marigold … *Calendula officinalis*

Sea cabbage … *Crambe maritima*

Sea holly … *Eryngium maritimun*

Sea kale … *Crambe maritima*

Sea spinach … *Tetragonia tetragonoides*

Seakale beet … *Beta vulgaris* ssp. *cicla*

Seapink … *Armeria maritima*

Seaside eryngo … *Eryngium maritimun*

Scarlet runner bean … *Phaseolus vulgaris*

Shallot … *Allium cepa* Aggregatum group

Silver beet … *Beta vulgaris* ssp. *cicla*

Silver dollar … *Lunaria annua*

Snapdragon … *Antirrhinum majus*

Soapwort … *Saponaria officinalis*

Spinach … *Spinacia oleracea*

Spinach beet … *Beta vulgaris* ssp. *cicla*

Spinks … *Cardamine pratensis*

St. Benedict's thistle … *Cnicus benedictus*

St. Johnswort … *Hypericum perforatum*

St. Peter Keys … *Primula veris*

Stock … *Matthiola incana*

Strawberry … *Fragaria moschata, F. vesca, F. virginiana*

String bean … *Phaseolus vulgaris*

Succory … *Cichorium endivia*

Summer savory … *Satureja hortensis*

Sunflower … *Helianthus annuus*

Swede … *Brassica napus* Naprobrassica group

Swedish turnip … *Brassica napus* Naprobrassica group

Sweet Alice … *Lobularia maritima*

Sweet Alison … *Lobularia maritima*

Sweet alyssum … *Lobularia maritima*

Sweet cicely … *Myrrhis odorata*

Sweet corn … *Zea mays*

Sweet marigold … *Tagetes lucida*

Sweet marjoram … *Origanum majorana*

Sweet pansy … *Viola odorata*

Sweet pea … *Lathyrus odoratus*

Sweet pepper … *Capsicum annum*

Sweet violet … *Viola odorata*

Sweet William … *Dianthus barbatus*

Swiss chard … *Beta vulgaris* ssp. *cicla*

Table beet … *Beta vulgaris* ssp. *vulgaris*

Tansy … *Tanacetum vulgare*

Thrift … *Armeria maritima*

Thyme … *Thymus vulgaris*

Tobacco plant … *Nicotiana alata, N. sylvestris*

Tomato … *Solanum lycopersicum*

Turnip … *Brassica rapa* Rapifera group

Turnip beet … *Beta vulgaris* ssp. *vulgaris*

Turnip greens … *Brassica rapa* Rapifera group

Turnip-rooted cabbage … *Brassica napus* Naprobrassica group

Turnip-rooted celery … *Apium graveolens* var. *rapaceum*

Turnip tops … *Brassica rapa* Rapifera group

Valerian … *Valeriana officinalis*

Vegetable fennel … *Foeniculum vulgare*

Watermelon … *Citrullus lanatus*

Weld … *Reseda luteola*

White mallow … *Althaea officinalis*

White turnip … *Brassica rapa* Rapifera group

Winter savory … *Satureja montana*

Witches' gloves … *Digitalis purpurea*

Witloof … *Cichorium intybus*

Yellow turnip … *Brassica napus* Naprobrassica group

Zucchini … *Cucurbita pepo, C. moschata*

THE VEGETABLE DIRECTORY

THE VEGETABLE DIRECTORY

ALLIUM

ONION & SHALLOT

BOTH ONIONS AND SHALLOTS are hardy biennials, native to Central and West Asia. The method of cultivation of onions and shallots is well described in all good gardening books. In general, onions prefer an open situation on rich loam soil, but they will survive on any well-cultivated soil. Plenty of farmyard manure should be incorporated, because onions and shallots are heavy feeders.

A. cepa
'AILSA CRAIG'

CULTIVATED BY 1887

Raised by Mr. D. Murray, Head Gardener to the Marquis of Ailsa at Culzean Castle, near Maybole, Scotland, it was cataloged by Sutton & Sons in 1895. The skin is a pale straw color and the flesh white with a mild taste. Bulbs are irregular in form, some being globe shaped, others inclined to a flat oval.

A. cepa
'BEDFORDSHIRE CHAMPION'
or 'Sutton's Globe'

CULTIVATED BY 1869

Introduced by Sutton & Sons of Reading, England, it should probably be classified as a hybrid of the American variety Danvers Yellow Globe. A solid and large globe-shape onion that stores well over winter.

A. cepa Aggregatum group
'CUISSE DE POULET DU POITOU'

CULTIVATION DATE UNKNOWN

Also known as a banana shallot because of its large, long bulb with a coppered skin and firm pink flesh. The flavor is delicate, fine, and very mild. An excellent type for pickling and making shallot chutney. Long since cultivated in kitchen gardens of the Lencloître region of western France, where it is found for sale in local markets.

A. cepa
'GIANT ZITTAU'

CULTIVATED BY 1876

A handsome late-keeping variety, thoroughly recommended to those who require a sound keeping type. Large, semi-globular bulbs with a strong flavor and an attractive brown skin. High yielding. Also good for pickling.

A wooden mold scuttle.

A. cepa
'JAUNE PAILLE DES VERTUS'
or 'Brown Spanish'

CULTIVATED BY 1793

Much of the winter supply of onions in Europe was dependent on this French variety for well over two centuries. Also known as Brown Spanish by French seed house Vilmorin, in 1885, they said, "The winter supply of Paris and of a great part of Europe consists chiefly of this variety, which may be often seen hanging up in dwelling houses in long hanks formed by interlacing and braiding the withered leaves together." An excellent keeper with flavorful flesh.

A. cepa
'PARIS SILVERSKIN'

CULTIVATED BY 1786

This is the type if you require crisp cocktail onions, but they are equally satisfying used whole in soups or casseroles. The thin-neck, perfectly globular bulbs have sweet, pure white flesh covered with a silvery skin. Pulled early, they also make excellent scallions.

THE ONION CURE
Any gardener who is stung by a bee or wasp when working in the vegetable plot should try the old remedy of rubbing a raw onion on the affected part. It is said to bring great relief.

A. fistulosum
JAPANESE BUNCHING ONION
or Hollow Leek, Perennial Welsh Onion

CULTIVATION DATE UNKNOWN

"When the leaves wither, the roots very much resemble shallots. Generally planted very thick in beds, in a convenient corner of the garden; one bulb, in a season, will increase and form a cluster from 6–10 or more, as the soil and situation may suit their growth." *Journal of the Royal Horticultural Society*, Mr. Thomas Milne, 1819. In mild climates, gardeners may find that the foliage remains present throughout winter, extending its use as a kitchen herb, prepared in much the same way as chives. The whole plant is edible, including the pretty white flowers.

A. ursinum
RAMSONS
or Wild Garlic

CULTIVATION DATE UNKNOWN

The sixteenth-century botanist John Gerard noted, "The leaves may be stamped and eaten of divers, with fish for a sauce, even as we do eat green sauce made with sorrel. The same leaves may be eaten in April and May with butter, of such as are of a strong constitution, and laboring men." A seasonal favorite among woodland walkers in the British Isles, where the plant grows wild.

A. cepa
'ROSSA DI FIRENZE'
or 'Long Red Florence,'
'Italian Torpedo'

CULTIVATED BY THE
NINETEENTH CENTURY

A reliable, traditional torpedo-shaped red onion with attractive deep purple-red bulbs. The flavor is mild and sweet, making them ideal for salads or roasting, but be aware that its storage life is not as long as other onions. The Royal Horticultural Society of London has awarded this onion its prestigious Award of Garden Merit.

A. cepa
'WHITE LISBON'

CULTIVATED BY 1787

In 1891 Mr. Charles Strachen wrote, "This has been called the early Lisbon and the White Lisbon. It varies in shape, but is, for the most part, globular, it attains to a large size, and is of a bright color. Its skin being smooth and thin. It grows about two-thirds below the surface of the ground, and has very strong fibers, with a coarse thick neck, and large, leaves which preserve their verdure late." Very popular today as a scallion, the pungency of the flavor intensifies as the bulbs swell.

A. cepa
'YELLOW SWEET SPANISH'

CULTIVATED BY 1866

Large and round, dark yellow or golden bulbs often weighing 1 pound (450g) or more with a sweet and mild flavor. Very successful if sown early in the season, when they will outperform set onions. Popular with growers because they seem to put on weight well with very little attention from the gardener. Good storers with some tolerance to thrips and mildew.

LOST, RARE, OR SIMPLY FORGOTTEN?

An active army of backyard gardeners are helping to keep the rare l'itou multiplier onion (*A. cepa* var. *aggregatum*) alive and well for future gourmets. Named after l'itou, the Elder Brother deity of the Tohono O'odham people, and harvested on l'itou Mountain (Baboquivari Mountain) in Arizona, these onions probably first arrived in North America in the seventeenth century, brought from Spain by Jesuit priests. Once planted, they multiply fast and can be used as scallions or small shallots. The leaves are harvested like chives, although their taste is stronger.

The large White Lisbon onion.

ALLIUM

LEEK

THE LEEK IS KNOWN TO HAVE BEEN a cultivated vegetable in the British Isles since the time of the Saxons. In fact, their kitchen gardens were often referred to as "leac tuns," in the same way that today we might refer to a "cabbage patch." Conventional wisdom suggests that this fine vegetable originated in the East Mediterranean region, or perhaps the Near East, although the modern garden leek does not appear to have a wild counterpart.

A fine specimen leek with fanlike leaves and a thick stem.

A. porrum
'BLEU DE SOLAISE'

CULTIVATED BY 1942

A very cold-hardy variety with blue-green leaves that turn violet in cold weather. Requires a long growing season. Considered something of a rare delicacy by American gourmets.

A. porrum
'LYON'

CULTIVATED BY 1883

Introduced by Messrs. Stuart & Mein, seedsmen and nurserymen of Kelso, Scotland. Their ad in *The Gardeners' Chronicle*, January 1883, states, "The Lyon Leek is unquestionably the finest in existence, being of enormous size, splendid mild flavor, and perfectly hardy. The blanched part is firm, crisp, and white as snow, 14–20 inches (35.5–51cm) in length, and 3–4 inches (7.5–10cm) in diameter. Weight of Leek 2–5 pounds (0.9–2.25kg). It is splendid for exhibition as well as general use." Two years later Mr. G.T. Myles wrote,

"A few years ago, a gentleman in Scotland was good enough to send me a few seeds of this splendid variety of leek, since that time I have grown a breadth of it each year, and I may safely venture to say, that considering its size and quality, and its merit of not running to seed so readily as other kinds which are more commonly cultivated, that it is the best kind of Leek with which I am acquainted, either for general use or for the exhibition table."

A. porrum

'MONSTRUEUX DE CARENTAN'

or 'Giant Carentan'

CULTIVATED BY 1874

Vilmorin in *The Vegetable Gardener*, 1885, has this as a selection of the Large Rouen Leek, "of which it is probably only an improved form, but a very distinct one, on account of its greater size, and the very dark color of its leaves."

A. porrum

'MUSSELBURGH'

or 'American Flag,' 'Scotch Flag'

CULTIVATED BY 1824

Raised by Mr. James Hardcastle, seedsman, of Fisher Row, Mussleburgh, Scotland. "A reliable old favorite that tastes excellent, produces white stems, and is the mainstay of vegetable production through the lean winter period. A heavy cropper." *An Encyclopedia of Gardening*, JC Loudon, 1882.

A. porrum

'PRIZETAKER'

or 'Lyon 2 Prizetaker'

CULTIVATED BY 1885

Recognized as a superior selection of the Lyon leek, it appeared in catalogs during the 1890s and was described thus: "Stems have been grown 1 foot (30cm) long and 5 inches (13cm) in diameter. They are solid, pure white, with a mild agreeable flavor."

TO BLANCH A LEEK
Place a stiff brown-paper sleeve about 6 inches (15cm) long over the plant soon after setting out. Support with canes at each side. Unlike celery, leeks are blanched in stages as they grow and not when completely mature.

BEST IN SHOW

In England, the growing of leeks for competitive showing dates back to the 1880s, and none takes the challenge more seriously than the National Pot Leek Society (NPLS) of County Durham. First prize secures for the winner not only the championship trophy and NPLS Silver Medal but also the princely sum of £500. Each leek grower has his or her "secrets" for achieving maximum size (copious amounts of farmyard manure is usually a prerequisite), while preparations on the day of the show may include careful washing of the leeks in milk. The leek is measured in cubic inches, and a complicated table is used to calculate the volume from the length and circumference.

APIUM

CELERY

WILD CELERY IS CERTAINLY a native British plant, and as such has probably been grown since early times. The variety sold as leaf celery is actually the oldest domesticated type, known as smallage or krul. Cultivated celery probably originated in Italy sometime in the sixteenth or seventeenth century. Precisely when it arrived in North America is unknown, but at least four varieties were commercially listed by 1806.

A. graveolens var. *dulce*
'AMSTERDAM'
or 'Soup Celery'

CULTIVATED BY 1793

This Dutch variety has been little improved by cultivation and is probably a reversion toward the wild state with its darker green fronds. Grown mainly for its leaves, which are cut like parsley and used for soups and seasoning, hence the alternative name Soup Celery.

A. graveolens var. *dulce*
'GIANT RED'
or 'Brydon's Prize Red'

CULTIVATED BY 1835

More flavorful than green celery, a description from January 1876 finds it a "Plant of strong and vigorous growth, attaining an average height of 3 feet (1m); leaflets broad green; heads compact, average girth 12 inches (30cm); the outer leaf stalks are moderately broad, slightly shaded with red;

hearts very solid; the stalks broad, thick and fleshy blanching for about 12 inches (30cm); a very excellent sort, stands the winter well. This is the largest variety." From "Trials of Celeries at Chiswick" in *The Garden*, January 1876. Highly desirable.

A. graveolens var. *dulce*
'GOLDEN SELF-BLANCHING'

CULTIVATED BY 1886

"This grand variety has justly become very popular. The stems are broader and heavier than those of the White Plume, but it is nearly as early. Produces large small bunches blanching to a deep golden yellow." *The Vegetable Garden*, Vilmorin-

Golden Self-Blanching celery, an old Victorian favorite.

Andrieux, 1885. It has stood the test of time but requires heavy watering and feeding, as well as a long season, for the best results.

APIUM

CELERIAC

or CELERY ROOT, KNOB CELERY, TURNIP-ROOTED CELERY

THAT CELERIAC WAS GROWN in the eighteenth century can be proved through the meticulous notes of our dear friend the Reverend Gilbert White: "Made a second Hot-bed: sowed within the frame, common Cucumbers, Horn Do, Squashes, Melons, Balsams, French Marygolds, Purslain: without the frame; common Celeri, Celeriac, or turnip-rooted Celeri, Nasturtium, Sun-Flowers and Purslain." *Garden Kalendar*, Reverend Gilbert White, 1751. Celeriac has long been favored by home growers for its flavor and ease of cultivation. It is a tough and hardy root vegetable that requires a long growing season. Water liberally and mulch to help retain moisture.

A. graveolens var. *rapaceum*

'GIANT PRAGUE'

CULTIVATED BY 1871

Globular roots with a slightly flattened base, topped by medium green foliage. The variety stores well and is packed full of good flavor. Harvest from early fall onward. With a creamy texture similar to potato, it is delicious if mashed together with them. It can also be used in soups, imparting a distinctive celery-like flavor.

HISTORICAL NOTE

Any gardener who begins to research the origins and history of old varieties of edible plants will very soon discover the wonderful tome *The Vegetable Garden* by Messieurs Vilmorin-Andrieux. This highly illustrated and endlessly entertaining publication dates back to the mid-nineteenth century and is a mine of information and advice, much of which is still relevant today.

Its origins began in 1734 with the founding of a business that later became the Vilmorin-Andrieux Seed Company, which remained a family concern until 1972. The first English edition of *The Vegetable Garden* was published in 1885 and contains a preface by the influential garden writer William Robinson, who enthused how the work "classified, described, and illustrated what are the most important of all plants to the human race."

ASPARAGUS

ASPARAGUS

A HARDY, DECIDUOUS PERENNIAL also known as sparrow grass, wild asparagus grows in waste places and on sand dunes. Known to the ancient Greeks, it has always been considered a luxury vegetable, becoming cultivated widely in the nineteenth century. "It is well known how much the Asparagus is improved in time since Gerard's time, and it might still be further improved if our gardeners were to import roots of this plant from the borders of the Euphrates." *History of Cultivated Vegetables*, Henry Phillips, 1822.

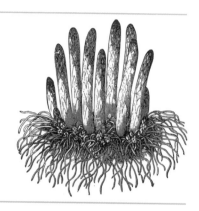

A. officinalis
'ARGENTEUIL EARLY'
or 'Precoce d'Argenteuil'

CULTIVATED BY 1853

An early French variety, long since identified with the Argenteuil commune, an important asparagus region close to Paris. One of three strains (early, mid, and late), it is highly esteemed for its large, sweet-tasting spears. Thick stems with purple lips.

A. officinalis
'CONNOVER'S COLOSSAL'

CULTIVATED BY 1867

Raised by Mr. Abraham van Siclen of Long Island, New York, and introduced into cultivation by a Mr. Connover. Claims of its size do not appear to have been exaggerated.

In "Agricultural Lectures" of the New York State Agricultural Society, 1866–67, it was noted, "From S. B. Connover, Esq, of West Washington, NY, a box containing 200 plants of his colossal asparagus. This is a new variety of asparagus, remarkable for the size of its shoots." While Mr. J. W. May wrote to *The Gardeners' Chronicle* in May 1873, "At the time of sowing I must say that I felt rather dubious as to the colossal dimensions of this new Asparagus as mentioned in seed catalogs and advertisements. I have now pleasure in saying that in point of size it is a colossal variety."

A. officinalis
'MARY WASHINGTON'

CULTIVATED BY 1919

One of the most popular varieties, as this claim from 1929 attests: "Marvelously productive. The most vigorous of all existing kinds. Yields a crop two years ahead of all other varieties; rust resistent; largest, sweetest, most tender, and succulent shoots. We strongly recommend this variety for planting in the home garden or on the farm." *Steele Briggs Seed Company Catalogue*, 1929.

FORCING ASPARAGUS
These view and section pictures show the French method of forcing asparagus in frames, as practiced in the market gardens of Paris in the nineteenth and early twentieth centuries.

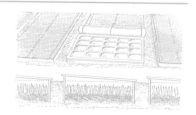

BETA

SWISS CHARD

or CHARD, CHILEAN BEET, LEAF BEET, SEAKALE BEET, SILVER BEET, SPINACH BEET

"Leaves used like Spinach, the very broad leaf stems may be steamed or boiled and used as an alternative to Seakale." *The Gardener's Dictionary*, Philip Miller, 1741. A close sister to beet, without the thick root, but instead with a thick crop of juicy leaves that bear comparison to spinach. Much easier to grow than spinach, because it does not possess the former's tendency to run to seed at the slightest hint of drought. Gardeners will see it listed under a variety of names. How its name has become linked to the Swiss or Chileans is a mystery, but kitchen growers with a good tongue and ready eye will pick up on its earthy and colorful links to the beet. Sown in spring, the crop will yield well through its first year, and may even stand through winter before it goes to seed the following year. It tolerates frequent harvesting.

B. vulgaris ssp. *cicla*
'BRIGHT LIGHTS'
or 'Five Colored,' 'Rainbow'

CULTIVATION DATE UNKNOWN

Use both the leaves and stems of this variety to give a colorful addition to your vegetable choices. Includes white, yellow, orange, pink, and red stem varieties, and green or red leaves. Although the exact date of cultivation is unsure, Mr. John Claudius Loudon in 1849 wrote of this variety, "Swiss chard, varieties with white, yellow, and red midribs."

B. vulgaris ssp. *cicla*
'FORDHOOK GIANT'

CULTIVATED BY 1727

With superb bolt resistance, vigorous growth, and good tolerance to low temperatures, which result in a very long period of harvest, Fordhook Giant may well be the King of Swiss Chard, reigning supreme over what is already regarded as a near-perfect vegetable. What it lacks in color it makes up for in size—its dark green leaves with white ribs stand nearly 2-feet (60cm) tall.

B. vulgaris ssp. *cicla*
'PERPETUAL SPINACH'

CULTIVATED BY 1790

An excellent and long-standing alternative to spinach, a very old variety that lives up to its name. That it is still in our gardens points adequately to its excellence. Noted as being very valuable on dry soil (where true spinach mostly runs to seed), Perpetual Spinach will produce a very heavy crop, and it is said that it will produce more greens per square foot than any other vegetable.

B. vulgaris ssp. *cicla*
'RHUBARB CHARD'
or 'Ruby'

CULTIVATED BY 1856

Grown for its bright color, as well as its culinary uses, this is perhaps the "Chilean beef" of Vilmorin-Andrieux. To many growers, it is less romantically known as red chard, but it is certainly pretty in the vegetable garden, especially over winter with frost crested over its puckered leaves. Unfortunately, the color is lost during cooking, but used raw in salads, this is a leaf bestowed with much taste and color.

Wrought-iron wheelbarrow.

B. vulgaris ssp. *cicla*
WILD SEA BEET

CULTIVATION DATE UNKNOWN

This wild relative of both the leaf and root beets is a short-term perennial that can be allowed to self-seed and establish itself in the vegetable bed, where it will give a nearly continuous supply of dark green leaves that are somewhat fleshier than commercial types. Pull up and remove the previous year's plants after they have been allowed to set seed. It does not form an edible root, but the crop is early and very hardy.

GARDEN GHOSTS

At first glance, the rustic writings of an eighteenth-century English curate might appear to have limited interest for a present-day gardener. However, many of the horticultural experiments made and meticulously noted by Gilbert White (1720–93) in his Hampshire village garden have continued to make fascinating reading for later generations of fruit and vegetable growers. White recorded his successes and failures in his *Garden Kalendar,* including his growing of potatoes, which was an innovative practice at the time. Of course, today he is best remembered for his *Natural History and Antiquities of Selborne,* which has never been out of print since it was first published in 1789.

BETA

FODDER BEET

or MANGEL, MANGELWURTZEL, MANGOLD, TURNIP BEET

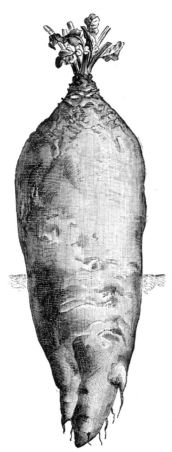

The lumpy appearance of the fodder beet may account for its noted lack of popularity with cooks.

A STURDY ROOT VEGETABLE, the fodder beet was originally used as fodder feed for animals. Going by many names, it is believed to originate from the Lower Rhineland in Germany in the sixteenth century, where it is known as the mangelwurtzel, which literally means "root beet," and it has also come to be known as the mangold. In his *An Account of the Species and Varieties of Beets*, 1818, William Morgan wrote, "The well known, kind, called here mangel wurzul, or root of scarcity . . . was introduced into this country [England] from Germany in 1786." Planted to provide cheap food, and eaten by people as well as cattle, it was probably never destined to be among the most popular of vegetables, although the Pennsylvania Dutch variety Deacon's Dan is enjoying a small revival with American home growers. Harvest the roots before the first frost or they will spoil.

B. vulgaris ssp. *vulgaris*
'MAMMOTH RED'

CULTIVATED BY 1869

A large red fodder beet that can quickly bulk up to a tremendous size: 20 pounds (9kg) and more. Perhaps best used small for the kitchen, either baked, stewed, or pickled, but if you keep livestock, this is a high-yielding crop that will provide much feed for the winter. The flesh inside is white, remaining sweet and tender even when large.

B. vulgaris ssp. *vulgaris*
'YELLOW ECKENDORF'

CULTIVATED BY 1893

A variety much prized by wine makers, because of its high sugar content, and those who keep horses, ponies, and goats. The Henry Fields catalog of 1927 describes these as, "Giant, smooth, long roots of cylindrical shape, weighing up to 20 pounds (9kg) each and growing two-thirds above ground. Solid white flesh with high food value." The flavor is described as very favorable, and the spinachlike leaves also have merit on the table.

BETA

BEET

or BEETROOT, GARDEN BEET, GOLDEN BEET, RED BEET, TABLE BEET

THE DEEP RED DYE OF THIS VEGETABLE is legendary, although white and yellow forms also exist. "It appears to be a native of Sicily, as the Greeks according to Pliny, had as well as the black, a white beet, which they also called Sicilian Beet. The beet was first cultivated in this country [England] in the year 1548, a period when many valuable plants were introduced to gratify a luxurious Monarch." *History of Cultivated Vegetables*, Henry Phillips, 1822. Manure the ground well before sowing in spring, and thin out the crop when the roots swell to the size of a billiard ball. Those remaining can be left to swell to the size of a baseball before pulling.

B. vulgaris ssp. *vulgaris*
'ALBINA VEREDUNA'
or 'Snow White'

CULTIVATION DATE UNKNOWN

An old Dutch variety with ice-white flesh and a very sweet and delicate yet distinctive beet flavor. The curled and wavy leaves are also a great delicacy and rich in vitamins. Perfect for tidy cooks who want to avoid staining their surfaces.

B. vulargis ssp. *vulgaris*
'BULL'S BLOOD'

CULTIVATED BY 1840

North American variety with outstanding dark red leaves and roots. Vilmorin-Andrieux mentions a *rouge a feuillage* ornamental like this in 1885, saying, "This variety is distinguished by the dark red color of its leaves which are broadly crimped and have an almost glazy luster." Indeed, the foliage is so striking it could also be grown in the flower border. The baby leaves are a most delightful salad ingredient.

B. vulgaris ssp. *vulgaris*
'BURPEE'S GOLDEN'

CULTIVATED BY 1940

Golden yellow throughout, and best harvested when small, this beet has turnip-shaped roots with the distinct advantage that they do not bleed. Though it appeared in the Burpee Catalog in the United States in 1940, similar sounding beets were also documented earlier in the nineteenth century. Regarded as the best yellow form.

B. vulgaris ssp. *vulgaris*
'CHELTENHAM GREEN TOP'

CULTIVATED BY 1883

Bred by Mr. A. H. Cook of Cheltenham and distributed by seedsmen Harrison & Sons of Leicester, England. A contemporary account states, "This is a valuable variety of beet, and scarcely any other is grown in the market gardens around Cheltenham. It is a moderate-size root with a smallish top and green leaved, as its name implies. Retains a good color when boiled." Another source laments, "I should have grown it in larger quantities but the seed was rather difficult to obtain."

B. vulgaris ssp. *vulgaris*
'DETROIT RED GLOBE'
or 'Crimson Globe,' 'Detroit Dark Red'

CULTIVATED BY 1892

Once extolled as "the world's greatest main-season beet," it is thought the original selection of this oxblood red beet was made by Mr. Reeves of Port Hope, Ontario, Canada. While still popular with gardeners, Detroit 2 Crimson Globe is considered to be a slight improvement on the original form with higher yields.

B. vulgaris ssp. *vulgaris*
'EGYPTIAN TURNIP-ROOTED'
or 'Egyptian Flat'

CULTIVATED BY 1871

Turnip-shaped roots described as having "Fine deep red flesh, strongly recommended for shallow soil and cold frames. Valuable for summer salads as it comes to maturity early." *Gardener's Calendar and General Directory*, Moore and Abercrombie, 1813. An unusual variety with flattened roots that grow almost entirely aboveground, hence their suitability for thin soil.

B. vulgaris ssp. *vulgaris*
'ROUGE CRAPAUDINE'
or 'Crapaudine,' 'Toad'

CULTIVATED BY 1856

This is perhaps one of the oldest varieties, and it is easily distinguished from all others by the peculiar appearance of its carrot-shaped roots that are covered by a black skin, broken by small cracks and crevices. Still available commercially, but rare. Superior flavor.

B. vulgaris ssp. *vulgaris*
'TONDA DI CHIOGGIA'
or 'Bassano,' 'Bullseye,' 'Candystripe Beet,' 'Chioggia,' 'Chioggia Pink,' 'Dolce di Chioggia'

CULTIVATED BY 1841

Italian form with flattened globes, with mild and sweet, ringed flesh. "Skin reddish, flesh white, with concentric rose-colored rings. It appears to be the same as those met with in the markets of North Italy. Called 'de Chioggia' in Venice, from the name of the place whence it comes from. It forms its roots chiefly on the surface, so may be grown on thinner land." *The Gardener's Assistant*, 1859. It was introduced into North America in 1841.

Tonda di Chioggia beet.

BRASSICA

RUTABAGA

or NEEP, SWEDE, SWEDISH TURNIP, TURNIP-ROOTED CABBAGE, YELLOW TURNIP

THE REPUTATION OF THE RUTABAGA has suffered unfairly in Great Britain from being known as a "wartime" vegetable, that is a root that was eaten only when other delicacies were rationed. However, its yellow flesh is subtle and sweet and should be eaten more often. Diced or mashed rutabaga, known in Scotland as "neeps," is the traditional accompaniment to haggis at Scottish Burns Night celebrations (January 25). It lacks popularity in the United States, too, but it makes an excellent winter vegetable from spring sowings; harvest the roots from early fall through late spring. Harvest before they get too large, otherwise they become tough and woody.

B. napus Naprobrassica group

'CHAMPION'

or 'Yellow Purple-Top'

CULTIVATED BY 1852

Vilmorin-Andrieux noted, "In Great Britain where Swedish Turnips are grown on a very large scale, the purple-top rutabaga is most in favor. Of these forms the most noteworthy are the Skirvings, the Fettercairn, and Sutton's Champion." This variety was the recipient of two silver cups presented by His Royal Highness Prince Albert at London's Smithfield Show, first in 1855, then again in 1856.

B. napus Naprobrassica group

'GERMAN GREEN-TOP'D YELLOW'

CULTIVATED BY 1840

"The Green Top'd Yellow is longer standing than the Purple Top'd, and where the same care is taken in selecting the roots grown for seeds, the green-topped may be considered as being equal in merit to the purple." *Description des Plantes Potageres*, Vilmorin-Andrieux, 1855.

An asparagus knife.

THE RUTABAGA CURLING CHAMPIONSHIPS

On the last market day of the year the International Rutabaga Curling Championships are held at Ithaca Farmer's Market in New York. This highly skilled competition, dating from the late 1990s, involves participants hurling hefty rutabagas over great distances. According to the rules, "any projectile besides a rutabaga" is strictly prohibited. A more genteel version of the sport, called the Turnip Toss, exists for those aged eight and under.

BRASSICA

KALE

KALE IS A VERY HARDY and most ancient member of the cabbage family, resembling in many ways the true wild cabbage *Brassica oleracea*. For people in the Middle Ages, kale would have formed a large part of the diet, and while it may have fallen out of use as a major commercial crop, its usefulness in the kitchen garden is beyond dispute. It is not difficult to have a supply of kale over winter and into early spring, plugging a hole in the "hungry gap" before the spring crops come to harvest. Kale grows well on most soil but requires protection in the form of a fine mesh net or floating row cover from birds and caterpillars. The name borecole is sometimes used instead of kale, and is an English adaptation of the Dutch word *boerenkool*, meaning "peasant's cabbage."

B. oleracea Acephala group
'DWARF GREEN CURLED'
or 'Bloomsdale's Kale,' 'Dwarf Curlies'

CULTIVATED BY 1779

With sweeter and more tender leaves after having been exposed to frost, "A fine winter and spring food for cattle, no frosts can destroy it, therefore it will supply when Cabbages and Savoys are gone." *An Account of the Best Directions for Raising Turnips, Rape, Cabbages etc.*, 1779.

A Dwarf Green Kale appears in the Flanagan and Nutting seed listing of 1835, but the first reference to the above named appears to be the James Carter seed catalog for 1849. The note detailed above, however, does suggest little doubt that this variety is probably much older and most likely introduced in the mid- to late eighteenth century.

B. oleracea Acephala group
'FLANDERS PURPLE'
or 'Caulet de Flandre'

CULTIVATED BY 1817

"The Purple form of the Jersey Tree Cabbage. Not so tall, but more hardy than the green. Leaves often undulated and, as it were, puckered at the edges." *Catalogue des Vegetaux de Tous Genres Cultives dans les Jardins et Pepinieres du Sieur Audibert,* 1885. Like the tree cabbage mentioned (see panel, right) it tends to need support, growing to quite a height, and the leaves, which have a strong kale flavor, are harvested from the bottom up, leaving a tall bare stem or "stick." Seeds are scarce.

B. oleracea Acephala group
'NERO DI TOSCANA'
or 'Black Cabbage,' 'Cavolo Nero'

CULTIVATED BY 1792

A striking dark color form that originated in Italy. With its popularity on the increase among gourmets in North America and the British Isles, seeds are easy to find. "Up to 6 feet (2m) in height, terminating, in a cluster of leaves, which are nearly entire on the borders, blistered on the surface & which sometimes measure 3 feet (1m) in length by 4 to 5 inches (10–13cm) in width." W. Hamilton, 1827.

B. oleracea Acephala group
'RED RUSSIAN'
or 'Rouge de Russie'

CULTIVATED BY C.1818

An ancient Russian heirloom, very hardy. "Before the plant begins to shoot in the spring, it appears purple, the back and edges of the leaves being tinged with that color, which of course are more in view in their growing state than when expanded. It is equal in value to

A daisy rake.

any variety of borecole, sweet and well flavored." *Page's Prodomus*, W. Page, 1818.

B . oleracea Acephala group
'RUSSIAN HUNGRY GAP'

CULTIVATED BY 1831

An account in the 1830s described it thus: "Coming in July, Hungry Gap kale is true to its name. Vegetables are at their lowest ebb in that month. This is an exceptionally heavy bearer." Similar in appearance to Red Russian, but with broader leaves, a lighter coloring, and more ragged leaves. Vigorous and very hardy, as seems appropriate for a plant that has fed people on the brink of starvation.

B. oleracea Acephala group
'THOUSAND HEAD'
or 'Branching Borecole,' 'Chou a Mille Tetes'

CULTIVATED BY 1801

Of this kale Mr. G. W. Watson wrote the following in *The Cottage Gardener*, 1817: "Extolled as an article in Agriculture. May be also considered as belonging to the garden. I know from experience that it will withstand the severest frost and will survive to be useful." Fairly unremarkable in its appearance, Thousand Head is nonetheless highly reliable and useful and can be harvested from an early stage, with leaves cut as required, allowing the side shoots to proliferate. Ultimately it will reach a height of 4 feet (1.2m) or more with widely spread foliage.

THE STRANGE CASE OF THE JERSEY TREE CABBAGE

It is true that many heritage vegetables display unusual or slightly eccentric qualities, but few are as odd as the Jersey Cabbage (*B. oleracea* var. *longata*). The sturdy stem of this plant can grow as high as 18 feet (5.5m) and is topped by edible cabbage-like foliage. Traditionally, it was fed to sheep because it was thought to make their fleeces particularly fine and silky. Once harvested, the stem was cut, dried, and varnished to produce handsome walking sticks, a practice still alive on the Channel Island of Jersey today. It gained a mention in the 1771 French catalog *Raisonne de Grains Etc.* Other names for this strange plant include Giant Cow Cabbage, Giant Jersey Kale, Tree Cabbage, and Walking Stick Kale.

BRASSICA

CAULIFLOWER

ASIDE FROM SPROUTING BROCCOLI, the main distinction between "heading" broccoli (or calabrese) and cauliflowers is that the former usually includes cold-tolerant varieties, whereas the latter are solely spring and fall varieties. To add to this confusion, certainly some of the varieties described below were listed by nineteenth-century seed merchants as broccoli. The strange white "curds" for which cauliflowers are valued are an evolutionary curiosity, developing somehow from the flowerheads of a distant cabbage relative and kept in cultivation since. The place of origin is said to be China, making its entry into Spain in the twelfth century, and much later still to the rest of Europe. Cauliflowers do best in fertile soil and need water at regular intervals to avoid any stunt in growth that can lead to deformed heads. Once the crop starts to form curds, make sure the heads are well protected, and cut before the florets begin to separate.

B. oleracea Botrytis group

'ALL THE YEAR ROUND'

or 'All Seasons'

CULTIVATED BY 1933

As the name suggests, this variety can be sown in some regions at any time of year, because it succeeds equally well in frames or in the open, but winter-sown seeds should be sown under glass for reliable germination. The large milky-white heads are protected by dark green leaves that are slightly curled. Their high quality make them popular for showing.

B. oleracea Botrytis group

'AUTUMN GIANT'

CULTIVATED BY 1838

A popular and reliable main-season variety with large, white, firm, and compact curds that mature over a long period and last well. Sow seeds and transplant in fall for a spring crop, or in spring for a fall crop. As the name suggests, the heads can reach a large size, but they are best harvested when they reach no more than 6 inches (15cm) across. The earliest written descriptions are from Canadian seed catalogs.

B. oleracea Botrytis group
'DI SICILIA VIOLETTO'

CULTIVATED BY 1812

"Packets of seeds, first sent here from Italy, which appear to me to have produced the same variety, have been sold for two seasons by Mr. Grange, in Covent Garden and Piccadilly (London)." *Journal of Natural Philosophy, Chemistry and the Arts*, 1812. This is, in fact, a remarkable selection by virtue of its deep purple curds that would catch the attention of any passing gardener. The color, unfortunately, is lost in cooking, turning instead to green, but the taste remains excellent. A regional variety from Sicily. Allow plenty of room for the plants to develop.

B. oleracea Botrytis group
'DWARF ERFURT'
or 'Snowball'

CULTIVATED BY 1830

Although cauliflowers were in cultivation in NorthAmerica by the late seventeenth century, it is the pure white varieties, such as Dwarf Erfurt, that have remained the most popular, not the purple and green types so often seen in the markets of mainland Europe. It is easy to see why, because they are more compact, easier to grow, and can be grown at closer spacings. This type—commonly known today as Snowball—should be harvested when the heads are just about at that size, when they fit nicely into your cupped hand.

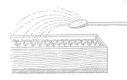
Watering seedlings.

B. oleracea Botrytis group
'PURPLE CAPE'

CULTIVATED BY 1808

Possibly developed in South Africa in the eighteenth century, certainly by the early 1800s it had been introduced into England by Mr. Marmaduke Dawney. A contemporary source noted, "This has a close, compact head, of a purple color. The plants grow from 1–1½ feet (30–45cm) in height, with short, erect leaves, regularly surrounding the head. The head is exposed to view in growing; and, as it enlarges, the projecting parts of the flower show a greenish white mixed with the purple color. Green when boiled."

B. oleracea Botrytis group
'ROMANESCO'
or Romanesco broccoli

CULTIVATED BY 1951

A contender for the most fantastic vegetable with its bright lime green heads made up of intricate fractal whorls of florets. Strictly it is a type of cauliflower, but it is often sold as a broccoli; this is easily forgiven— its dense green heads appear to be neither one nor the other. Growers may think this miracle of nature too beautiful to cook, but it is worth enjoying lightly steamed for its mild and sweet flavor.

B. oleracea Botrytis group
'VEITCH'S SELF-PROTECTING'
or 'Veitch's Self-folding'

CULTIVATED BY 1874

The seed company Veitch advertised their prized cultivar, "A valuable early variety. Produces close compact white heads, of delicious flavor. The protective covering of leaves is very pronounced. Sow under glass in March and in open ground in April." The self-protecting leaves are a desirable trait, protecting the curds from weather damage. A rare variety with seeds difficult to come by.

BRASSICA

CABBAGE

IN THE NINETEENTH CENTURY, **Mr. Charles Darwin** was moved to write the following notes upon the humble cabbage: "The principal kinds of cabbage existed at least as early as the sixteenth century, so that numerous modifications of structure have been inherited for a long period. This fact is the more remarkable, as great care must be taken to prevent the crossing of different kinds. I raised 233 seedlings from Cabbages of different kinds, which had purposely been planted near each other, and of the seedlings, no more than 155 were plainly deteriorated and mongrelized; nor were the remaining 78 all perfectly true. It may be doubted whether many permanent varieties have been formed by intentional or accidental crosses, for such crossed plants are found to be very inconstant." *The Variation of Animals and Plants Under Domestication*, 1868. The modern gardener may not find it necessary to cross-pollinate his or her own crop of cabbages, but heed Mr. Darwin's advice if you intend to save seeds from one crop for use the following year not to allow your crop to cross-pollinate with another.

B. *oleracea* Capitata group
'BRUNSWICK'
or 'Chou de Brunswick a Pied Court,' 'Early Drumhead'

CULTIVATED BY 1800

A very big Drumhead cabbage, a cattle or fodder type, but do not let that deter you from growing it, because it produces large and solid, medium-green heads with a good standing ability. Sown in spring, it will be ready to harvest from late summer, but manure well before planting to be sure of maximum growth.

B. *oleracea* Capitata group
'CHRISTMAS DRUMHEAD'

CULTIVATED BY 1889

Most probably raised and distributed by Barr & Sugden of Covent Garden, London, who described it as "a compact cabbage with dense blue-green heads sown May–July and harvested from October to Christmas." Its name, therefore, is slightly misleading, but because its heads stand well over winter, it will be a gift that keeps on giving. Sow in spring into a well-prepared bed. Drumhead type with a crisp texture.

B. oleracea Capitata group
'COPENHAGEN MARKET'

CULTIVATED BY 1884

A contemporary account describes it thus: "A valuable early cabbage, producing a large, globe-shape head. Stands longer in the field than any other variety. Produces fine, large heads of light green color, averaging 5 pounds (2.25kg); uniform in shape and size and very solid with few loose leaves." It was introduced from Denmark into the United States by H Hartman & Company in 1909. Still readily available, it is valued for its small stature, so recommended for smaller gardens. For the table, it makes wonderful coleslaw or sauerkraut. Store in a cool, frost-free place; the heads do not stand well over winter in cold climates.

B. oleracea Capitata group
'COUER DE BOEUF DES VERTUS'

CULTIVATED BY 1771

"Bears early frost pretty well. It is said that 'mountains' of this cabbage are sent to Market at Paris during the winter." *The Vegetable Garden*, Vilmorin-Andrieux, 1885.

A green cabbage.

A delicious French Ox-heart type cabbage that has tall, pointed green heads that are ready from early summer and are tender. A classic market variety.

B. oleracea Capitata group
'D'AUBERVILLIERS'

CULTIVATED BY 1783

In *Correspondence Rurale* M. de la Brettonaire wrote of this French savoy cabbage, "Early variety, easy to grow, very productive with leaves of blue green color. The interior leaves are white yellowish. It is a vegetable with very short stem and a flattened, very tender head." Sown in spring, it is ready to harvest from early winter, standing well in cold weather. The flavor of its wonderfully crinkled leaves is said to be excellent, but it is a rare type, and seeds may be hard to come by.

B. oleracea Capitata group
'FILDERKRAUT'
or 'Pomeranian'

CULTIVATED BY 1828

"A late variety succeeding better when sown in Spring and keeping well for some time in Winter ... It appears to be productive without being excessively late," wrote Vilmorin-Andrieux, but he seems to be literally missing the point, because this is a pointed cabbage with such an exaggerated shape that it is a feature impossible to ignore. Originates from the Filderstadt region just south of Stuttgart in Germany. Each head is large and heavy, and it is the variety of choice for making sauerkraut.

LOST, RARE, OR SIMPLY FORGOTTEN?

Shetland Cabbage (*B. oleracea*) is believed to be the oldest known Scottish local vegetable variety. It has been grown on the island of Shetland since at least the sixteenth century. Traditionally planted within the sheltering protection of a small, stone-walled, circular structure known as a plantie crub (some survive on the island today, although often as ruins), once established, it was then replanted within a larger area. This cabbage is open-hearted in form and has a distinctive, peppery taste. In the past, it was most often cooked in mutton stew with the discarded leaves used as animal fodder. Seeds of Shetland Cabbage are not commercially available, and its continued survival is totally dependent on farm-saved seeds.

B. oleracea Capitata group

'FLOWER OF SPRING'
or 'Offenham 2'

CULTIVATED BY 1885

Bred by Sutton & Sons of Reading, England, the following description comes from their 1897 catalog: "Successive annual trials in our Experimental Gardens have proved this to be the best cabbage for August sowing. It not only comes very early in spring, and produces finer heads than any other August-sown cabbages but shows no disposition to run to seed. Dwarf and compact; heart firm and quality excellent." Harvest for early spring greens or allow to form its pointed head.

B. oleracea Capitata group

'GOLDEN ACRE'
or 'Derby Day,' 'June Giant'

CULTIVATED BY 1889

An excellent ball-headed cabbage of light green color, producing an early summer crop of tightly wrapped cabbage heads, which will keep right up until fall. With its relatively compact size, it is suitable for confined areas, with plantings spaced at 12 inches (30cm) apart. The flavor is very good, and it is a favorite for making sauerkraut. North American bred.

A Savoy cabbage.

B. oleracea Capitata group

'JANUARY KING'
or 'De Pontoise'

CULTIVATED BY 1867

A French savoy variety that is sown in spring for cutting in February and is particularly suited to cold regions as it is one of the hardiest cabbages. A contemporary source noted, "Extremely cold hardy yet also grows well in the summer months. Dense, green, round to slightly flattened heads, have attractive, purple-tinged outer leaves." Its good looks are hard to beat, taking a deeper purple tint as the cold intensifies.

B. oleracea Capitata group

'JERSEY WAKEFIELD'

CULTIVATED BY 1800

Forming a compact, somewhat conical head with glaucous-green leaves, this wonderful early heading variety occupies little garden space, ready from early summer. The American seed

merchant Mr. Peter Henderson reported that this variety was first grown in the United States by Mr. Francis Brill of Jersey City, New Jersey, in the 1840s, but it may have originated in Yorkshire, England.

B. oleracea Capitata group

'MR. WHEELER'S IMPERIAL'

CULTIVATED BY 1844

Raised by Mr. George Wheeler of Warminster, Wiltshire, England, who described it as, "Dark green leafy heads, compact plants with harvest time of mid-April onward. Suitable for spring sowing for fall use." The habit is indeed neat and compact, with pointed heads made up of tender leaves. A fall-sown crop will yield an earlier harvest of spring greens from the very onset of spring.

B. oleracea Capitata group

'ORMSKIRK'
or 'Irish Gaint Drumhead'

CULTIVATED BY 1899

A cold-tolerant savoy-type cabbage with attractive leaves. Raised and distributed by JL Clucas Ltd of Ormskirk, Lancashire, England, who promoted it as "an extra late green savoy with crinkled leaves and firm rounded heads. Very hardy and reliable that you can be harvesting for Christmas dinner." With a solid center it produces a fine head with a blue-green outer and a pale green inner. It stands well into spring once it begins to mature in mid-fall.

B. oleracea Capitata group
'RED DRUMHEAD'
or 'Red Dutch,' 'Rubine,'
Seven Hills'

CULTIVATED BY 1771

In *Modern Gardener* by James Meader, 1771, the Red Dutch was described as, "The most familiar, as well as the most popular of the red varieties. The head is somewhat large, round, hard, and solid; the leaves composing the head are of an intense purplish red; the outer leaves are numerous, red, but with some intermixture or shades of green." Its heads begin to mature from late summer, although it is best to wait until the first frosts before harvesting. It stores and pickles well with a sweet flavor. Introduced to the Americas from Germany around 1867.

B. oleracea Capitata group
'WINNIGSTADT'

CULTIVATED BY 1803

A very old German variety, described in *The Gardeners' Assistant*, 1859, "Stem dwarf, head large, broad at base, sharply conical, heart compact, boiling tender. The leaves, till blanched by hearting are a glaucous hue, like those of the cauliflower, or broccoli. A good late cabbage." Ready to harvest from late summer from a spring or fall sowing, seeds can be hard to come by for this rare variety. Its outstanding flavor makes it ideal for salads, sauerkraut, and coleslaw.

LOST, RARE, OR SIMPLY FORGOTTEN?

Lamenting the loss of rare varieties is not the sole preserve of modern-day growers. As far back as the 1820s John Claudius Loudon described the Vanack cabbage as "an old variety, which has now fallen into neglect." *Register of Rural and Domestic Improvements, Vol. 2*, JC Loudon, 1827. The Countess of Bridgewater's gardener, a Mr. Torbon, had been growing this splendid-sounding cabbage since 1776 on her Ashridge Estate, Hertfordshire, England, and was quoted in *The Gardener's Magazine* as saying, "By timely sowings it is always in season; it makes excellent spring coleworts, becomes a white-hearted cabbage very early, and pushes fine sprouts from the stump after the cabbages are cut. In quality it is inferior to none of the best cabbages." What a sad shame it is not a regular feature of today's seed catalogs.

The German late cabbage Winnigstadt.

A hand vaporizer.

BRASSICA

BRUSSELS SPROUT

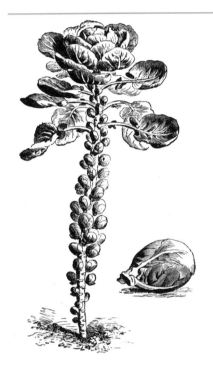

WHILE THE ORIGIN OF THE brussels sprout is perhaps uncertain, the Early Ulm savoy cabbage was known to produce sprouts at its leaf axils, and it may be that the brussels sprout is derived from this source. In addition, there is a distinct similarity between Brussels Tops (a much maligned and overlooked source of spring greens) and some of the looser varieties of savoy cabbage. History notes that sprouts were grown around the area of Brussels in Belgium in the Middle Ages, although how much they resembled modern-day sprouts is a matter of discussion. Another historical claim is that the true brussels sprout originated from a plant grown in the Brussels region in the eighteenth century. All brassica crops grow best in firm, fertile, and free-draining but moisture-retentive soil, preferably with a neutral or slightly alkaline pH. Protect from birds and caterpillars. The flavor is said to improve after the first frosts.

B. oleracea Gemmifera group
'EVESHAM SPECIAL'

CULTIVATED BY 1920

Distributed by HJ Speed & Co. of Evesham, Worcestershire, England, who described it as "a good all rounder, producing large quantities of good quality medium-size solid sprouts from September to December." From the market gardens of the Vale of Evesham, this has become a firm favorite among British growers, valued for

providing a plentiful crop from early fall right up until Christmas.

B. oleracea Gemmifera group
'LONG ISLAND IMPROVED'
or 'Catskill Strain,' 'Half Dwarf Improved,' 'Paris Market'

CULTIVATED BY 1890

A hardy plant, compact in size with a good yield, and its flavor truly improves after the first frosts. Its

diminutive size may make it a good choice for an exposed site. Despite the confusion of name this variety is not the same but is similar to the Catskill introduced in 1941 (thought to be named after Catskill Park, in New York State). This was once one of the most important commercial varieties, and it is still a great pick today.

B. oleracea Gemmifera group
'RUBINE'

CULTIVATION DATE UNKNOWN

A beautiful and productive brussels sprout with purple-red sprouts, a few gardeners even grow it for foliage effect in garden borders. Taste-wise, the sprouts have a delicious nutty flavor, and because they retain their color when cooked, try mixing them in with some green sprouts for your Christmas dinner. Unusual and rare.

B. oleracea Gemmifera group
'SEVEN HILLS'

CULTIVATION DATE UNKNOWN

This old favorite English variety is not very tall, so it tolerates cold, wet, and windy weather well and can even withstand a little snow. It is from late-maturing, open-pollinated stock, so the plants come into crop at different times giving sprouts over a long period from December onward.

BRASSICA
KOHLRABI

THIS UNUSUAL VARIETY of the cabbage family is grown for the swollen ball-shaped stem, which grows just above the soil surface. Early seed listings differentiated this species from the ordinary turnip by referring to it as "turnip above the ground." Its seeds were commercially available in North America in the early nineteenth century, and it came to be much loved by the Victorians for its cabbage taste, which was to be enjoyed without the associated cabbage smell. "The crop will be fit for use when the stems are the size of a cricket ball; when larger they are tough, and only fit for cattle. In the varieties grown in the fields, the bulbs sometimes attain an immense size, weighing in some cases as much as 14 pounds (6.3kg)." *The Gardeners' Assistant*, 1936.

B. oleracea Gongylodes group
'PURPLE VIENNA'

CULTIVATED BY 1849

"Though this is generally thought to be a farm rather than garden vegetable, there are two varieties, viz., the Early Green Vienna and the Early Purple Vienna both of which attain a moderate size only, and the bulbs, if used when about the size of a medium-size turnip, make a fine substitute for that vegetable when through drought or fly, they have failed." *The Garden*, January 17, 1880.

B. oleracea Gongylodes group
'WHITE VIENNA'
or 'Green Vienna'

CULTIVATED BY 1849

This type is smaller than Purple Vienna but grows faster (it can be ready to harvest less than two months from sowing). With light green skin and tender creamy white flesh the taste is sweet and mild. High yielding and cold hardy.

BRASSICA

BROCCOLI

or CALABRESE

NOTABLE HISTORIANS HAVE SUGGESTED that the Mediterranean island of Cyprus is the true home of broccoli. It has certainly been in cultivation in the British Isles for more than three hundred years. Although the sprouting broccoli varieties mentioned below may well have been developed from "reselected" stock, the basic nature and attributes of the original varieties must, we trust, still feature significantly. What is referred to as calabrese is strictly Calabrese Broccoli, or if you prefer Calabrian Broccoli, taking its name from that region of Italy. Unlike sprouting broccoli, which bear many small sprouting heads, calabrese types have a large single head. Gardeners will find sprouting types much easier to grow, requiring any fertile, well-drained but moisture-retentive soil. Birds and caterpillars are almost always a problem, so conventional wisdom is to grow the crop under a net of fine mesh or floating row cover. Broccoli is usually an overwintered crop, bearing its heads the following spring, whereas calabrese is a summer crop, bearing its large heads in the same year as it is planted.

B. oleracea Italica group
'GREEN SPROUTING'
or 'Italian Green Sprouting'

CULTIVATED BY 1784

A very prolific and hardy variety, noted in *The English Garden Displayed*, 1784, as "A distinct variety forming good-size green heads. After these are cut a number of sprouts developing on the axis forming smaller heads." Very easy to grow, with a great many uses in the kitchen, because the stems, buds, and leaves are also edible.

A fine head of broccoli.

B. oleracea Italica group
'NINE STAR PERENNIAL'

CULTIVATED BY 1928

Bred and introduced by Charles Lewin Curtis, a seedsman from Cambridgeshire, England, who described it thus: "Is now within the reach of every grower. Seeds sown in April or May planted out in June, July, or August (or even September), 4 feet (1.2m) apart each way on well-manured land. By the March and April, a permanent bed of Broccoli will be produced, each plant of which will give a crop of from 5 to 15 heads of good saleable size and of excellent quality year after year. It is a distinct form occasionally grown in gardens, with a branching stem producing several heads and capable of persisting and heading for several years." Unfortunately, this is no longer quite "within the reach of every grower," because it is increasingly scarce. However, enthusiastic perennial vegetable gardeners are helping to keep it alive.

B. oleracea Italica group
'PURPLE SPROUTING'

CULTIVATED BY 1777

This variety featured in *The Day Book of Cockmanning's Nursery*, 1777 (of Orpington, Kent, England). Sown in April, it will produce from November to February. Sown in June, it will produce sprouts in March and April. Heavy and long-bearing crops of excellent flavor make it an extremely rewarding crop. There is also a white form.

Purple Sprouting broccoli.

HISTORICAL NOTE

First cultivated by the Greeks and Romans, broccoli continued to be grown in Italy but only appeared in France in the sixteenth century. England did not enjoy its health-giving properties until around 1700, where it was known as "sprout colli-flower" or "Italian asparagus." In North America, it was referred to as "Roman or Italian Brocoli" in John Randolph's *A Treatise on Gardening by a Citizen of Virginia* (1765), a publication that Thomas Jefferson held in his gardening library. Jefferson grew broccoli not just as a vegetable but also as an ornamental, alternating green, purple, and white varieties in his garden at Monticello.

BRASSICA

TURNIP

or RAPINI, TURNIP GREENS, TURNIP TOPS, WHITE TURNIP

A SOMEWHAT NEGLECTED VEGETABLE, the turnip deserves something of a kitchen revival. Today, it is the root that is most favored in the northeastern states, while the green leafy part is more often cooked farther south. "A hardy biennial, native of Europe, including Britain. It has been cultivated for its roots from time immemorial, and the leaves are also frequently used as Greens, or sometimes blanched as a substitute for Sea Kale." *The Gardeners' Assistant*, 1859.

B. rapa Rapifera group
'GOLDEN BALL'
or 'Jaune Boule d'Or,' 'Orange Jelly'

CULTIVATED BY 1853

A small and compact round turnip with golden skin and flesh and a sweet and mellow taste. "This variety was raised by Mr. Chivas, of Chester, (England) and it is a Turnip of most excellent quality, the skin being thin and smooth, and the pulp solid, sweet, and good … Tested in the kitchen, it was found to be everything that the best kind of Turnip should be." *RHS Journal*, 1853.

Golden Ball turnip.

B. rapa Rapifera group
'LONG WHITE VERTUS'
or 'Jersey Navet,' 'Navet des Vertus Marteau'

CULTIVATED BY 1856

This French variety has long white roots with a swollen lower part and tender sweet flesh. It may become hollow with age.

B. rapa Rapifera group
'MANCHESTER MARKET'
or 'Green Topped Stone,' 'Marble Top Green'

CULTIVATED BY 1821

A globe-shaped turnip, with white roots and a green crown. One of the most useful varieties for late sowing, because it is very hardy and will stand well into the winter; it has firm, tender and juicy flesh.

B. rapa Rapifera group
'SNOWBALL'
or 'Boule de Neige,' 'Model White,' 'White Egg,' 'White Stone'

CULTIVATED BY 1800

A mild and tender, egg-shaped turnip from Europe that can be eaten raw. "The difference between varieties arises through selection of seeds, the tendency being to become more pointed, the correct form being nearly round, with a small tap root." From a report on growing turnips by the Royal Horticultural Society, London, 1877.

B. rapa Rapifera group
'VEITCH'S RED GLOBE'
or 'Blanc Globe a Collet Violet,' 'Purple Top White Globe'

CULTIVATED BY 1838

"This excellent variety should be grown in every garden. It is far superior to Red American Stone, both in flavor and shape, and has the additional very real advantage of remaining a long time fit for use." From an advertisement for the seeds of Messrs. James Veitch & Sons, January, 1871.

B. rapa Rapifera group
'WHITE AMERICAN STONE'
or 'Early White Milan,' 'Milan White'

CULTIVATED BY 1858

A very early European variety with white skin. The roots are flat, of medium size, and quite smooth. The flesh is creamy white.

CAPPARIS

CAPER

IT IS THE UNOPENED FLOWER BUDS of the caper bush that provide the basis for pickled capers. In cool climates, they need the protection of a greenhouse. Of the caper, Vilmorin-Andrieux wrote, "Under the name of 'Capers,' the flower buds, gathered when they are as large as Peas, are pickled in vinegar. They are valued in proportion to the smallness of their size." Mr. Etty suggests that the seeds are initially immersed in warm water and then soaked for one day. They should be wrapped in a moist cloth, placed in a sealed jar, and kept in an Ice-house (or new-fangled "refrigerator" if you prefer) for two or three months. After such cooling, soak the seeds again in warm water overnight. Plant the seeds about ½ inch (1.3cm) deep in loose, well-drained soil. There is also a wild form of caper seed that can be procured, but both forms are slow to germinate.

A caper bush.

C. spinosa
CAPER

CULTIVATION DATE UNKNOWN

Although in cultivation since the early decades of the seventeenth century, capers have been gathered in the wild since ancient times. The caper bush has small green leaves and short-lived white flowers with long purple stamens. They favor a sunny position in well-drained soil.

CAPSICUM

SWEET PEPPER

or BELL PEPPER, PEPPER

CULPEPER GAVE THIS FULSOME ACCOUNT of the pepper in the seventeenth century: "There are several kinds. It grows with an upright, firm, round stalk, with a certain pith within it, about 2 or 3 feet (60–90cm) high, spreading into many branches on all sides, from the very bottom, which divide themselves again into other smaller branches, at each joint two long leaves upon short foot stalks, with several veins, not dented about the edges, and of dark green color: the flowers stand severally at the joints, consisting usually five or sometimes six, white, small-pointed leaves, standing open like a star, with yellow threads in the middle after which come the fruit, either great or small, long or short, round or square, as the kind is, either standing upright or hanging down, as the flowers show themselves: the seeds are numerous, kidney shaped and a little compressed: the root annual and fibrous spreading plentifully in the ground, but perishing after it has ripened all its fruits." *Complete Herbal*, Nicholas Culpeper, 1653.

C. annuum
'BULL NOSE RED'

CULTIVATED BY 1759

It is suspected this blunt-ended bell pepper was introduced into North America from India before 1759. Jefferson grew it at Monticello; it was then listed in the 1863 catalog of the American seed company Fearing Burr and also

pops up in the *Amateur's Guide in Horticulture* (1879) by the English seed company Sutton & Sons.

C. annuum
'CALIFORNIAN WONDER'

CULTIVATED BY 1928

This North American variety is a large stuffing pepper with

extremely thick, mild, sweet flesh. The glossy dark green fruit, which turns red as it matures, is indistinctly four-lobed, upright, and shapely. It is prolific and productive over a long season.

C. annuum
'GOLDEN MARCONI'

CULTIVATION DATE UNKNOWN

These Italian sweet peppers produce golden yellow vegetables that grow up to 12 inches (30cm) long and are very productive. Their taste is sweet and mild. Harvest early when still light green to let mature to a golden yellow.

C. annuum
'LONG RED MARCONI'

CULTIVATED BY 1880

Originating in Italy, this variety has thin, long red pods with a sweet flavor. It is mild and yields well. If the sweet peppers are still on the plant as the weather starts to cool, cut and hang upside down indoors to completely ripen.

Green sweet peppers taste sharper than the sweeter red varieties.

C. annuum
'SPANISH MAMMOTH'
or 'Doux d'Espagne'

CULTIVATED BY 1824

An early-maturing variety with large, sweet-flavored peppers shaped like a cone and truncated at the end. It produces well and displays good resistance to disease.

C. annuum
'SWEET NARDELLO'

CULTIVATED BY 1880S

This prolific pepper was taken to Connecticut by the Nardello family in 1887 from the Basilicata region of Italy. It is a classic frying pepper that is also good eaten raw. The long, slim peppers are thin-walled and crunchy.

HISTORICAL NOTE

In *The Young Gardener's Assistant*, published in 1847, the American gardener, seedsman, and florist Thomas Bridgeman writes of the bell pepper: "This family of plants are native of the East and West Indies; some of their capsules or pods, are yellow, and others red, when at maturity; they are much used for pickling, and should be gathered for that purpose before they are fully ripe." He goes on to advise that "One ounce of seeds will produce about three thousand plants"—which will be somewhat beyond the requirements of most home growers.

CAPSICUM

CHILI PEPPER

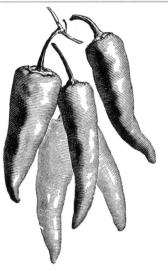

THE *Gardener's Assistant* GAVE THIS somewhat alarming warning regarding the chili pepper in 1936: "The frequent adulteration of this condiment with red-lead and other poisonous substances renders the cultivation of the Capsicum in gardens for a homegrown supply very desirable." Although such commercial practices are no longer prevalent, the sheer diversity of chili peppers means that every gardener should make room for at least one or two varieties to suit their tastes, of course. Of their ease of cultivation, *Beeton's Dictionary of Every-Day Gardening*, 1910, notes: "Their culture is simple and easy: the plants must be raised from seed sown in a hot-bed, or placed over gentle bottom heat, and as they increase in size they must be shifted singly into small pots at first, and thence into larger pots."

C. annuum
'BULGARIAN CARROT'
or 'Shipkas'

CULTIVATION DATE UNKNOWN

This is a very unusual European heirloom variety that is said to have been smuggled across the Iron Curtain in the late 1980s. It produces "baby carrotlike" hot peppers up to 4 inches (10cm) in length. The bright glossy vegetable crops heavily in clusters close to the stem and has a crunchy flesh. A compact grower, it is ideally suited to growing in pots, scoring up to 30,000 on the Scoville scale.

C. chinense
'CHOCOLATE HABANERO'
or 'Black Habanero,' 'Brown Congo,' 'Congo Black'

CULTIVATION DATE UNKNOWN

This Caribbean chili pepper is one of the hottest of the Habanero range. The hot vegetables are about 1½ inches (3.8cm) long and only slightly longer than they are wide; they mature from green to a chocolate brown. They are slower growing than other varieties so are more suited to glasshouse cultivation in cool climates.

C. annuum
'HUNGARIAN HOT WAX'
or 'Hot Banana Hungarian,' 'Hungarian Yellow Wax'

CULTIVATED BY THE 1930S

A chili pepper plant with a vigorous habit and long and pointed, bright yellow, waxy medium-hot fruits that ripen to a rosy red. It ranges from 2,000 to 8,000 on the Scoville scale. An early maturing variety suitable for cool climates.

The hot Long Red Cayenne chili pepper.

C. annuum
'LONG RED CAYENNE'

CULTIVATION DATE UNKNOWN

Pre-Columbian in origin, this chili pepper was named after the Cayenne River in New Guyana and was spread around the world by Portuguese traders. This is the standard red chili pepper for pickles. Its slender, twisted pods grow to about 4 inches (10cm) long and are deep green when young, turning to bright red when ripe, with a relatively high heat up to 50,000 on the Scoville scale.

C. annuum
'PASILLA BAJIO'
or 'Chile Negro'

CULTIVATION DATE UNKNOWN

Pasilla means "little raisin" in Spanish, referring to its deep

brown dried pods and raisin-like aroma. The pods are 6 to 8 inches (15–20cm) long by 1 inch (2.5cm) wide. It is delicious fresh or dried and forms the basis for the rich complex flavor of Mexican mole sauces, from where it originates. The fruits are a glossy, deep forest green maturing to dark chocolate brown. They have a gentle heat, scoring up to 1,500 on the Scoville scale.

C. annuum
'PIMIENTOS DE PADRON'

CULTIVATION DATE UNKNOWN

This chili pepper was brought from the New World to Spain in the eighteenth century, when Franciscan monks first attempted to cultivate the pepper seeds at their monastery in Herbon, near Padron. Frequently fried in oil, salted, and served in tapas bars throughout Spain. Eating them is considered a form of culinary Russian roulette, because some are sweet, while others are hot enough to keep you humble. Measuring up to 12,000 on the Scoville scale.

C. annuum
'SATAN'S KISS'
or 'Ciliegia Picante'

CULTIVATED BY 1828

Small, cherrylike chili peppers with pods that are pretty hot when eaten raw but, unusually, they lose around 60 percent of their heat when cooked. They are quick to crop, maturing at between 40,000 and 50,000 on the Scoville scale.

SOME LIKE IT HOT

The Scoville scale is named after Wilbur L. Scoville (1865–1942), who in 1912 devised the Scoville organoleptic test to measure the concentration of the chemical compound capsaicin in chili peppers. Capsaicin is the substance that burns the mouth. The Scoville scale and the associated SHU (Scoville heat units) are still in use more than a hundred years later, although high-pressure liquid chromatography can now establish heat with greater accuracy. Growers be aware that it is not just the variety of chili pepper you grow that determines its ultimate heat, but also environmental factors, such as sunlight, soil type, moisture, and growing temperatures.

C. chinense
'SCOTCH BONNET'
or 'Red Scotch Bonnet'

CULTIVATION DATE UNKNOWN

This is similar to and of the same species as the Habanero group of chili peppers. It ranks among some of the hottest chili peppers in the world and is grown mainly in the Caribbean Islands and the Maldives. Its heat measures up to 350,000 on the Scoville scale.

CICHORIUM

CHICORY

or BATAVIA, BATAVIAN ENDIVE, CURLY ENDIVE, ESCAROLE, FRISÉE

CURLY ENDIVE (OR FRISÉE) AND ESCAROLE are types of chicory. In his nineteenth-century *History of Cultivated Vegetables,* Mr. Henry Phillips wrote, "The Garden Endive [chicory] appears to have been first cultivated in England in . . . 1548; but the wild endive or succory, intybus, being indigenous to the soil was sown in all probability at a much earlier period" as an "herb and as a salad."

C. endivia
'BROAD LEAVED WINTER OF BORDEAUX'
or 'Cornet de Bordeaux'

CULTIVATED BY 1856

This is a hardy old French variety. The loose and curly foliage is bright green, paler in the center of the head, and can be harvested as a cut-and-come-again crop. It is less bitter than some other chicories.

C. endivia
'FINE DE LOUVIERS'

CULTIVATED BY 1857

The following fulsome description appeared in an 1878 seed catalog: "Leaves short, very deeply cut, and lacinated; of a dull glaucous green color. Forms close full hearts of excellent quality, which blanch naturally to a good extent. This variety will not tie up and requires covering to blanch thoroughly; very hardy."

C. endivia
'FRISEE DE MEAUX'

CULTIVATED BY 1771

A hardy variety suitable for growing for a fall harvest. The dark green leaves have particularly frilly edges but are paler in color at the heart.

C. endivia
'GREEN CURLED RUFFEC'

CULTIVATED BY 1863

A contemporary account sang its praises thus: "Leaves from 7 to 8 inches (18–20cm) long, resting close to the ground with a broad fleshy midrib, the edges toothed and much curled; of a deep green color. Forms very large full hearts, which blanch without much tying. Crisp, fleshy, and excellent."

CICHORIUM

BELGIAN ENDIVE

or BLUE DANDELION, FRENCH ENDIVE, SUCCORY, WITLOOF

APART FROM ITS USE AS A SALAD VEGETABLE, endive (called chicory in Europe) can also be used as a substitute for coffee. In the past, the large-rooted variety Madgeburg was particularly favored for this purpose. The practice dates back to the Napoleonic Wars, when the British Fleet blockaded the French ports and cut the supply of coffee.

C. intybus
'BARBE DE CAPUCIN'

CULTIVATED BY 1767

L'Ecole du Jardinier Fleuriste described this as the semi-wild ancestor of all chicories," …much esteemed by the French as a winter salad; and when blanched, is known under the name of Barbe du Capucin. For winter leaf use."

C. intybus
'ROSSA DI VERONA'

CULTIVATION DATE UNKNOWN

Endive has traditionally been grown in the area of Verona in northern Italy since the early twentieth century. This loose-head endive has a firm texture and strong red color. The leaves are heart shaped, with a spicy and bitter taste that mellows when cooked. It can also be eaten raw.

C. intybus
'ROSSA DI TREVISO'
or 'Red Treviso'

CULTIVATED BY 1899

A very attractive plant, its deep red leaves are contrasted with the pure white ribs. They can be eaten raw or lightly cooked. In the Italian region of Treviso, it is grown in winter and both the leaves and roots are eaten.

ABOVE RIGHT *Endive Witloof (see page 62).*

HOW TO BLANCH ENDIVE

"The lifted roots should be placed in deep boxes or in one corner of the mushroom house, or some suitable place where the light can be excluded and where there is little heat. They should be planted in old potting soil that contains just sufficient moisture to keep the root fibers in action. An occasional syringing with tepid water may be given. In planting, the crown should stand at least ½ inch (1.3cm) above the soil, and any loose soil should be removed from about the leaves with a syringe, in order that the young foliage may be perfectly clean when cut. In about three weeks the leaves will have made growth, and if they have been kept in perfect darkness the color will be a delicate creamy white." *The Gardener's Assistant*, 1936.

CRAMBE

SEA KALE

or SEA CABBAGE

C. intybus
'VARIEGATA DI CASTELFRANCO'

CULTIVATED BY 1700S

This ancient variety of endive has green leaves heavily blotched with red and is thought to have been developed in the eighteenth century in the Castelfranco region of northern Italy. It is forced in the same manner as Witloof.

C. intybus
'VARIEGATA DI CHIOGGIA'
or 'Rossa di Chioggia'

CULTIVATED BY THE 1800S

A popular variety with large, loose leaves that turn into tight heads that ripen to a bright crimson red with white ribs and veins. In cool weather, the color lessens in intensity.

C. intybus
'WITLOOF'
or 'Large Brussels'

CULTIVATED BY 1872

"Leaf growth makes one of the most delicious winter salads or it can be cooked in the same manner as Sea Kale. In fall the roots are taken up, the leaves trimmed to 1½ inches (3.8cm) from the neck, and the end of the roots shortened … to a length of 8 to 9 inches (20–23cm). The roots are planted in earth in a dark, cool place in the cellar or under a greenhouse bench." *Gardeners' Year-Book and Almanack*, R. Hogg, 1872.

A EUROPEAN NATIVE PERENNIAL, the actual date when sea kale was taken into cultivation is uncertain. It is known to have been grown and popularized in London by a Dr. Litton of Grove Hill in about 1767, and it was also cultivated in gardens near Dublin, Ireland, as early as 1764. In 1853 the publication *Scientific American* noted, "Why the culture of the crambe maritima this delicious vegetable, should have been so long neglected, we do not know, but from the frequency with which it is met in the New York markets for two years past, it seems that its value is better appreciated now than it was a few years ago." Sea kale is one of only a few vegetables that are regarded as being better flavored when they have been forced.

C. maritima
'LILYWHITE'

CULTIVATED BY 1895

This variety was announced as "new" in the catalog of the English seed company Carter's in 1895: "A delicate, good flavored Seakale, and when forced pure white in color. It is not as hardy as the common variety and the crowns should be protected from frost."

HISTORICAL NOTE

Vilmorin-Andrieux commented on the popularity of sea kale. "Like Rhubarb, the use of Sea-Kale is at present almost confined to the English people at home and abroad. It has gone to America and the antipodes, but has not crossed the Channel! In a few gardens in France it may be seen, but they belong to those who have learned to care for the plant in England."

CUCUMIS

CUCUMBER & GHERKIN

THE WILD CUCUMBER ORIGINATES FROM INDIA and was grown around the Mediterranean region of Europe by the ancient Greeks and Romans. It was widely cultivated by the sixteenth century and arrived in the New World with Christopher Columbus. The long types with smooth skin are favored for salads and are sometimes referred to as English, European, hothouse, or slicing cucumbers. Smaller varieties, known as cornichons or gherkins, have a tart taste and are best used for pickling.

C sativus

'CRYSTAL APPLE'

or 'Apple Shaped,' 'Lemon'

CULTIVATED BY 1894

This unusual cucumber has pale creamy white fruits that are 3 inches (7.5cm) long with a circumference of 2 inches (5cm). In 1903 the *RHS Journal* noted, "Messrs. Hobbies, Dereham (England), brought Lemon Cucumbers, the fruit being small and roundish oval, with a pale lemon-colored skin, but exactly similar in flavor to the ordinary Cucumber," although many growers are said to detect a faint lemon taste when the fruit is fully mature. It was introduced into the United States in 1894, appearing in the seed catalog of Samuel Wilson, Mecanicsville, Pennsylvannia.

C. sativus

'LONG GREEN RIDGE'

or 'Bedfordshire Prize Ridge,' 'Long Green Prickly Cucumber'

CULTIVATED BY 1767

Abercrombie and Moore listed this as Long Prickly in *Every Man His Own Gardener,* 1834, and described it thus: "From 7 to 10 inches (18–25cm) long, of a green color, with few prickles. A good bearer; and upon the whole, this is accounted the best cucumber for the general summer crop, the pulp being very crisp and pleasant."

The much sought-after long, straight cucumber.

A trug basket.

CURVACEOUS CUCUMBERS

It seems that the desire to correct the natural curve of the cucumber has reoccurred several times throughout its long cultivation. The Romans grew theirs in hollow reeds while the Victorians manufactured a similar device in glass. In 1995 the European Union introduced Commission Regulation No. 2257/94, which stated that cucumbers offered for sale should be "practically straight," bent by a gradient of no more than one-tenth. I propose that in my experience, growers of heritage varieties like to raise their cucumbers unfettered and curvy.

A cucumber glass.

C. sativus
'NATIONAL PICKLING'

CULTIVATED BY 1924

This variety was developed by G. E. Starr at the Michigan College of Agriculture, to the specifications of the National Picker's Association. The vegetable matures early, is dark green and square-ended, and grows to about 6 inches (15cm) in length.

C. sativus
'ROLLISSON'S TELEGRAPH IMPROVED'

CULTIVATED BY 1864

This is a "special selection" of nurseryman William Rollisson's earlier Telegraph Cucumber. An enthusiastic correspondent to *The Gardeners' Chronicle* in 1868 wrote, "Gardeners who are expected to produce cucumbers in quantity in winter should get this kind; and when they have once grown it will not grow any other sort."

C. staves
'SMALL GREEN PARIS'
or 'Improved Bourbonne,'
'Paris Pickling'

CULTIVATED BY 1876

"This is a French variety known in Europe as Improved Bourbonne and used exclusively for the manufacture of gherkins and cornichons much in the same way as the West India gherkins are used in America. When the variety was brought to America for the first time is not known, although Gregory lists it as early as 1892." *The Curcubits of New York*, U. P. Hedrick, 1937.

C. sativus
'WHITE WONDER'
or 'Long White'

CULTIVATED BY 1890

Mr. U. P. Hedrick also makes mention of this cucumber in his extensive work *The Curcubits of New York*, saying, "The Seeds of a white cucumber were sent to W. Atlee Burpee of Philadelphia from a customer in Western New York in 1890. In trial this was thought to have considerable merit and was accordingly introduced by the firm in 1893."

GROWING CUCUMBERS
Victorian gardeners constructed special houses in which to grow their cucumbers. These included an open water tank to help keep the air moist.

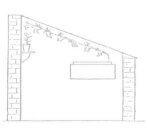

Cross section of a cucumber house.

CUCURBITA

ZUCCHINI

or COURGETTE, MARROW

Cucurbita pepo HAS BEEN CULTIVATED for centuries, and traces have been found in Mexico dating back to 8750 BCE. Traces as old as 4000 BCE have been discovered in Missouri and as far back as 1400 BCE in Mississippi. It is perhaps their undemanding nature that has helped them survive for so long, as Vilmorin-Andrieux noted, "[They] will grow anywhere if supplied with plenty of manure and moisture at the root." Be warned, however, that zucchini will expand to become what the British call "marrows," if left to grow (they can be stuffed and baked), and may split open.

C. pepo
'BLACK BEAUTY'
or 'Black Milan'

CULTIVATED BY 1927

A type with dark green vegetables of superior quality and a compact bush. It has the advantage of an open habit that makes harvesting the vegetables much easier. Produces large crops over a long period.

C. pepo
'COUCOURZELLE'

CULTIVATED BY 1826

In *Le Bon Jardinier Pour L'Année*, 1826, M. Poiteau notes that this variety was, "Sent from Italy to the Duke of Orleans, in 1820 … forms a dwarf bush, with short, reclining stems, and upright leaves, which are deeply lobed. The vegetables are used when the flowers are about to drop from their ends. They are 4 to 5 inches (10–12cm) long and 1½ to 2 inches (3.8–5cm) round. Pale yellow, heavily striped with

green. Bears abundantly, and being a bush may be grown closer than the true Marrow."

C. pepo
'LONG GREEN TRAILING'

CULTIVATED BY 1879

As its name suggests, this vigorous zucchini variety is only for those growers for whom space is not an issue. The vegetable is green or light green, attractively striped with a darker hue.

C. pepo
'LONG WHITE BUSH'
or 'Blanche non Coureuse'

CULTIVATED BY 1883

Like most zucchini, this productive, light green variety will expand to an impressive size if left to grow. "At the risk of seeming boastful I must note that here at Mr. Etty and Company our chief clerk grew a fine specimen of this variety, measuring some 27 inches (68.5cm), which won first prize at the Horton Village Largest Marrow Competition in August 2011!"

A selection of squashes.

C. pepo
'TONDO CHIARO DI NIZZA'
or 'De Nice à Fruit Rond,' 'Ronde de Nice'

CULTIVATED BY 1903

Of this variety from the South of France a contemporary source noted, "Trailing vigorous plant with a peculiarly spherical vegetable of light green. Pick when tennis ball size and before the skin begins to darken in color."

C. moschata
'TROMBONCHINO'

CULTIVATED BY 1800S

A very interesting trailing or climbing variety, with long and thin vegetable that curves at the end into a bell shape, reminiscent of a trombone. With a good flavor, it is treated as a zucchini when picked small, or stored like a squash if allowed to ripen fully. A decorative as well as a useful plant.

C. pepo
'VERTE PETITE D'ALGERS'
or 'Gray Zucchini,' 'Grise de Algiers'

CULTIVATION DATE UNKNOWN

An early-maturing variety, originally from Algiers, much appreciated by connoisseurs. The slightly bulbous vegetables are light green with pale gray mottling. Very productive.

LOST, RARE, OR SIMPLY FORGOTTEN?

Slow Food USA is part of the global Slow Food movement (see www.slowfoodusa.org). As part of their fight to save biodiversity in all things food-related, they produce the *Ark of Taste*, which they describe as "a living catalog of delicious and distinctive foods facing extinction. By identifying and championing these foods we keep them in production and on our plates." The Boston Marrow squash, the Hidatsa Red bean, and Roy's Calais corn are just a few of the vegetable cultivars with strong cultural or regional connections that appear on the list and, sadly, are currently endangered in the United States. Likewise, the global *Ark of Taste* extends to food products from all over the world, be they fruits, vegetables, cheeses, fish, or rare breeds of animals. The only way to keep these precious foods alive and well is to grow, nurture, and eat them. Take up your trowel without delay!

Fern trowel (above) and garden trowel (below).

CUCURBITA

PUMPKIN & SQUASH

THE SPECIES AND VARIETIES OF THESE GOURDS are very numerous. They are tender or half-hardy annuals, native to the warmer parts of both hemispheres, and particularly India. They are, however, hardier than their allied genera, the cultivated cucumber and melon, and succeed very well in the open ground in ordinary warm summers in temperate climates. The varieties cross with each other very readily, so that it is difficult to keep any one distinct if other kinds are growing in the neighborhood and flowering at the same time. It is best, therefore, to obtain seed from a reputable seed merchant, to be sure that the desired variety may be expected.

C. maxima
'BUTTERCUP'

CULTIVATED BY 1919

Introduced by Oscar H. Wills & Co. of Bismark, North Dakota. It produces small, medium to early squash and has thick, fine-grain flesh, which is dry, mealy, and excellent in flavor when baked.

C. pepo
'CONNECTICUT FIELD'
or 'Big Tom,' 'Large Yellow,' 'Yankee Cow Pumpkin'

CULTIVATED BY 1700

Mr. Thomas Bridgeman mentions it in his *Young Gardener's Assistant* of 1847, and it is also listed in Mr. J. B. Russell's catalog of 1827, Boston, Massachusetts. "A big, yellow pumpkin, often producing vegetables weighing 25 pounds (11kg) or more. It is grown extensively and may be used for pies, canning, or stock feeding." Lindenberg's Seed Catalogue, Canada, 1950.

C. pepo
'DELICATA'
or 'Sweet Potato'

CULTIVATED BY 1894

Stores for up to a year. "A squash with small medium late vegetables suitable for baking in the half shell. In comparison to Table Queen or Acorn, Delicata is larger, smoother, sweet, and has moister, less stringy flesh when baked. Long narrow vegetables are orange-yellow striped with dark green. Considered by many to be the choicest baking Squash on the market. Maturity is too late for districts with a real short season." McFayden's Seed Catalogue, Canada, 1937.

C. pepo
'EARLY WHITE FLAT CUSTARD'
or 'Custard Marrow,' 'Cymling,' 'Patisson Panache,' 'White Scallop Squash'

CULTIVATED BY 1591

This pattypan type is one of the most popular of the early squash with white skin. They have a disk shape and scalloped edges and should be picked when small. Thomas Jefferson noted in 1803 that he was growing this, under the name Cymling.

C. maxima
'GOLDEN HUBBARD'

CULTIVATED BY 1896.

Introduced by Mr. Harrison of Painesville, Ohio, who described it thus: "A new and valuable sport of Hubbard. It has the shape and virtues of its parent, but is earlier and more productive. The color of the skin is deep yellow or orange red. Flesh richer in color than Hubbard, and of equal quality."

C. maxima
'GREEN HUBBARD'

CULTIVATED BY 1798

First mentioned by Mr. James J. F. Gregory in *Magazine of Horticulture*, December 23, 1857. "Of the origin of the Hubbard Squash we have no certain knowledge. The facts relative to its cultivation in Marblehead, Massachusetts, are simply these.

Upward of 20 years ago, a single specimen was brought into town, the seed from which was planted in the garden of a lady now deceased; specimen from this yield was given to Captain Knott Martin, of this town, who raised it for family use for a few years when it was brought to our notice in the year 1842, or '43.

We were first informed of its good qualities by Mrs. Elizabeth Hubbard, a very worthy lady, through whom we obtained seed from Captain Martin. As the squash, up to this time, had no specific name to designate it from other varieties my father termed it Hubbard Squash."

In a subsequent publication, Mr. Gregory states that "the first specimen was brought to Marblehead in 1798, from Boston, by a market man named Green."

There are numerous heirloom squashes bearing the name Hubbard, including the splendid Hubbard Green Warty.

C. argyrosperma
'GREEN STRIPED CUSHAW'

CULTIVATED BY 1820

A classic pear-shaped pumpkin grown in Europe since the 1820s. Pumpkins are creamy white, marked with green lines. Because it is recommended for warm areas, it is best grown in a greenhouse or tunnel in cool climes.

C. maxima
'MAMMOTH'
or 'Large Yellow Gourd,' 'Yellow Potiron'

CULTIVATED BY 1834

The staggering gourds of Maxima can often weigh more than 100 pounds (45kg). "This is the largest-fruited variety known. In a very rich compost, above a large quantity of manure, and under favorable conditions of climate, it grows to an enormous size: fruit weighing 120 pounds (54kg) is by no means

LOST, RARE, OR SIMPLY FORGOTTEN?

From 1827 onward, the squash Canada Crookneck (*Cucubita moschata*) was a common sight in the vegetable gardens of New England. Today, it is now teetering on the verge of extinction and appears on Slow Food USA's Art of Taste list of endangered cultivars. Certainly one wonders why it has become so unpopular when reading this description: "The Canada is unquestionably the best of the Crookneck sorts. Vines are remarkably hardy and prolific, yielding almost a certain crop both North and South. The variety ripens early; the plants suffer but little from the depredations of bugs or worms; and the fruit, with trifling care, may be preserved throughout the year." *The Field and Garden Vegetables of America*, Fearing Burr, 1865.

uncommon. In North America, it has weighed 226 pounds (102.5kg); and at Sutcome in Devonshire (England), one weighing 245 pounds (111kg) was produced. This we believe is the heaviest on record. It is only used in a fully grown or ripe state, in which it will keep for several months and even during the winter if preserved in a dry airy place, where it may be suspended in a strong net." *The Gardener's Assistant*, 1857.

C. maxima

'ROUGE VIF D'ETAMPES'
or 'Cinderella'

CULTIVATED BY 1830

This is a French variety, in which country it has been grown since the early 1830s. If there were a model for the legendary Cinderella's coach this would surely be it. This variety was introduced into North America in 1883, by Mr. Atlee Burpee.

C. pepo

'SMALL SUGAR'
or 'New England Pie,' 'Sugar Pie'

CULTIVATED BY 1860

In *Field and Garden Vegetables of America*, 1863, Fearing Burr noted, "The variety is the smallest of the sorts usually employed for field cultivation. It is however a most abundant bearer, rarely fails in maturing its crops perfectly, is of first rate quality, and may be justly styled an acquisition."

C. maxima

'TURK'S TURBAN'
or 'American Turban,'
'Turk's Cap'

CULTIVATED BY 1817

A squash so aptly named, because it resembles nothing more than this. French records suggest it has been grown since the early nineteenth century, and probably before. Fine eating (the flesh is moister than most squashes) despite this somewhat off-handed description by Mr. Thompson in *The Gardener's Assistant*, 1859: "Fruit middle-size, flat, with a

Turk's Turban squash.

rounded margin, and elevated center, which is deep green, the rest is yellow or pale cream. Flesh firm. This variety is chiefly grown for ornamentation in this country."

C. moschata

'WALTHAM BUTTERNUT'

CULTIVATED BY 1944

Raised by Dr. C. E. Young at the Waltham Experimental Station in Massachusetts. High yielding, it has a uniform shape and yellow-orange flesh with a nutty flavor.

A SELECTION OF TOOLS TO BE FOUND OF USE IN EVERY GARDEN

THE HUMBLE SPADE

"Of all garden implements, the spade is universally admitted to be the most generally useful. With it alone the roughest soil may be gradually brought to a fine tilth and a state of fertility. Although long-handle straight spades are used in some countries, there is no better and no more efficient spade in existence than the neat short-handle variety, with a D-shape top, such as is generally used in English gardens."

The Gardener's Assistant, 1859.

KEY

A: Spade
B: Shovel
C: Mattock
D: Grubbing Ax
E: Pitchfork
F: Drag
G: Garden Trowel
H: Verge Cutter
I: Hand Fork
J: Daisy Rake
K: Dibble
L: Turfing Iron
M: Trenching Fork
N: Digging Fork
O: Manure Fork
P: Draw Hoe
Q: Dutch Hoe
R: Rammer

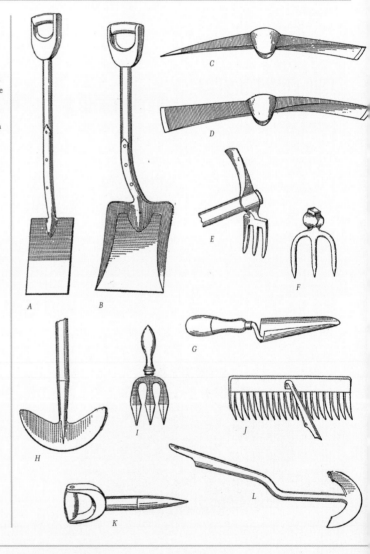

A SELECTION OF USEFUL TOOLS

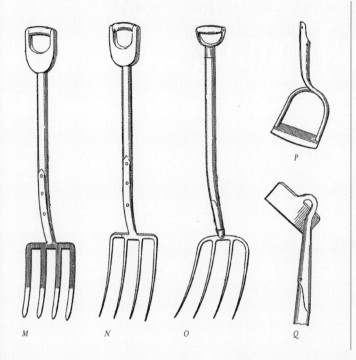

M   N   O   P   Q

HOE KNOW-HOW

"Hoes are used for drawing furrows or drills, stirring the soil, piling up soil, etc. Draw hoes have the blade attached to a socket by a solid neck, more or less curved. The blade should be made of steel, welded on an iron neck. The length of the plate for the largest need not exceed 9 inches (23cm); hoes for onions etc., are required as small as 2 inches (5cm). A very useful crane-neck hoe is in use in the midland counties, with movable steel plates 5 to 7 inches (12–18cm) long. The Dutch or thrust hoes are useful for cutting down weeds, and for shallow work on an even surface; but they are not so good as the draw hoe when the ground is stiff and lumpy. The Dutch hoe can be used to a considerable extent without going out of the alleys, so that the ground is not trodden as it is in using the draw hoe. For light work, and in flower gardens, these hoes are most useful."

The Gardener's Assistant, 1859.

THE USEFUL RAMMER

"The rammer is useful for firming the soil about posts, tree-guards etc., and for consolidating sod and gravel. It is generally made of wood, in the form of a half cone, attached to an upright stem."

The Gardener's Assistant, 1859.

R

EXTENSION LADDER

"Various kinds of ladders are useful in gardens and orchards. For wall-trained trees, a stepladder, with boards for steps, is far preferable to one with rounds. In the glasshouse, a set of small folding steps is useful. Extension ladders, as shown here, are useful for work requiring a self-supporting ladder."

The Gardener's Assistant, 1859.

CYNARA

CARDOON

CLOSELY RELATED TO THE GLOBE ARTICHOKE, cardoons are grown for their blanched leaf stems, which can be eaten like celery, or used to flavor soups and stews. The English naturalist John Tradescant wrote to the Royal Apothecary John Parkinson that he "saw 3 acres of land about Brussels, planted with this kind which the owner whited, like endive, and then sold them in the winter." Later in 1830 a correspondent to *The Gardener's Magazine* wrote the following: "The Cardoon (*Cynara cardunculus*) is much cultivated in Kitchen Gardens in Montpellier, and in Provence (France); the blanched foot stalks of the leaves being boiled, and used at table. The dried florets of this plant have the property of coagulating milk and are sold for that purpose at Montpellier."

C. cardunculus
'PLEIN BLANC PUVIS'
or 'Artichole-Leaved'

CULTIVATED BY 1750

In the nineteenth century, this was praised thus: "The Puvis Cardoon is remarkable for its strong growth, the large size it attains, and the thickness of its ribs, which are almost solid. The leaves are thick, not prickly, or only very slightly so. It is a fine variety."

C. cardunculus
'PLEIN BLANC INERME'
or 'Smooth Solid Cardoon'

CULTIVATED BY 1750

This variety is favored for its spineless leaves, which are far less prickly than others. It can reach the dizzying height of 5 feet (1.5m) and is often seen in the ornamental garden as well as the potager.

The cardoon is a thirsty vegetable and must be watered in dry spells.

A garden syringe.

CYNARA

GLOBE ARTICHOKE

THE GLOBE ARTICHOKE is a hardy perennial, native to southern Europe, and was known to both the ancient Greeks and the Romans. It is generally agreed that it was introduced to the British Isles from Italy in 1548. One wonders who first thought of eating this strange, thistlelike vegetable, because its edible parts consist of the fleshy base of the leaf bracts and the fleshy receptacle at the base of the young flower head. The tender central stems can also be eaten like the cardoon, but they must be blanched first. Artichoke heads can also be pickled.

C. cardunculus Scolymus group
'GREEN GLOBE'

CULTIVATED BY 1791

In North America, this variety was available from about 1829 in the seed catalog of Mr. Thorburn. It was still popular in the 1920s, as this excerpt from the *The Gardener's Assistant* shows: "The best undoubtedly is Green Globe, which has incurved scales. It is generally grown for the French and London markets, being prolific and of excellent quality, but it is the least hardy of all."

C. cardunculus Scolymus group
'GROS VERT DE LÂON'
or 'Large Green Paris,' 'Tête de Chat'

CULTIVATED BY 1771

This traditional French globe artichoke is not an early variety but is the best for its very reliable yields of large and fat heads every year. Although less hardy than other types, it is considered to have the best flavor. As with all globe artichokes, plant in full sun in well-drained soil and stake if exposed to excessive winds.

C. cardunculus Scolymus group
'PURPLE GLOBE'
or 'Purple Italian'

CULTIVATED BY 1835

Generally considered to be hardier than Green Globe, it is of medium size and fair quality. "Has a very rich purple color with large round heads without thorns and excellent taste. The best variety for Northern regions." *The British Cyclopedia of Natural History,* C. F. Partington, 1835–37.

DAUCUS

CARROT

THIS HARDY ESCULENT-ROOTED BIENNIAL was introduced, in the cultivated form, from Holland during the sixteenth century. The now familiar orange carrot is, in fact, not the true and original color of the carrot. Before the seventeenth century, carrots were available in purple, white, and yellow; the modern deep orange varieties, which were selected by Dutch market gardeners, are actually a mutation of the purple form.

D. carota

'AUTUMN KING'

or 'Flakkee Long Red Giant,' 'Norfolk Giant,' 'Vita Longa'

CULTIVATED BY 1900

This handsome main-season variety is a long and cylindrical, heavy, stump-end carrot, with rich, deep orange flesh. Of excellent quality, it is ideally suited to soil that is not deep enough to grow the longest types.

D. carota

'BLANCE DE KUTTINGEN'

CULTIVATION DATE UNKNOWN

This is a Swiss heirloom carrot with conical white roots that are often green at the shoulder. The shape is similar to that of Chantenay. It is long keeping and flavorful.

D. carota

'CHANTENAY RED CORED'

CULTIVATED BY 1829

An old seed catalog describes this carrot thus: "The tops are short and the foliage finely cut. The tops are not brittle and are strong enough to bunch easily. Roots are refined in appearance with small collars, evenly stumped with very small tails. The root surface is smooth and free from large eyes and side rootlets. Exterior color a rich orange." This is a fine French variety that was introduced into the United States in 1929 by the Burpee Company.

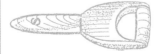

A dibble.

D. carota

'EARLY HORN'

or 'Early Scarlet Horn'

CULTIVATED BY 1610

In *Field and Garden Vegetables of America*, 1865, Mr. Fearing Burr Jr. wrote, "Root 6 inches (15cm) in length, 2½ inches (6cm) in diameter, nearly cylindrical and tapering abruptly to a very slender taproot. Skin orange-red but green or brown where it comes to the surface of the ground. Flesh deep orange-yellow, fine grained, and of superior flavor and delicacy. The crown of the root is hollow and the foliage short and small … as a table carrot, much esteemed, both on account of the smallness of its heart and the tenderness of it fiber." This is a rare cultivar of great age, having been noted before 1610. It is time perhaps to dispel the notion that the variety name is derived from the shape of this carrot. My own research has, in fact, revealed that the variety arose in the vicinity of the Dutch town of Hoorn, and it is to this that it owes its name.

D. carota
'EARLY NANTES'
or 'Scarlet Nantes'

CULTIVATED BY 1867

In his dissertation entitled "The Carrots," published in *The Garden Magazine*, May 1, 1887, Mr. Guiheneuf wrote the following: "This is a recent French introduction. The root is deep red in color, 4½ inches (11.5cm) long, from 1½ to 2 inches (3.8–5cm) thick, and bluntly cylindrical in form: the top is greenish in color with a hollow crown. The leaves are of medium size; the flesh is very superior in flavor and quality, the heart being far less developed and much more tender than in other varieties, and both for sauces and stews it is a most desirable kind."

D. carota
'JAUNE OBTUSE DU DOUBS'
or 'Yellow Intermediate'

CULTIVATED BY 1851

A contemporary account reads thus: "A variety well suited for feeding livestock, but also an excellent kitchen vegetable, popular in France. It combines a sweet flavor with good winter storage."

D. carota
'PARIS MARKET'

CULTIVATED BY 1875

This short, almost round carrot is one of the very earliest, making it a favorite among market gardeners. It is sweet, tender, and excellent for forcing. An old French variety, it has long been popular in Europe and is now gaining favor in North America. Due to its small size, it is useful for container growing.

D. carota
'ROUGE SANG'
or 'Violette'

CULTIVATED BY 1897

Dark green foliage, with squat and conical roots and an interesting and unusual red and violet skin. A real "rustic carrot" from France, it is well suited to growing in difficult conditions.

D. carota
'TOUCHON IDEAL RED'

CULTIVATED BY 1900

Another fine French carrot that was traditionally popular with home and commercial growers. It is quick growing (to about 8 inches/20cm), sweet, tender, and crisp; it also stores well.

D. carota
'WHITE BELGIUM'
or 'Green-Topped White'

CULTIVATED BY 1600S

An old Dutch type, this carrot is not a particularly hardy variety, because, we are told, it becomes "disorganized by the slightest frost." Originally derived from the old Long White, which had been in commerce from the 1600s, it was previously considered to be only of use as a forage carrot. Its mildness of flavor and unusual color has, however, led it to be considered more than fit for use "at table."

White Belgium carrot.

ERUCA

ARUGULA

or ROCKET, RUCOLA, RUGOLA, ROQUETTE

IN 1978 THE COOKERY WRITER Jane Grigson wrote the following in her wonderful *Vegetable Book*: "Arugula as an unremarkable item of salads is now eaten only in Mediterranean countries, John Evelyn grew it once in his kitchen garden, along with corn salad, clary, purslane, and all the other greens we have sadly allowed to disappear from our salad bowls." How times change! Arugula is now almost as ubiquitous as lettuce on many menus.

E. sativa
'SALAD'

CULTIVATION DATE UNKNOWN

Stephen Switzer wrote in *Practical Kitchen Gardiner* of 1727 (when printers were wont to sometimes print the letter *s* as if an *f*, in imitation of an elegant hand): "The Eruca, was held in fo great efteem heretofore, as to its efficacy in conjugal performances, that many of the ancient authors both in poetry and profe, make mention of it purely for that purpose."

B. orientalis
'TURKISH'

CULTIVATED BY 1762

Vilmorin-Andrieux wrote of this cultivated form: "The young leaves and shoots are eaten either boiled or as a salad ... It commences to grow very early in spring, when other fresh green vegetables are exceedingly scarce, and it resists both cold weather and drought remarkably well."

Water arugula plants frequently to prevent the flavor from becoming too peppery.

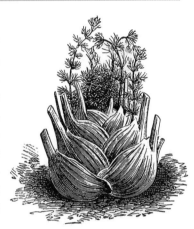

FLORENCE FENNEL

or FINOCCHIO, VEGETABLE FENNEL

A simple contrivance for striking cuttings.

D. tenuifolia
WILD ARUGULA

CULTIVATION DATE UNKNOWN

Wild arugula belongs to *Diplotaxis*, a different genus to the cultivated kinds, and it has a more pungent taste. Because they are of different genera, the wild and cultivated types above can be grown alongside each other without fear of hybridization. The wall arugula, *D. muralis*, is sometimes also used. In *Flora Londinensis*, 1777, William Curtis wrote: "[Wild arugula] grows very plentifully in and around London and is, I believe in general growth in moft of the old walls and Castles throughout England. With us it particularly grows on the walls around the Tower at the back of Bedlam and Near Hyde Park."

THIS DELICIOUS VEGETABLE was noted in *The Gardener's Assistant,* 1936, as being "a perennial, native of South Europe" and that the Florence type was known as common, sweet, or finocchio fennel. Its history is long; both the ancient Greeks and Romans used it not only as food but also for medicinal purposes and as an insect repellent.

F. vulgare var. dulce
'SWEET FLORENCE'

CULTIVATED BY 1677

An unknown writer made these fulsome culinary notes: "A distinct

A bottle trap for wasps.

dwarf, very thick set herb. The large, finely cut, light green leaves are borne on very broad, pale green or almost whitish stems, which overlap at their bases, somewhat like celery, but much more swelled at edible maturity, to form a kind of head or irregular ball, 'the apple,' as it is called, sometimes as large as a man's fist. Usually boiled and served with butter or cream dressing. It suggests Celery in flavor, but is sweeter and even more pleasingly fragrant. A native of Italy."

LACTUCA

LETTUCE

"NATIVE OF INDIA OR CENTRAL ASIA. Annual. The origin of the cultivated Lettuce is not known for certain, any more than the time when it was first introduced into Europe; neither can we be sure that the ancients knew anything about it. However, the great number of varieties of it which now exist in cultivation, and the very permanent manner in which some of these varieties appear to be established, afford good grounds for the opinion that the plant has been cultivated for a very long time." *The Vegetable Garden,* Vilmorin-Andrieux, 1885.

L. sativa
'ALL THE YEAR ROUND'
or 'Black Seeded Tennis Ball,' 'Blonde de Berlin'

CULTIVATED BY 1825

"Popular for home and market garden. Heads are large, handsome, and very solid, with broad, pale green leaves. Inner leaves beautifully blanched and of delicious quality, crisp, and of the buttery character so much liked." *Manuel Complet du Jardinier,* Louis-Claude Noisette, 1825.

L. sativa
'BALLOON'

CULTIVATED BY 1882

First noted by Vilmorin-Andrieux, this romaine-type lettuce has large outer leaves that surround the heart to give the balloon-like appearance reflected in the name.

L. sativa
'BLACK-SEEDED SIMPSON'

CULTIVATED BY 1850

This lettuce may date back as early as 1813, but it arrived in the United States somewhat later. It was noted as being "new" in the *American Agriculturalist* as late as 1880: "Splendid loose leaf or curled leaf lettuce of great popularity with market and home gardeners. Grows large leaves, the inner ones forming a semi-compact head, very tender, crisp, fine quality, and sweet flavor. Reliable and easily grown."

L. sativa
'BLONDE DE PARIS'
or 'Batavia Blonde,' 'Iceburg,' 'White Silesian'

CULTIVATED BY 1751

It should be noted that this is not the inferior Iceburg now seen so often for sale, but a much older variety that is associated with the same name. It was described in glowing terms in the Burpee catalog of 1894: "There is no handsomer or more solid Lettuce in cultivation, it is strikingly beautiful. The unusual solidity of the heads is ensured by the large, white ribs of the leaves, each of which, curving strongly into the center, acts like a truss, making it impossible for the leaves to open outward and expose the center, which is thoroughly blanched.

Verte Maraichere lettuce (see page 80).

It matters not whether in the early spring or the hottest days of summer, the quality is simply perfect."

L. sativa

'BRUNE D'HIVER'

CULTIVATED BY 1855

A French butterhead type, suitable for fall sowing. The attractively buckled green leaves are flushed with red and the color intensifies the more sun the plant is exposed to. Hardy, compact, and of excellent quality.

L. sativa

'DRUNKEN WOMAN'

or 'Frizzy Head,' 'Ubriacona Frastagliata'

CULTIVATION DATE UNKNOWN

This is a large bicolor lettuce with red and green leaves. Even without its excellent flavor and resistance to bolting, it would be worth growing for its name alone (see panel, right).

L. sativa

'FAT LAZY BLONDE'

or 'Grosse Blonde Paresseuse'

CULTIVATED BY 1856

"A fine Lettuce, large-size and productive. It grows well and keeps the head perfectly in hot weather. Plants 7 to 9 inches (18–23cm) in diameter." *Description des Plantes Potageres*, Vilmorin-Andrieux, 1855 (see panel, right).

L. sativa

'FRISÉE DE BEAUREGARD'

or 'Reine de Glaces'

CULTIVATED BY 1883

A black-seed lettuce, the leaves are dark green, wavy, and indented. It is crisp with a tight heart.

L. sativa

'LITTLE GEM'

or 'Sucrine'

CULTIVATED BY 1880

Of this romaine-type of lettuce, *The Gardener's Assistant* in 1936 wrote, "Dwarf and compact in growth and a beautiful color." A lettuce of good quality and reliability.

WHAT'S IN A NAME?

The name of the French heirloom lettuce Fat Lazy Blonde (or Grosse Blonde Paresseuse) is actually a descriptive term rather than one of judgment. "Fat" because it is indeed large, "lazy" because it is slow to bolt, and blonde alluding to the light green color of its center. The soubriquet Drunken Woman (a.k.a. Frizzy Head and Ubriacona Frastagliata) may also be descriptive to some extent because this lettuce has frizzy leaves streaked with red, a possible reference to the wayward hair and high color of an inebriated woman.

L. sativa

'LOBJOIT'S GREEN COS'

CULTIVATED BY 1856

W. J. Lobjoit was a former head gardener to the Rothchild family and, in 1828, founded a firm of market gardeners in Hammersmith, London. This is one of their introductions: "Heads in the form of an inverted cone; green, with a grayish tone about the top; compact, and forming well without tying. Exterior numerous, deep green, erect, firm, and prominently blistered."

Marvel of the Four Seasons lettuce.

L. sativa

'WHEELER'S TOM THUMB'

or 'Commodore Nutt,' 'Stone Tennis Ball'

CULTIVATED BY 1830

This was probably bred and introduced by Wheeler's of Warmister, Wiltshire, England. It was then introduced into North America in 1868 by Mr. Gregory of Marblehead, Massachusetts. It is small, compact, and delicious.

L. sativa

'MARVEL OF THE FOUR SEASONS'

or 'Red Besson'

CULTIVATED BY 1880

"A markedly dark, reddish brown variety. One of the darkest colored varieties within the group of butterhead lettuce … Plants are large and spreading. Rather large head, which is firm and closes well. Heart leaves light green with only light tingeing." *Varieties of Lettuce*, H. Basse, 1960.

L. sativa

'TROCADERO'

or 'Big Boston,' 'Lorthois'

CULTIVATED BY 1882

An attractive French lettuce, the outer leaves are tinged with russet. In 1890 Mr. Henderson introduced this variety into the United States, renaming it Big Boston.

L. sativa

'VERTE MARAICHERE'

or 'Buckland,' 'Green Paris Cos'

CULTIVATED BY 1850

On May 18, 1878, *The Garden* magazine described this romaine, or cos, type thus: "A leading white-seed variety, much hardier than the White Cos which it resembles. Its outer leaves are large, erect, dark green, and hooded at the margin, forming a fine plant that hearts and blanches without trying. This variety grows a little larger than the White Cos, and the heart is crisp and tender." It may date back to 1786.

L. sativa

'WEBBS WONDERFUL'

or 'New York Iceburg'

CULTIVATED BY 1856

This variety was raised and distributed by Messrs. Webbs of Wordsley, Staffordshire, England, who described it as having an interior "beautifully blanched, creamy white, crisp, tender, and delicious."

L. sativa

'WHITE PARIS COS'

CULTIVATED BY THE 1700S

"This is unquestionably the finest Cos lettuce that can be grown for summer use. Though tall, the outer leaves are hooded so as to close at the top and blanch the heart without being tied." *The Gardeners' Chronicle*, February, 13, 1841. This was introduced into the United States in 1802 by Mr. McMahon as White Cos.

L. sativa

'WINTER DENSITY'

CULTIVATED BY 1909

This was first offered by Messrs. Toogood of Southampton, England, who described it as having "glossy dark green leaves, hardy, very delicious. Lovely firm, semi-cos hearts. Slow to bolt."

LOTUS

ASPARAGUS PEA

NOW PRIZED FOR ITS NUTTY, asparagus-like flavor, the pods seem not to have been quite so valued in the nineteenth century, as this excerpt from *Gardener's and Botanist's Dictionary*, Philip Miller, published in 1807 by Thomas Martyn, shows: "It was formerly cultivated as an esculent plant, for the green pods, which are said to be still eaten in some parts of our Northern counties, but they are very coarse. This plant is now chiefly cultivated in flower gardens for ornament. It is a native of Sicily, where Ray found it in the hills above Messina; and was cultivated in 1596 by Gerard. Parkinson calls it Crimson-blossomed or square-codded pease. In Johnson's edition of *Gerard's Herbal,* it is named Square crimson-velvet Pease. Ray called it Square Codded Vetch. None of its authors speak of the pod's being esculent." Sow in open ground in mid- to late spring. The dried seeds may also be used as a coffee substitute.

L. tetragonolobus
'ASPARAGUS PEA'

CULTIVATED BY 1596

The unusual and attractive, cinnamon red, pealike flowers make it an interesting addition to the flower garden as well as the kitchen garden. "A curious pea-like vegetable with a decorative habit of growth, reddish brown flowers and rectangular pods, which should be gathered when an inch long and cooked whole." *The Compleat Seedsman's Monthly Calendar,* 1738.

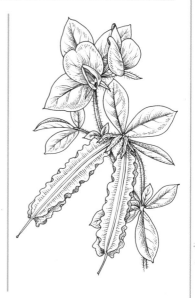

TYPES OF LETTUCE
The cabbage type of lettuce (shown in the lower picture) is more suited to late-winter and fall sowings than the romaine (cos) type (shown top). It is traditional to loosely tie romaine lettuce before it reaches maturity so that the heart can develop wihin.

PASTINACA

PARSNIP

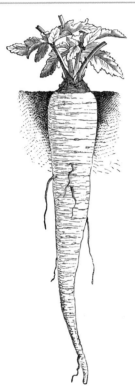

THE PARSNIP IS NATIVE to the British Isles as well as occurring throughout the rest of Europe and the Caucasus. It has been cultivated since Roman times, although the fleshy rooted varieties do not appear to have been developed until the Middle Ages.

P. sativa
'HARRIS MODEL'
or 'Harris Early Model'

CULTIVATION DATE UNKNOWN

This North American variety may date back to the 1940s. With a very white smooth skin, a sweet and nutty taste, and fine flesh, this parsnip is understandably a long-time favorite with growers.

P. sativa
'HOLLOW CROWN'
or 'Long Jersey'

CULTIVATED BY 1803

Described in Mr. Sutton's seed catalog of 1857 as "a good sort," Hollow Crown is an "improved" variety that arose from reselection of the original and was offered for sale in the late nineteenth century. "In this variety the leaves are shorter and not so numerous as those of the common Parsnep. The leaves are oblong. About 18 inches

A parsnip fork.

(45cm) long, more swollen at the top and not tapering gradually, but ending somewhat abruptly with a small taproot, which is about 4 inches (10cm) in diameter and at the shoulder; the crown is short and quite sunk into the shoulder, so as to form a hollow ring around the insertion of the foot stalks, and grows mostly below the surface of the soil." Mr. Mathews, *Transactions of the RHS*, December 6, 1825.

P. sativa
'THE STUDENT'

CULTIVATED BY 1861

"Our ennobled examples of these were considered so perfect that it was thought advisable to consign the whole of the seed of 1859 to Messrs. Sutton of Reading (England), as new varieties of any cultivated crop plant are always desirable, and more especially when, as in the present case, the new form has been directly derived, not from original wild stock." Annual Report, Royal Horticultural College, Cirencester, England, 1861.

P. sativa
'ALL AMERICAN'

CULTIVATION DATE UNKNOWN

This is a tender parsnip with white flesh and a mild, sweet, and nutty flavor. Growing to 10 to 12 inches (25–30cm) and 2 to 3 inches (5–7.5cm) wide, it is hardy and stores well. Harvest it in early fall when the taste is especially sweet.

PHASEOLUS

GREEN BEAN

or BUSH BEAN, FIELD BEAN, FLAGEOLET BEAN, FRENCH BEAN, HARICOT BEAN, KIDNEY BEAN, POLE BEAN, STRING BEAN

THE CLIMBING BEAN forms one of the components of the fabled Three Sisters: squash, corn, and bean interplanted together in a mutually beneficial system. The corn acts as a support for the bean, the bean fixes nitrogen into the soil, while the squash provides shade and mulch. This harmonious and sustainable method was developed by the Native American Iroquois people.

P. vulgaris
'BLUE LAKE WHITE SEEDED'

CULTIVATED BY 1885

Although listed by 1885, this is most certainly a much older bean, said to have originated with Native Americans. It is a high-yielding climbing bean that matures early with stringless green pods.

A Dutch hoe.

P. vulgaris
'BORLOTTO LINGUA DI FUOCO'
or 'Coco Rouge de Prague'

CULTIVATED BY 1805

A beautiful bean, with pods white-flushed and dappled with red, its Italian name translates as "tongue of fire." When young, it can be eaten raw or cooked, or shelled and dried as it matures. A climbing type, "Tall, late, but very productive in fine falls. Pods tender; seeds round, purplish red with variegations. Thick-skinned, mealy, and of good flavor." *The Gardener's Assistant*, 1859.

P. vulgaris
'CANADIAN WONDER'
or 'Red Canada,' 'Rognon de Coq,' 'Rose,' 'Summer's Canadian Wonder'

CULTIVATED BY 1873

The Gardeners' Chronicle of April 17, 1886, noted of this bush kidney bean, "Probably the true credit of introducing this bean is due to the late Mr. James Cutbush, of Highgate (London), who cataloged it for many years, under the name Cutbush's Giant French Bean, but did not appear to make it known beyond his own business circle. It was, in all probability, a fine selection of Red flageolet of the French." Mr. Hedrick, in *The*

Beans of New York, added the following to the debate in 1928: "The history of the Canadian Wonder is uncertain but it is undoubtedly of Canadian origin, some time previous to 1873 when mention is made of it in an English periodical."

P. vulgaris
'DE ROQUENCOURT'

CULTIVATED BY 1948

This bush bean appeared in the *Revue Horticole Journal d'Horticulture Practique* in the 1940s but it is almost certainly earlier: "An old variety with straight 5 to 6-inch (12–15cm) yellow pods; productive; good for regions where summers or night temperatures are cool."

HISTORICAL NOTE

The climbing French bean Cherokee Trail of Tears commemorates the march, the Trail of Tears, that the Cherokee Indians made when they were forcibly removed from their lands. The enforced march over the Smoky Mountains of Oklahoma lasted from October 1838 until the following March. In the harsh winter conditions more than 4,000 Cherokees died. It is believed that they carried seeds of this bean with them on their journey to a new homeland, very much as displaced settlers from all over the world have carried their own heirloom seeds throughout time.

P. vulgaris
'FLAGEOLET CHEVRIER'

CULTIVATED BY 1872

A bush type, "This selection from Green Flageolet originated about 1872 at Bretigny-sur-Orge, near Paris, with Gabriel Chevrier a market gardener whose name it bears. It was commercially distributed in 1880." *The Beans of New York*, U. P. Hedrick.

P. vulgaris
'KENTUCKY WONDER'
or 'Old Homestead,' 'Texas Pole'

CULTIVATED BY 1850S

This is an enduringly popular climbing bean. In 1913 Mr. Wickson wrote in *California Vegetables*: "The best climbing bean for most California situations is the Kentucky Wonder or Old Homestead, which bears a mass of pods when grown to a 6-foot (1.8m) pole …wonderfully prolific, the veins being actually loaded from top to bottom with pods from 6 to 9 inches (15–23cm) in length; as string beans the pods are nearly round, tender, and very solid."

P. vulgaris
'LAZY HOUSEWIFE'
or 'Sophie,' 'White Coco'

CULTIVATED BY 1829

This climbing bean grows in clusters so is easy to pick. It is also entirely stringless, making it easy to prepare, hence its name. This may also have helped to make it the third most popular bean in

the United States in 1907. In his *The Beans of New York*, 1931, U. P. Hedrick wrote the following: "Maule, in 1894 says Lazy Wife originated in Bucks County, Pennsylvania, but was probably brought there by German Settlers. When comparison is possible it corresponds in every way with Martens' 'Sophie,' which he says was noted by Savi in 1882 as San Domingo bean; and Tracy says the variety was known in America as early as 1810 as White Cherry Pole, or White Canterbury Pole. In France the type is known as Coco Blanc." If we hold Mr. Hedrick to be correct, then it should be noted that Messrs. Crombie and Cormack list a Dwarf Canterbury French Bean in their catalog of 1800.

P. vulgaris
'MASTERPIECE'
or 'Glory of St. Andrew,' 'Saint Andreas'

CULTIVATED BY 1907

Before the advent of the refrigerator car, and, therefore, previous to the development of large areas in the south of England for the growing of green produce to ship to northern markets, there was a place for bean varieties suitable for forcing in greenhouses. This bush variety is another of the group that was chiefly used for that purpose. It was originally introduced by the French seed company Vilmorin-Andrieux as Jeaune de Pereux about 1907. In the United Kingdom, Sutton's listed it in 1910 as a novelty under the name Sutton's Masterpiece, "The 1st place for size, form, and flavor … a strong grower, the plants are short-jointed and bear a heavy, long continued crop of fleshy, juicy beans, 8 inches (20cm) long, ¾ inch (2cm) wide, and over ¼ inch (0.6cm) thick; stringless until too old for use. A winner on the exhibition or dining table."

P. vulgaris
'MONT D'OR'
or 'Merveille de Venise'

CULTIVATED BY 1885

Raised near Lyon, in France, this climbing bean is very early, the thick fleshy pods are pale sulfur yellow, stringless, and very tender. It has black seeds.

P. vulgaris
'NUN'S BELLYBUTTON'
or 'Spread Eagle,' 'St. Esprit ou a la Religieuse'

CULTIVATED BY 1856

This bush bean is so named because of the purple marking on the seed at the hilum, which, it is said, resembles an eagle in flight and, to some scallywags, a certain part of a nun's anatomy.

P. vulgaris
'TENDERGREEN'

CULTIVATED BY 1922

A contemporary account of this bush bean praised it thus: "Meaty, smooth, dark green, round, tender pods 6 to 7 inches (15–18cm) long, straight, too slightly curved, and of the most delicious flavor. Absolutely stringless. Pods mature early and are borne profusely. Ideal for canning."

LOST, RARE, OR SIMPLY FORGOTTEN?

The Carr bean has an excellent flavor and has proved reliable in cool regions; unfortunately, it is now rare. It was reintroduced by the American Abundant Life Seed Foundation, who tell the story of its fascinating history. "In 1998 Harry Morgan was 93 and still growing a garden. He has been growing the Carr Bean most of his life, and got it from his mother who got it from the Martin family in about 1900. They brought it to Colorado in the 1880s as they fled religious persecution in southwestern Virginia. It's called Carr Bean after a family in that area. Harry and dozens of other people grew this bean at 8,200 feet (2,500m) of elevation where the nights are cool even in summer and it was one of the few dependable crops they could grow."

Beans growing up a pole tripod.

PHASEOLUS

RUNNER BEAN

or OREGON BEAN, MULTIFLORA BEAN, SCARLET RUNNER BEAN

THE RUNNER BEAN is a native of South America and, like its cousin the bush or green bean, is much more tender than its other (more distant) relative the fava bean. Runner beans were first introduced into Europe in the mid-sixteenth century. It is not widely known nor practiced, but this bean is a perennial with tuberous roots and can, in fact, be dug up and overwintered in frost-free conditions, much as you would with dahlias.

P. coccineus
'CZAR'
or 'The Czar'

CULTIVATED BY 1888

This bean was certainly listed in England by 1901 by Messrs. Thompson and Morgan although it is considered by many to be much older. It has white flowers that are said to be less attractive to birds, who often strip the flowers of other runners from their stalks. It also has white beans.

P. coccineus
'PAINTED LADY'
or 'Yorkshire and Lancashire'

CULTIVATED BY 1633

A mysterious lady indeed. In 1887 a correspondent to *The Gardeners' Chronicle* wrote: "In 1817 the Painted Lady Runners do not appear to have existed. It is known also as York and Lancaster, because its blossoms are scarlet and white, blending in one the colors of the opposing roses [the rival Houses of York and Lancaster who waged the Wars of the Roses 1455–87]. How did the Painted Lady originate? It is generally regarded as a sport from the Scarlet Runner; but it has also been claimed as a true species."

Fast into the fray comes milady's champion in the form of the *Royal Horticultural Society's Dictionary of Plants* 1956, which describes four varieties of runner beans introduced in 1633. The Painted Lady with red and white flowers was one of these. It is my contention that the gracious lady who was cataloged by Carter's in 1847 is actually hiding her true age of more than 350 years.

P. coccineus
'SCARLET EMPEROR'

CULTIVATED BY 1633

In their *Vegetable Growers Guide*, 1908, Messrs. John and Horace Wright state that "Carter's Scarlet Emperor is a selection from the old Scarlet Runner," a fact verified by Mr. Hedrick in *The Beans of New York*, 1931, who calls the variety a synonym of Scarlet Runner. If this is the case, then Scarlet Emperor (or Scarlet Runner) shares the same date of introduction as Painted Lady, 1633. Either way it was formerly known as Mammoth Exhibition and renamed in 1906.

PISUM

PEA

PEAS WERE CULTIVATED for their edible seeds more than two thousand years ago. Their botanical name, Pisum, is derived from Pisa, a town in northern Italy once famous for its peas. The origin of the pea is unknown, beyond that it is probably Asiatic, and that it was certainly introduced into Europe in about 1548. The end of the eighteenth century was an important era in the evolution of the garden pea. In 1787 Mr. Thomas Andrew Knight, President of the London Horticultural Society (later the Royal Horticultural Society), made some experiments in crossing different forms of pea, including "a white pea," which possessed the remarkable property of "shriveling excessively when ripe." Of his experiments he wrote in 1817, "The Pea which I have always planted for fall crops is a very large kind, of which the seeds are much shriveled and which grows very high; it is now very common in the shops of London, and my name has, I believe, been generally attached to it. I prefer this variety because it is more saccharine than any other, and retains its flavor late into fall."

P. sativum
'ALDERMAN'
or 'Admiral Dewey'

CULTIVATED BY 1891

This main-season pea is thought to be a selection from Duke of Albany. Laxton Brothers catalog describes it as: "Late, large podded variety, 5 feet (1.5m) tall. Producing dark green, long, well-formed pods. Peas are large, sweet, and of an exceptional quality. A home garden variety that will not stand up under an intense period of drought."

P. sativum
'CARLIN'
or 'Black Badger,' 'Marlin'

CULTIVATION DATE UNKNOWN

A carlin is a dried pea with a soft nutty brown color, also called a pigeon pea. Carlin is taken from the German *Karr*, meaning "atonement." In the northeast of England, the tradition of eating them dates back to the mid-seventeenth century (they may originally have been washed ashore from a shipwreck). It used to be the custom to eat them on the fifth Sunday of Lent. The bloom is a striking purple color, reminiscent of a sweet pea instead of the traditional white pea flower.

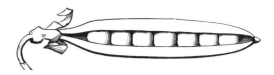

P. sativum
'CAROUBY DE MAUSSANE'

CULTIVATED BY 1891

A sugar snap pea with large pods up to 4 inches (10cm) long. It has an excellent taste and grows tall with attractive purple flowers.

P. sativum
'DAISY'
or 'Small Telephone'

CULTIVATED BY 1892

A second early pea introduced by the English seed company Carter's. It grows to about 2 feet (60cm) high. The large and straight pods are usually in pairs, containing five to nine seeds, which are large,

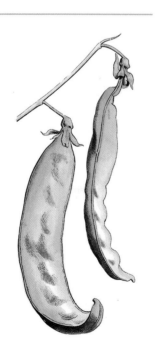

compressed, wrinkled, and of fine quality and flavor. In 1947 Pike's of Edmonton, Alberta, Canada, described it in their catalog as, "The most famous dwarf second early marrowfat."

P. sativum
'KELVEDON WONDER'

CULTIVATED BY 1938

A first early pea that can be sown in fall or spring. It was introduced by Hurst & Sons of Kelvedon, Essex, England, who described it as: "An early wrinkle seeded pea that has become extremely popular. Superb flavor, prolific, and early. Ideal for successional sowing. To 18 inches (45cm)." Awarded an Award of Garden Merit by the Royal Horticultural Society.

P. sativum
'LITTLE MARVEL'
or 'Improved American Wonder,' 'Sutton's Little Marvel'

CULTIVATED BY 1900

A cross between Carter's Daisy and William Hunt, this first early pea has dark green pods. It was introduced into the United States a few years later by Mr. J. H. Gregory. The peas are delicate and tasty, growing on hardy and high-yielding plants.

P. sativum
'ONWARD'
or 'Unwin's Onward'

CULTIVATED BY 1899

This is one of the best and finest flavored of all main-season peas. A tremendous cropper, it has blunt-end pods that are dark green in color. It bears an Award of Garden Merit from the Royal Horticultural Society.

P. sativum
'PETIT PROVENCE'
or 'Sharpe's Meteor'

CULTIVATED BY 1922

A French heirloom bush first early pea that is very hardy. It can be sown anytime from early fall to late spring, depending on the local climate.

P. sativum
'PRINCE ALBERT'

CULTIVATED BY 1837

Although this first early pea was probably introduced before 1837, the following 1842 advertisement is the first reference to it to appear in the press: "Cormack & Oliver Seedsmen and Nurserymen of New Cross near the Croydon Railway Station and Bedford Conservatory, Covent Garden, London, have the

Harvesting peas.

honor to offer to the notice of Noblemen, Gentlemen, and others, the above NEW PEA, as one of the earliest and best sorts extant; in proof thereof, a quantity put into open earth on the 14th of March was ready for use the 25th April, being only 'forty-two days from sowing to the date of gathering for the table' it is moreover a good bearer of excellent flavor and highly advantageous for early forcing." Thomas Jefferson must have concurred with this assessment, because he, too, grew it at Monticello.

P. sativum

'PROGRESS NO. 9'

CULTIVATED BY 1939

A second early pea, this variant was introduced by Laxton Brothers of Bedford, England, who lauded it as: "An early wrinkle seeded pea that has become extremely popular. Superb flavor, prolific, and early. Ideal for succession sowing."

P. sativum

'TALL TELEPHONE'

CULTIVATED BY 1878

This second early pea is a sport from Telegraph. Introduced by Messrs. Carter who proclaimed: "Pods very large and broad, sometimes 4 inches (10cm) long, straight, and slightly curved toward the end like a blade of a pruning knife, rather swollen each containing 8 to 10 very large green peas, squarish in shape, and when ripe, either perfectly white or more or less tinged with green."

P. sativum

'THE LINCOLN'

CULTIVATED BY 1884

An early main-season crop that is especially good in cool climates. It is one of the finest peas for small vegetable gardens.

BE KIND TO BIRDS

An old gardening encyclopedia advises, "Birds sometimes do considerable damage to the growing plants and to the pods, but a few strands of black cotton stretched along and among the sticks is usually sufficient to keep them off." This is now considered poor practice, because the bird can become trapped; a pea guard is a much kinder deterrent.

PEA GUARD

The wire pea guard, also known as a pea protector, is placed over young peas to protect the crop from birds.

RAPHANUS

RADISH

ALPHONSE DE CANDOLLE IN 1883 WROTE of the radish, "There is no doubt that the species is indigenous in the temperate regions of the old world; but it has been cultivated in gardens from the earliest historic times, from China and Japan and Europe, and because it sows itself frequently round cultivated plots, it is difficult to fix upon its starting point."

R. sativus
'BLACK SPANISH LONG'

CULTIVATED BY 1707

Noted in Mr. J. London's *The Retir'd Gardener* of 1707. An earlier date of 1548, however, may be attributed to the Black Spanish radish, although whether it refers to the long or the round variety (see below) is not known. In 1834 a Mr. F.F. Ashford, writing to the *Gardener and Forester's Record,* contends that "the Radish Black Spanish was originally brought, with the type, from China in 1548."

R. sativus
'BLACK SPANISH ROUND'

CULTIVATED BY 1548?

"Its bulb is oval, or rather regular pear shape. Grows 3 to 4 inches (7.5–10cm) or larger in diameter with a firm, white flesh and nearly black, thin skin. Flesh is crisp and pungent." Philip Miller, 1768.

R. sativus
'CHINA ROSE'
or 'Chinese Rose,' 'Rose d'Hiver de Chine'

CULTIVATED BY 1843

An American correspondent tells us that this variety was reportedly introduced from China by Jesuit missionaries. This variety may possibly have started life as the New Chinese Rose Colored Winter Radish, and is listed as such by Mr. Carter in 1845.

R. sativus
'FRENCH BREAKFAST'
or 'Flamboyant'

CULTIVATED BY 1865

Although probably much older, this French cultivar made its first appearance in the United Kingdom in Mr. Carter's Seed Catalogue of 1865. "A new quick growing variety; very much liked in Paris, and considered the best for early forcing. It is of an oval form, colors Scarlet, tipped with White; and for its good flavor and ornamental appearance it is decidedly an acquisition for salads and other purposes."

R. sativus
'LONG SCARLET'
or 'Rose Longue'

CULTIVATED BY 1868

We hesitate to say that this is indeed Mr. Wood's Early Frame

Radish, but beg to lay before you the evidence. The EEC Common Catalogue lists a radish variety called Long Scarlet or Rose Longue, and Vilmorin-Andrieux offers Radis Long Rose as a synonym for Wood's Early Frame. Furthermore, *The Gardener's Assistant* states: "Long scarlet—roots long rose red; flesh white, transparent, crisp, and of good flavor…there are several forms of it, such as Scarlet short-top, Early Frame, and Wood's Early Frame—the best for forcing." We must leave you to decide. If not Mr. Wood's variety, this is still a very old radish, known since at least 1868.

R. sativus
'LONG WHITE ICICLE'
or 'Ladies Finger'

CULTIVATED BY 1896

Most probably predating 1896, this variety was noted for its pure white flesh and appreciated both for its shape and excellent quality.

R. sativus
'SCARLET GLOBE'

CULTIVATED BY 1885

A contemporary source noted, "A very early forcing Radish, and one which does equally well outside. Handsome in both form and color—a beautiful oval and a rich scarlet; the roots are of a fair size, with a very small amount of foliage; flesh always crisp, tender, juicy, and mild. An ideal Radish for the home gardener or market purposes."

BLACK SALSIFY
or BLACK VEGETABLE OYSTER, SCORZONERA, SERPENT ROOT, VIPER'S GRASS

"NATIVE OF SPAIN. PERENNIAL. This plant is cultivated as an annual or a biennial. It has a fleshy taproot, resembling that of the Salsafy [salsify] in size and flavor, but distinguished from it by the black of the skin … The Scorzonera is grown in exactly the same manner as the Salsafy, with this difference, that it is not absolutely necessary to pull up all the plants that remain after the first year's growth, because the roots will continue to increase in size without becoming less tender or less fit for use, even though the plants may have produced some stems and flowers in the course of the summer. The roots are eaten boiled, like those of the Salsafy; the leaves also may be used as salad." *The Vegetable Garden,* Vilmorin-Andrieux, 1885.

S. hispanica
'DUPLEX'

CULTIVATED BY 1951

This variety has a delicious oyster-like flavor, with long roots of a fine texture. It is very hardy and has a good resistance to bolting.

SAVING YOUR OWN SEEDS

Collect seeds from the healthiest and most productive specimens in your garden and you increase your chance of growing future generations of plants that thrive well in your particular situation (see page 11). Seeds from these parent plants will already have some degree of acclimatization to your garden. The resulting plants, therefore, will probably be better suited to your soil type and the vagaries of your climate, such as seasonal variations in temperature, rainfall, and wind.

Peppers are self-pollinating, so their seeds will always come true.

A GUIDE TO SAVING SEEDS

🌿 Always collect seeds from open-pollinated varieties (see page 11). This ensures the resulting plants will be like their parent, often known as "coming true." Never save seeds from F1 hybrids, because the offspring will not come true.

🌿 Be sure that any plant that you save seeds from is not protected by Plant Breeder's Rights or Patents.

🌿 Seeds collected from self-pollinating plants (such as beans, peas, peppers, and tomatoes) are the easiest to grow, because they will always come true.

🌿 Many plants, for example, brassicas (such as cabbage) and corn, can cross-pollinate with other nearby species, resulting in plants that differ from the parent. These types of plants must be isolated to ensure their purity, either by distance (often impractical in a garden) or, more usually, by netting or bagging.

🌿 Always select the very best plants to save seeds from. Your choice will depend upon which characteristics are most desirable; these could be productivity, disease resistance, height, or flower color.

- Label the chosen plants carefully and note separately which you have selected and why.

HOW TO COLLECT SEEDS

- To collect seeds from plants that produce dry seeds (such as lettuce and poppies) wait until the flower has died and the petals fallen away. Choose a dry and sunny day to cut off the seed heads or pods, leaving 8 inches (20cm) of stem attached, if possible.
- Place in a paper bag and mark with the name of the plant.
- Seal the bag around the stems with string and hang up in a dry, well-ventilated place indoors for about three weeks.
- Separate the seeds from the chaff, then store.
- To collect seeds from plants that produce wet seeds (such as cucumbers and squash), open the fruits and scrape out the seeds. Wash and strain them several times to remove the surrounding pulp.
- Let wet seeds dry on a clean dry surface for several days before storing.

Squash produce "wet" seeds.

Poppies produce large seed heads.

Always label plants accurately.

STORING SEEDS

Only store seeds that have been properly dried.

Always store seeds in a sealed container; seeds exposed to the air will absorb moisture, which can do harm.

Store seeds in a cool, dark, dry place. A refrigerator is ideal.

Always label seed containers clearly with the name of the plant and the date it was stored.

SOLANUM

TOMATO

or LOVE APPLE

NATIVE OF ECUADOR, tomatoes reached Spain in about 1525, having been brought back from Mexican gardens. When first introduced, the tomato was grown only as an oddity; the fruit was certainly not eaten, because it was thought by our puritanical forefathers to be an aphrodisiac. In her book *The Heirloom Gardener,* Carolyn Jabs tells of an event that helped turn the fortunes of the tomato around. "The turning point for the tomato came in 1820, when Colonel Robert Johnson, an eccentric but enthusiastic gardener announced that he would eat a basketful on the steps of the courthouse at Salem, New Jersey. A large crowd gathered, expecting to see Johnson 'foam and froth at the mouth and double over with appendicitis' as his own physician had predicted. Instead Johnson downed the entire basket, lived, and inspired an American passion for tomatoes."

Thanks in part to the popularity of farmers' markets, heirloom tomatoes have become much more widely available in recent years and can also be seen on many menus. To get the best range of varieties, however, you really do need to grow your own. Tomatoes usually exhibit two growth types: indeterminate (also known as vine or cordon) or determinate (or bush). The most common form is the indeterminate habit, and these forms will need to have their side shoots nipped out as they grow and be trained up a support to make a long, tall plant bearing fruit trusses along its length. Determinate types require none of this training, naturally forming a compact shape, perhaps with a little support, if necessary.

S. lycopersicum
'ALICANTE'

CULTIVATED BY 1963

A superior and traditional indeterminate variety popular with gardeners. It is early and reliable, with fleshy tomatoes with smooth skin and a fine flavor.

S. lycopersicum
'ALISA CRAIG'

CULTIVATED BY 1907

An indeterminate, this old favorite was bred by Mr. Alan Balsch of Forres, Ayrshire, Scotland, before 1907. It was rightly praised as, "The favorite for glasshouse cultivation. Fruit of medium size, bright red, tough skinned, rarely cracks, a great cropper under forcing treatment. Out of doors grows against a south wall."

S. lycopersicum
'BANANA LEGS'

CULTIVATED BY 1984

An extremely prolific determinate heritage variety producing 4-inch (10cm)-long yellow tomatoes with a thick meaty flesh and few seeds late in the season. The tomatoes have a slightly pointed end, ideal for salads or as a paste tomato. Introduced by the US seed company Tater Mater.

S. lycopersicum
'BEEFSTEAK'
or 'Red Ponderosa'

CULTIVATION DATE UNKNOWN

Considered to be the original heirloom Beefsteak tomato, popular since the mid-1800s. The Beefsteak has vigorous indeterminate vines that will need to be securely staked to hold the 10 ounces to 2 pounds (280–900g) of tomatoes. Although the tomatoes are so large, it is still an abundant producer. With its flat, solid, meaty, juicy, and bright red tomatoes, this variety does not disappoint hard-core tomato lovers. It is also an excellent slicer.

S. lycopersicum
'BIG RAINBOW'

CULTIVATION DATE UNKNOWN

An American indeterminate heirloom variety that is striking when sliced, because the yellow tomatoes have neon red streaking through the flesh. A Beefsteak-sized tomato that delivers tomoates up to 1 pound 5 ounces (600g) each, it is best grown under glass.

S. lycopersicum
'BLACK CHERRY'

CULTIVATION DATE UNKNOWN

A modern, dark-colored indeterminate cherry tomato that crops on large and sprawling, vigorous plants. The yield is large in huge clusters, with the tomatoes about 1 inch (2.5cm) in diameter, deep purple to mahogany brown. The bite-sized tomatoes

are delicious, with a sweet, rich, complex flavor.

S. lycopersicum
'BLACK CRIMEA'
or 'Black Krim'

CULTIVATED BY 1990

This Russian heritage variety was found in 1990 on the island of Krim in the Black Sea. It is indeterminate with large, dark red-purple, juicy tomatoes, and a rich sweet flavor.

S. lycopersicum
'BLACK PRINCE'

CULTIVATION DATE UNKNOWN

This is a modern indeterminate medium-size tomato with dark maroon to almost black flesh and distinctive green shoulders. It is especially tender, and the tomato is good for slicing.

S. lycopersicum
'BRANDYWINE'

CULTIVATED BY 1886

This is thought to be an American Amish variety from Chester County, Pennsylvania; certainly it was introduced commercially in 1889 by Messrs. Johnson & Stokes of Philadelphia. A potato-leaved indeterminate Beefsteak, it has large tomaotes with red skin, pinkish red flesh, and a superb flavor. It does best grown in a greenhouse. Other Brandywine cultivars include the variously colored Brandywine Pink and Brandywine Yellow.

S. lycopersicum
'BROWN BERRY'

CULTIVATION DATE UNKNOWN

A relatively new indeterminate variety that delivers huge yields of unusual, chocolate brownish, cherry-sized tomatoes with a sweet and slightly smoky flavor, carried on herringbone-like trusses. It is highly resistant to splitting.

S. lycopersicum
'COSTOLUTO GENOVESE'

CULTIVATED BY 1957

A northern Italian indeterminate heritage plant with scarlet, slightly ribbed tomatoes. These develop to 3 inches (7.5cm) long, and with a weight of about 5 ounces (140g).

S. lycopersicum
'GERMAN ORANGE STRAWBERRY'

CULTIVATED BY 1900

A beautiful and unusual heritage variety from Germany, delivering large, deep orange, Oxheart-type, strawberry-shaped tomatoes. Expect each tomato to weigh 8 to 16 ounces (225–450g). They are loaded with a superb rich and sweet flavor. Indeterminate, with very few seeds, they are vigorous and high yielding.

S. lycopersicum
'GOLDEN QUEEN'

CULTIVATED BY 1882

Said to have been discovered at a fair by seedsman Alexander Livingston, who improved it, then introduced it commercially in 1882. An indeterminate type with a superior flavor and solid, always smooth tomato that is large and ripens early. The skin is rich golden-yellow with a tinge of pink on the blossom side.

S. lycopersicum
'GOLDEN SUNRISE'
or 'Carter's Golden Sunrise'

CULTIVATED BY 1894

Carter & Son of High Holborn, London, England, may have bred this indeterminate tomato. Certainly they were its distributor, and described it thus: "Has all the good qualities of the best red varieties and is of a beautiful golden-yellow color, making it invaluable for slicing and mixing with the red." Given an Award of Garden Merit by the Royal Horticultural Society.

THOMAS ETTY ESQ
THE HERITAGE SEEDSMAN & BULB MERCHANT

TOMATO
Orange Oxheart
An heirloom variety prized for its large bright orange-yellow, aromatic fruit. Originating in the Virginias, it is a favourite for sauces & canning. It has extensive vines & attractive, heart-shaped fruit.
15 seeds
CULTIVATION: Sow in seed trays in gentle heat from January (if growing in a greenhouse) to late April (for outdoor planting from late May until early June), prick out into small pots & grow on until 3 or 4ins. high. Harden off if they are to be planted outside & do not set out until all danger of frost is past, setting them 2ft apart in all directions. For greenhouse production plant directly into the greenhouse border allowing 15ins. between plants, or grow on in 10ins. pots.
Indeterminate varieties of tomatoes, also called "cordon" tomatoes, are varieties that need the side shoots nipped out. They generally will require support.
Carefully Hand-packed by
www.thomasetty.co.uk – 01460 298249
Seedsmans Cottage, Puddlebridge, Somerset TA19 0RL
EU Rules & Standards – Standard Seed
EU registered variety (FR)
Packed Year Ending August 2016
Registered Seed Packet - DEFRA Ref No 0000

S. lycopersicum
'GREEN ZEBRA'

CULTIVATED BY 1983

Bred by Thomas Wagner and released in 1983 in the Tater Mater catalog, these medium-sized indeterminate tomatoes ripen to a green color, heavily suffused with cream yellow spots and stripes. It has an excellent flavor—a mixture of sweet and acidic.

S. lycopersicum
'HARBINGER'

CULTIVATED BY 1891

Daniel Brothers of Nottingham, England, may have originally bred this indeterminate tomato, as well as distributing it. They described it thus: "Very early and a prolific bearer will be found extremely valuable for growing in the open air. The fruits are round, smooth, solid, and of a bright red. Although small they begin to ripen early."

S. lycopersicum
'ILDI'

CULTIVATION DATE UNKNOWN

This is a golden pear- or plum-shaped indeterminate tomato that produces fruit like bunches of grapes, with up to 100 tomatoes per truss. Naturally, each one is small, but they have a mild sweet flavor. The seeds can be slow to germinate.

Mortgage Lifter tomato.

S. lycopersicum
'LEMON TREE'

CULTIVATION DATE UNKNOWN

An unusual indeterminate heritage variety originating from St. Petersburg, Russia. Huge crops of bright yellow tomatoes shaped like lemons grow on vigorous 4- to 5-foot (1.2–1.5m)-tall plants. The flavor is light and crisp, with a solid flesh like a paste tomato.

S. lycopersicum
'MARGLOBE'

CULTIVATED BY 1917

A North American determinate heirloom variety, developed by Dr. F.J. Pritchard at the Bureau of Plant Industry from a cross between Globe and Marvel. The Burpee catalog of 1932 wrote, "Within a very short time growers all along the east coast, all the way down to Florida have quickly accepted this new tomato because of its outstanding features."

S. lycopersicum
'MARMANDE'

CULTIVATED BY 1939

A semi-determinate tomato that was developed by the French Vilmorin Seed Company. It has large scarlet tomatoes with a rich flavor. Very reliable for cool climates, and of good constitution, making it a perfect candidate for the Royal Horticultural Society's Award of Garden Merit.

S. lycopersicum
'MONEYMAKER'

CULTIVATED BY 1906

An indeterminate tomato bred and distributed by Stoner & Son of Southampton, England, who claimed it "can be relied upon to give a good account of itself under all circumstances." A productive and reliable plant, the bright red tomatores are medium size and uniform in shape with a great flavor.

S. lycopersicum
'MORTGAGE LIFTER'

CULTIVATED BY 1930S

It was Mr. M.C. Byles (a.k.a. "Radiator Charlie") of Logan, West Virginia, who developed this large, mild-flavored, and pink tomato in the 1930s. He sold so many plants at a dollar a piece that he was able to pay off his $6,000 mortgage. In grateful recognition of this, he renamed the variety in the 1940s.

S. lycopersicum
'NAPOLI'

CULTIVATION DATE UNKNOWN

This is an improved variety of Roma. Indeterminate in shape, it has cylindrical red tomatoes that finish at a point and grow five to six a truss. An ideal tomato for sauces, ketchups, preserves, and eating raw.

S. lycopersicum
'OMAR'S LEBANESE'

CULTIVATION DATE UNKNOWN

A vigorous heritage plant originating from a Lebanese hill town, this is an intermediate Beefsteak-type producing large, pink, irregularly shaped tomatoes. Individually, these typically weigh 1½ pounds (650g), yet some can reach 3 pounds (1.3kg). A good roasting tomato with rich complex flavors, it was taken to the United States by a Lebanese student.

S. lycopersicum
'OXHEART GIANT'
or 'Livingston's Giant Oxheart'

CULTIVATED BY 1925

In 1933, this indeterminate giant was hailed thus: "A newer variety which is positively the largest Tomato ever introduced. The skin is purplish scarlet. It is smooth and evenly colored. The individual Tomatoes weigh as much as 1½ pounds (700g) each, although not a heavy yielder. Excellent flavor."

Tomatoes trained up a trellis.

S. lycopersicum
'PANTANO'

CULTIVATION DATE UNKNOWN

This is a rare Italian heirloom with Beefsteak-sized, slightly ruffled tomatoes. Indeterminate, the tomatoes are an intense red, often with green shoulders, and have a rich deep flavor.

S. lycopersicum
'PINEAPPLE'
or 'Ananas'

CULTIVATION DATE UNKNOWN

A French cultivar with large, red-and-yellow striped tomatoes and a rich flavor. An indeterminate type, its abundant tomatoes can weigh up to 2 pounds (900g) each.

S. lycopersicum
'PRINCIPE BORGHESE'

CULTIVATED BY 1910

An indeterminate Italian variety with red, apricot-sized tomatoes with a sharp taste, very suitable for sun drying. It crops well, producing abundant clusters of tomatoes, and is a good keeper.

S. lycopersicum
'RED CHERRY'
or 'Red Currant'

CULTIVATED BY 1795

Originally from South America, Red Cherry was included in the 1868 edition of Carter's catalog. In 1877 the Royal Horticultural Society reported of it: "Fruit round red, of the size of ordinary cherries, borne on short racemes very profusely. Ripens freely. Plant of free growth, branching … a very free fruiting ornamental sort, but the fruit is too small for ordinary use." Indeterminate growth habit.

S. lycopersicum
'RED PEAR'
or 'Red Fig'

CULTIVATED BY 1861

A North American indeterminate tomato that may be older than thought. The Pennsylvannia Dutch used it as a "fig tomato," dipping it in hot syrup made from sugar and tomato juice, then dried in the sun.

S. lycopersicum
'ROMA'

CULTIVATED BY 1956

Developed in Maryland, this is a determinate outdoor plant whose tomatoes ripen early and nearly all at once. A fleshy plum type that is almost seedless, it is suitable for drying, juicing, and making ketchup sauces.

S. lycopersicum
'SAINT PIERRE'
or 'St. Peter'

CULTIVATED BY 1880

A traditional French tomato with an excellent taste. This is a midseason indeterminate slicing variety. It is productive and a good keeper, with red tomatoes the size of big plums.

S. lycopersicum
'SAN MARZANO'

CULTIVATED BY 1927

An Italian tomato about which a contemporary account waxed lyrical: "The best and most wanted Tomato for the manufacture of conserves in tins! Owing to their solid flesh and tenacious skin; the fruits are very apt to drying and the preservation of the entire fruit." An indeterminate type.

S. lycopersicum
'STRIPED STUFFER'

CULTIVATED BY 1967

A unique concept in tomato plants producing 3½-inch (9cm) tomatoes like sweet bell peppers, with strong walls and nearly empty cavities. The attractive bright red tomatoes have golden orange stripes and an excellent pure classic tomato taste. Created by the UK Glasshouse Research Institute before 1967.

S. lycopersicum
'TIGERELLA'
or 'Mr. Stripey'

CULTIVATED BY 1967

This is a tall-growing indeterminate plant that produces good crops of medium-size red tomatoes with clearly defined yellow-and-orange stripes. It crops reliably and heavily, growing well outdoors or in a glasshouse. As you would expect, it carries an Award of Garden Merit from the Royal Horticultural Society.

S. lycopersicum
'VALENCIA'

CULTIVATION DATE UNKNOWN

From Maine, this indeterminate heirloom variety is well suited to cool climates. The bright orange, round, and smooth tomatoes are nearly seedless, with a rich flavor.

S. lycopersicum
'VINTAGE WINE'

CULTIVATION DATE UNKNOWN

This is one of the most beautiful tomatoes available today, bearing Beefsteak-style tomatoes weighing up to 1½ pounds (650g). They have a bright red base and orange-and-yellow stripes. The pulp is thick.

S. lycopersicum
'YELLOW CURRANT'
or 'Yellow Cherry'

CULTIVATED BY 1795

An indeterminate plant with small yellow tomatoes borne in clusters. They are tiny, even for cherry tomatoes, averaging just ½ inch (1.3cm) across.

S. lycopersicum
'YELLOW PEAR'

CULTIVATED BY 1800

Possibly eighteenth century or older, this is a midseason indeterminate variety with a tall and vigorous habit that will tolerate heavy soil. The yellow, pear-shaped tomatoes are thin skinned with a mild flavor.

Tomatoes in a greenhouse.

LOST, RARE, OR SIMPLY FORGOTTEN?

The tomato Paul Robeson is a Russian heirloom named after the opera singer and human rights activist. Paul Robeson (1898–1976) was much admired in Russia, and just like his voice, the tomato has a distinct flavor: deep, rich, and smoky. The 3- to 4-inch (7.5–10cm) tomatoes are a very dark red with dark green shoulders. It appears on the Slow Food USA Ark of Taste list of cultivars in danger of extinction.

S. lycopersicum
'YELLOW PERFECTION'

CULTIVATED BY 1890

Bred and introduced by W. J. Unwin's of Histon, Cambridgeshire, England. The description reads: "Early and heavy cropping, this variety performs well outdoors or under glass. Bright yellow fruits of outstanding quality." An indeterminate growth habit that can be relied upon, hence the Award of Garden Merit from the Royal Horticultural Society.

SOLANUM

EGGPLANT

AUBERGINE

NOW CONSIDERED A DELICIOUS ADDITION to many dishes, the eggplant was regarded with much suspicion when it first arrived in England. In 1587 John Gerard in *The Historie of Plantes* wrote the following: "in Egypt and Barbary they used to eat the fruit of Mala Insana boiled or roasted under ashes, with oile and pepper, as people used to eat Mushrooms. But I rather wish English men to content themselves with the meate and sauce of our own country, than with fruit eaten with such peril, for doubtless these apples have a mischievous quality; the use whereof is utterly to bee forsaken. As we see and know many have eaten and do eat Mushrooms more for wantoness than for need; for there are two kinds thereof deadly, which being dressed by an unskilful cooke may procure untimely death: it is therefore better to esteem this plant and have it in the garden of your pleasure and the rareness thereof, rather than for any vertuie or good qualities yet knowne." It was perhaps because of Mr. Gerard's startling description of the humble eggplant that for many centuries cautious gardeners did no more than confine it to the "garden of your pleasure," cultivating it simply as an ornamental. That the eggplant ever came to be eaten after such a dire warning must, I surmise, only have occurred when English gentlemen traveled abroad upon their Grand Tour of continental Europe in the eighteenth century and sampled the culinary delights of other European countries.

S. melongena

'BLACK BEAUTY'

or 'Imperial Black Beauty'

CULTIVATED BY 1875

A cross between Early Long Purple and Black Peking, introduced in the United States in 1902. It has glossy dark purple, oval eggplants with a fine flavor.

S. melongena

'EARLY LONG PURPLE'

or 'Long Purple'

CULTIVATED BY 1805

Introduced into the United States in 1855; B. K. Bliss & Son of New York noted it in 1870, and it was later sold by the Peter Henderson Seed Company and by D. M. Ferry.

"The fruit is oblong, somewhat club shaped, from 5 to 8 inches (12–20cm) long, often straight but generally slightly bent. Deep purple in color but subject to some difference being sometimes pale purple, slightly striped, and often much variegated with longitudinal stripes, always more deeply colored on the exposed side.""On

POTATO

the Esculent Egg Plants," Andrew Mathews, *RHS Journal*, 1826.

S. melongena
'LISTADA DI GANDIA'

CULTIVATED BY 1850

This is a very attractive but unusual variety from either Spain or Italy. The eggplants are purple but heavily suffused with white stripes and streaks. It is fine fleshed and almost seedless, and it arrived in southern France in the early 1850s, where it was known as Striped Guadaloupe.

S. melongena
'WHITE EGG'
or 'Bianca a Uovo,' 'Japanese White Egg'

CULTIVATION DATE UNKNOWN

Originally from Japan and used in Asian cooking, it unsurprisingly has white eggplants that resembles a hen egg. These turn yellow on ripening, and the small eggplants may be pickled. The earliest eggplant to reach the United Kingdom was a white ornamental variety much like this, and in the United States the Boston seedsman John Russell offered Old White Egg for sale in 1828 as an ornamental for growing in the flower garden.

A draw hoe.

THE TRUE ORIGIN OF THE POTATO has been much debated, but in all probability the first edible plants grew at high altitude in the South American Andes and began to be eaten around 5000 BCE. By the time of the arrival of the Spanish conquistadores in the sixteenth century, the potato was already a domesticated crop, and the invaders took it back with them to Europe. There it gradually became widespread, although it often met with much resistance. For example, in France it was not declared edible until 1772, while English farmer William Cobbett referred to it as the "root of wretchedness." In 1621, the potato made the reverse journey back across the Atlantic Ocean with the Pilgrims, arriving in New England where it was hitherto unknown. Potatoes are mainly divided into three groups, depending on their time of harvest: first early, second early, and maincrop. First early types are ready soonest, from 100 days after planting; second early types come next, ready from 110 days; and maincrops take the longest, from about 125 days.

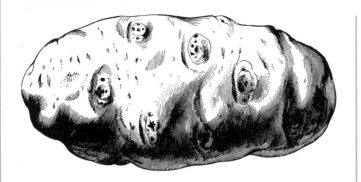

S. tuberosum
'EARLY OHIO'

CULTIVATED BY 1875

Introduced by DB Harrington, this early variety appeared in Vilmorin-Andrieux's *The Vegetable Garden* where it was noted, "For the last twenty years the Americans have been very actively engaged in sowing Potato seed for the purpose of raising new varieties, and rival the English raisers in the success which attended their efforts." The skin is flushed with pink and has the advantage of being less easily damaged when dug up than many other heirloom types of potatoes.

S. tuberosum
'EARLY ROSE'

CULTIVATED BY 1860

It was tradition for the Pennsylvania Dutch to begin planting their early varieties on March 17, St. Margaret's Day. Early Rose was introduced by Albert Bresee, a farmer from Vermont, and its tubers have smooth pink skin and attractive white flesh, streaked with pink. The 1899 catalog of Ross Brothers, Worcester, Massachusetts, introduced it thus: "This standard variety needs no description; it is sufficient to say that most new early varieties are compared with this in point of earliness and quality."

S. tuberosum
'IRISH COBBLER'

CULTIVATED BY 1876

Legend has it that an immigrant shoemaker from Ireland living in New Jersey selected this variety from Early Rose. It is a late variety with white skin and flesh that is excellent for mashing. Its nickname "old reliable" speaks volumes.

S. tuberosum
'OZETTE'
or 'Anna Cheeka's Ozette,' 'Makah Ozette'

CULTIVATED BY 1791

Colloquially, large and round potato tubers of a harvest are referred to as bakers or boilers, while the small and long ones are sometimes known as fingerlings. Ozette is a fingerling, with a nutty flavor, firm flesh, and creamy texture. It appears on the US Ark of Taste list and deserves to be grown much more widely as it is a superior variety. It is thought to have arrived in the United States via Spanish explorers from South America, and the Makah Indians cultivated it in Neah Bay, Washington, naming it after a Makah village.

S. tuberosum
'PURPLE MAJESTY'

CULTIVATION DATE UNKNOWN

There are several purple heirloom potato cultivars, but the consensus is that Purple Majesty is the darkest

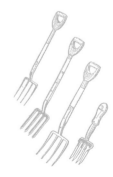

A border fork, a potato fork, a digging fork, and a weeding fork.

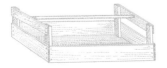

Box for storing potatoes.

of all. A late-season variety, it is purple throughout, with moist flesh with a buttery flavor that is particularly high in antioxidants.

S. tuberosum

'RUSSIAN BANANA'

CULTIVATION DATE UNKNOWN

A fingerling variety with pale yellow skin and rich yellow flesh with a firm texture. Originally from the Baltic, it was taken first to Canada then spread throughout North America. Russian Banana has gained notoriety, as some claim that the murderous bank robber and gangster John Dillinger (1903–34) carved a replica gun from this long and slim potato. The brandishing of this "weapon" helped him escape jail.

HISTORICAL NOTE

The historical event known as the Great Hunger of 1845–49 is one of the most potent arguments for the preservation of genetic diversity, and a grave warning of the dangers of monoculture food production. The wind-born water mold *Phytophthora infestans*, better known as potato blight, spread across northern Europe, arriving in Ireland in 1845. This was a country already severely impoverished, with much of the population subsisting on just one food crop: the potato. To compound matters, the vast majority of these potatoes were the variety known as Lumper, unremarkable except for its high yields and its susceptibility to blight. Serial potato crop failures resulted in famine, with an estimated one million deaths. What followed was an exodus of emigration, as people fled poverty and destitution.

POTATO DIBBLE
A traditional potato dibble has a cross tread higher than the depth at which the potato sets are planted. It is best done as a two-person job: one makes the holes with the dibble while the other drops the sets in the holes.

> **Warning:** Never eat a potato that has turned green. Potatoes contain the poisonous alkaloid solanin, and its toxicity levels become elevated if exposed to light. Potatoes, therefore, should always be stored in the dark and checked carefully for discoloration before cooking. The stems and leaves of potatoes are also poisonous, as is the case with their relative the tomato. In summer you may notice your main-season plants developing small green potaotoes after flowering; these too are highly toxic. Along with sweet and chili peppers, tomatoes, and eggplants, potatoes belong to the Solanaceae family of plants—which also includes the deadly nightshades.

SPINACIA

SPINACH

IN *The Practical Kitchen Gardiner*, 1727 (when printers were wont to sometimes print the letter *s* as *f* in imitation of an elegant calligraphic hand), Stephen Switzer commented: "Upon a careful infpection into some books of antiquity, I can't find that this ufeful fallet was known to the ancients." Certainly it was known during the previous century, as the *Receipt Book of Joseph Cooper* of 1654 (Mr. Cooper had been cook to Charles I) reports that the "juice of spinach" was used to color the root vegetable skirret green. John Parkinson, in his book *Paradisi in Sole Paradisus Terrestris*, printed in 1629, offers a method of cooking spinach learned from refugees from Holland. "Spinach is a herbe fit for sallets (salads) . . . many English that have learned it of Dutch people, doe stew the herbe in a pot or pipkin without any moisture than its owne, and after the moisture is a trifle pressed from it they put butter and a little spice unto it and make therewith a dish that many delight to eat of. It is used likewise to be made into Tartes and many other varieties of dishes, as Gentlewomen and their Cookes can better tell than myself."

Spinach leaves can be round or pointed.

S. oleracea
'AMERICA'

CULTIVATED BY 1856

A popular variety with dark green leaves and a good taste. It grows to 8 inches (20cm) tall and is slow to bolt.

S. oleracea
'BLOOMSDALE LONG STANDING'

CULTIVATED BY 1920

This variety arose from a single plant discovered in the 1920s.

Its dark and glossy green leaves are crumpled and blistered. It is vigorous, with tender, fleshy leaves and a rich flavor, and is slow to bolt.

S. oleracea
'GIANT WINTER'

CULTIVATED BY 1940

A prickly seeded variety from North America that is known for its large leaves and very long standing. It may be sown in spring as well as the autumn.

S. oleracea
'VIROFLAY GIANT'

CULTIVATED BY 1866

Introduced by the French Vilmorin-Andrieux seed company in 1866, it was listed in the United States in the same year. In May 1883, it received the Royal Horticultural Society Award of Merit. Its dark green leaves are giants, up to 10 inches (25cm) long and 8 inches (20cm) wide at the base. The plant can grow 2–2½ feet (60–75cm) in diameter.

TETRAGONIA

NEW ZEALAND SPINACH

or BOTANY BAY SPINACH, COOK'S CABBAGE, SEA SPINACH

THIS MOST VENERABLE PLANT WAS INTRODUCED by the renowned English plant hunter Sir Joseph Banks in 1770. It was discovered during Captain Cook's exploration of the coasts of New Zealand on the vessel *Endeavour* and was found to be effective at preventing scurvy. It was first grown at Kew Gardens, London, in 1772. While it is less hardy than its namesake, it does have the virtue of not bolting in hot weather, so is particularly useful in hotter regions.

T. tetragonioides
NEW ZEALAND SPINACH

CULTIVATED BY 1772

Although not related to the true spinach, this plant is a good substitute and has the considerable advantage of being resistant to heat. It featured in the 1937 McFayden Seed Company's catalog in the United States, where its similarity to spinach was highlighted: "The Hot Weather Spinach. This plant, when prepared for the table, so greatly resembles Spinach in appearance and flavor that most people will not be aware of the difference. Strong plants resisting heat and drought."

TRAGOPOGON

SALSIFY

or VEGETABLE OYSTER

THE ANCIENT GREEKS AND ROMANS grew this long and slender root vegetable. In North America, the Pennsylvannia Dutch cultivated it from the 1700s; the old varieties were red flowering, but these have been gradually replaced by the blue-flowered kinds. Its common name, vegetable oyster, acknowledges its flavor, which is said to resemble the mollusk.

A bunch of salsify.

T. porrifolius
'SANDWICH ISLAND'
or 'Mammoth Sandwich Island'

CULTIVATED BY 1860

This variety has slender, creamy white roots. It is a good winter crop because the flavor improves after the first frosts. It has been grown in North America since the 1860s and was distributed by the J. M. Thornburn Seed Company, among others. In 1889 *American Garden* announced that "We are now using this delicious vegetable." In England Messrs. Veitch sent seeds of Sandwich Island to trial at the Royal Horticultural Society in February 1899. Their verdict was: "This is one of the best winter root crops, although it seems little known. Prepared in soup, it is extra nice; also creamed, scalloped, or browned in deep fat it is one of the very choicest foods. Salsify is as easily grown as parsnips and the large, straight, fleshy roots more delicately flavored."

HISTORICAL NOTE

The 1867 catalog of the Massachusetts seed company Washburn lists the fava bean as the "English Bean" and comments, "The following varieties are much grown in England, but find little favor in this country." Among the three types listed is Broad Windsor (a.k.a. Green Windsor), recommended as being "much esteemed and extensively cultivated, remaining fit for use longer than any other variety. A sure bearer."

VICIA

FAVA BEAN

or BROAD BEAN

A HARDY ANNUAL, THE FAVA BEAN is thought to have originated in the Near East, possibly Egypt, and probably introduced to the British Isles (where it is known as broad bean) by the Romans, with a later reintroduction in the sixteenth century. John Gerard listed two varieties. The marvelous scent of the fava bean flower is something not to be overlooked; distilled, the blooms are said to make an effective lotion to improve the complexion. In the United States, the beans were popular during the colonial period, with seedsman Bernard McMahon of Philadelphia listing fourteen varieties in 1806. By the 1840s, however, they had begun to fall out of favor.

V. faba
'AQUADULCE CLAUDIA'
or 'Aquadulce Longpod'

CULTIVATED BY 1937

Aquadulce Claudia is a large fava bean with long pods. It is very hardy and suitable for growing in cool climates. The variety Aquadulce is the original nineteenth-century strain of which it was written: "A very fine long-pod bean of continental origin, named the Aquadulce, is not nearly so much grown by gardeners and exhibitors as it deserves to be, it is a variety bearing a very fine long symmetrical pod, without the coarseness we sometimes see in the Seville Long-pod. It is also known as the Leviathan Long-pod." *The Gardeners' Chronicle*, 1884.

V. faba
'BUNYARD'S EXHIBITION'

CULTIVATED BY 1835

Bred and distributed by Mr. Bunyard of Allington, near Maidstone, Kent, England. At the time it was described as: "Newly introduced, and apparently a superior variety; its pods are long, and contain six to eight beans, resembling in size and shape those of the Windsor."

V. faba
'CRIMSON FLOWERED'

CULTIVATED BY 1771

In *Everyman His Own Gardener* (1787), Thomas Mawe and John

Abercrombie described this attractive bean: "Height about 4 feet (1.2m); flower bright red approaching scarlet, but varying from pale to dark red, or almost black. Pods medium size, with, generally, four or five beans, similar in shape, but longer than the long-podded sort. An excellent bearer, when in bloom, it is very ornamental and often grown for that purpose."

V. faba
'GREEN WINDSOR'
or 'Broad Pod Windsor,' 'Broad Windsor,' 'English Windsor Broad,' 'Windsor'

CULTIVATED BY 1704

"In the Middle of January, if the Weather is open and good, you may plant your first crop of Windsor

A fava bean germinating.

plant your first crop of Windsor Beans, and every three weeks make a fresh plantation until the middle of May, in order to preserve a succession through the Season; Indeed there are some People who are very fond of Beans, which plant even in June, but unless the Soil is very strong and moist, or the Season proves wet or cold, they seldom succeed well." *The Retir'd Gardener*, 1704. One of the beans grown by Thomas Jefferson at Monticello, it is particularly useful for home growers who have cool and short summers.

V. faba

'MASTERPIECE GREEN LONGPOD'

or 'Carter's Masterpiece Green Longpod,' 'Land's Supreme'

CULTIVATED BY 1891

A contemporary account describes this fine bean as: "An exhibition

Bean. It combines the earliness of the Seville; partakes of the length of pod of the Agua-dulce; and possess the fine quality of flavor of the Green over the White Bean. It is most prolific, a great number of the pods hanging in pairs."

V. faba

'SUTTON DWARF'

CULTIVATED BY 1923

Bred and introduced by Sutton & Sons of Reading, Surrey, England, in the early 1920s, this bean is probably derived from the earlier Dwarf Fan. Their catalog described it as, "Attaining a height of only 9 to 12 inches (23–30cm). The plants are of more or less spreading habit, and so freely branch that a very large number of pods are produced each containing four to five beans of superior table quality."

NOTES ON THE CULTURE OF FAVA BEANS

"In the summer of 1826, my first crop of Mazagan and early long-pod beans was, by a very strong and violent wind, blown down; this was done when the Beans were in full blossom. The crop from the blossoms which the plant had possessed was very fine and abundant and gathered during July. In three weeks after, the beans were prostrated; each stem pushed forth from near the root one or more, in some instances four or six, fresh stems; these bloomed freely and produced an abundant crop, which was gathered during September.

Since that year, I have uniformly bent down, so as to break the stalk near the root, my first and second crop of Beans; I have by this means obtained four crops of Beans from two sowings, and which supplied me from July 1st to October 31st." *Harrison's Gardener and Forester's Record*, July 3, 1833.

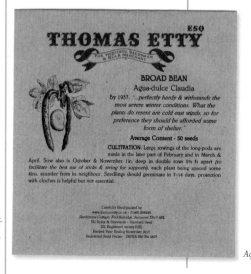

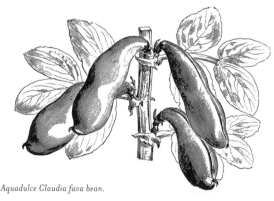

Aquadulce Claudia fava bean.

ZEA

SWEET CORN

or CORN, CORN ON THE COB, MAIZE

A NATIVE OF SOUTH AND CENTRAL AMERICA, the history of the cultivation of sweet corn stretches back as far as the Inca people. Seeds of sweet corn were sent back to Spain soon after the discovery of the New World, and probably arrived in Britain in the sixteenth century, although it was not until the eighteenth century that it began to be grown there in any quantity. Mr. William Cobbett is generally attributed with suggesting sweet corn as an agricultural crop on those shores, although this claim was disputed in the horticultural press at the time. In fact, the Reverend Gilbert White was growing it much earlier; in 1754 he noted, "Sowed in the new-garden hot-bed, rows of African Marygold, and Indian Corn."

Z. mays
'BLOODY BUTCHER'

CULTIVATED BY 1845

From Virginia, this dent corn has dark, bloodred kernels mixed with pink and yellow. The cobs are 8 to 12 inches (20–30cm) long and the plant has good drought tolerance.

This corn makes good flour, is good roasted, and can also be eaten fresh when young.

Z. mays
'BLUE HOPI'
or 'Sakwapu'

CULTIVATION DATE UNKNOWN

A staple of the Hopi people of northern Arizona, this is a flint corn that is ground to make the ceremonial bread piki. Alternatively, it can be eaten fresh when young. The ivory kernels dry to royal blue-black.

Z. mays
'COUNTRY GENTLEMAN'

CULTIVATED BY 1890

Developed by S. D. Woodruff & Sons of Orange, Philadelphia, this highly popular corn was introduced in 1891 by Peter Henderson & Company of New York. It is named after a nineteenth-century magazine. The cobs measure 8 inches (20cm) long and have creamy white seeds packed tightly and irregularly, with a rich and sweet flavor. Corn that has kernels arranged like this instead of in rows is known as "shoe peg" corn.

LOST, RARE, OR SIMPLY FORGOTTEN?

These three advertisements for corn appeared in the Ross Brothers (of Worcester, Massachusetts) spring and summer catalog for 1899. First of All corn, we are told, "still continues to be the first in the market without exception." With bold and confident exactitude, the image asserts that it should be ready to eat from the third week of June. Dibble's Mammoth Early Flint was a selection of the variety Longfellow and grew corns that measured an impressive 15 inches (38cm) long. White Cap Yellow Dent is adorned with a sash, much as a beauty queen might be, and this ambitious claim was made for it: "The grower and introducer of this wonderful corn says he will guarantee this corn to mature in ninety to ninety five days from planting and to grow a larger crop on poor soil, than any other corn in the world." Unfortunately, none of these varieties appear to be available to today's home or commercial growers.

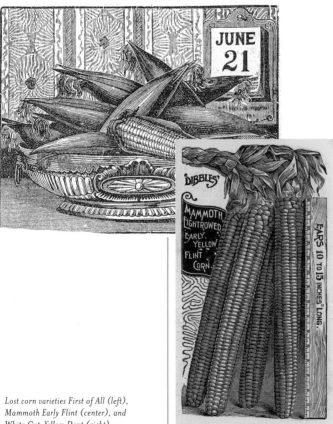

*Lost corn varieties First of All (left),
Mammoth Early Flint (center), and
White Cap Yellow Dent (right).*

Z. mays

'EARLY PEARL'
or 'Hobnail'

CULTIVATED BY 1932

Introduced by the North American Charles C. Hart Company, this is an early season variety with long and slender white kernels on compact cobs just 6 inches (15cm) long. It is productive over a long period of time.

Z. mays

'GOLDEN BANTAM'

CULTIVATED BY 1898

Although introduced commercially by the celebrated North American seedsman W. Atlee Burpee in 1902, in truth this variety was already old when (re)discovered in 1898 by Mr. E. L. Coy. It had originally been raised by a farmer in Greenfield, Massachusetts, who is believed to have selected it from an old nineteenth-century variety called Golden Sweet. Golden Bantam was one of the first yellow corns to be accepted as a food plant (as opposed to purely stock fodder).

Z. mays

'RAINBOW SWEET INCA'
or 'Inca Rainbow'

CULTIVATED BY 1970S

This is a beautiful variety developed by Dr. Alan Kapuler of Oregon. The 12-inch (30cm) cobs are made up of a lovely mixture of blue, purple, red, and yellow kernels.

Z. mays

'STOWELL'S EVERGREEN'
or 'True Gold'

CULTIVATED BY 1848

Developed by Nathan Stowell of New Jersey, this was introduced in 1856 by Thorburn & Company. Its name alludes to the length of time it stays fresh in the field, and if the plant and root is pulled before completely ripe, and hung in a cool pantry, then fresh corn can be picked into late winter. A great boon, therefore, before canning and freezing were available. "This variety is intermediate in its season, and if planted at the same time with earlier kinds, will keep the table supplied till October. It is hardy and productive, very tender and sugary, remaining in a condition suitable for boiling a long time." *Washburn & Company's Amateur Cultivator's Guide to the Flower and Kitchen Garden*, catalog, 1867.

A range of watering cans.

This spade is known as the London Treaded Spade.

CORN ON THE COB

"This is a very fine garden vegetable. The ear is stripped off the stalk just at the time when the grains are full of milk. The ears are then boiled for about twenty minutes; they are brought to the table whole; each person takes an ear, rubs over it a little butter and sprinkles a little salt, and bites the grains from the stalk to which they are attached, and which, in America is called the cob. In the Indian Corn countries, every creature likes Indian corn better than any other vegetable, not excepting even the fine fruits of those countries." *English Gardener*, William Cobbett, 1829.

NOTES ON THE CULTIVATION OF ESCULENT VEGETABLES

to be undertaken during the spring months.

This is the great season for sowing seeds, and the gardener must be up with the lark and go to bed with the robin, which is the latest of birds to bid farewell to a sunny day. "Now or never" is the motto for the man or woman who means it in the work of the garden. The first care should be to make good all arrears, especially in the preparation of seed beds, the sowing of seeds, and the cleaning of all plots that are in any way disorderly. Enthusiastic east winds now commit vast havoc, but a little protection provided in time will do wonders to ward off their effects, and the sunny days that are now so welcome, and that we are pretty sure to have, will afford opportunity for giving air to plants in frames, and for clearing away litter, and for the regular routine work of the season.

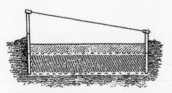

A cross section of a hotbed showing the layers of soil, manure, and subsoil.

HOTBED

To make one is easy enough, but it is of no use to half make it, for half acres in this department do not bear good corn.

🍂 In the first place, secure a good bulk of manure, and if it is long and green, turn it two or three times, being careful it is always moderately moist, but never actually wet, for that is ruin. If the stuff is dry, sprinkle with water at every turn, and let it steam away to take the rankest fire out of it.

🍂 Then make it up where required into a good square pile, being careful not to beat it down, but let it settle in its own way.

🍂 Now place the freestanding frame over the pile. Add the lights (windows), but wedge them open to allow ventilation.

🌺 Put on a 1-foot (30cm) depth of light rich soil after the frame is in place, and wait a few days to sow the seeds in case of a great deal of heat rising.

🌺 When the heat is steady and comfortable, sow on the beds or in pans as needful, the quantity required of each separate crop determining which course is to be taken.

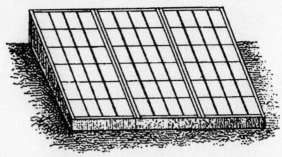

A glazed frame.

Do not attempt to hurry the growth of anything overmuch, for undue haste will produce a weak plant; instead, give air and light in plenty, but with care to prevent undue stunt of growth, and your plants will be short and healthy from the first.

The plants most needed to be sown in a hotbed now are celery, lettuce, peppers, tomato, zucchini, New Zealand spinach, eggplant, and melon. The earlier all these things are sown the better; to secure a long summer for their aftergrowth and maturation.

SOME VEGETABLES IN NEED OF THE GARDENER'S ATTENTION AT THIS MOST PROPITIOUS TIME OF YEAR

ARTICHOKE *Cynara scolymus*
Clear off protecting material as soon as the weather permits, and make fresh plantations of suckers in rows 4 feet (1.2m) apart, and the plants 2 feet (60cm) apart in the rows.

ASPARAGUS *Asparagus officinalis*
New beds should be planted in early spring. Established beds to be dressed, if not already done. If manure cannot be afforded, put on a sprinkle of wood ashes.

BEET *Beta vulgaris* ssp. *vulgaris*
Sow a few for an early supply, in well-dug, mellow soil.

HISTORICAL NOTE

Victorian gardeners forced on early crops such as melons, cucumbers, and strawberries in constructions known as hotbeds. At its most basic, a hotbed is a frame made from four pieces of wood, topped with glazed sashes known as "lights." A traditional frame was typically 12 feet (3.6m) long by 4 feet (1.2m) wide. The front side was 9 inches (23cm) high and the rear 18 inches (45cm), with sloping side panels. Each light was 4 feet (1.2m) long by 3 feet (90cm) wide. Permanent hotbeds were mounted on low brick walls, like a cold frame. A smaller freestanding portable version can easily be erected in a convenient part of the garden.

Where early-sown crops have evidently failed, sow again without complaining; seed costs but little, and a good plant is the earnest of a good crop; a bad plant will probably never pay the rent of the ground it occupies.

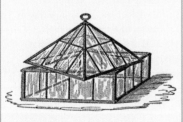

A square hand glass for protecting tender crops.

BROCCOLI *Brassica oleracea* Italica group
To be sown in quantity from early to late spring for planting out late spring to early summer. Plant out in mild weather from frames as soon as the plants are fit and well hardened.

BRUSSELS SPROUT *Brassica oleracea* Gemmifera group
For an early gathering of fine buttons, a sowing should be made now, on the warm border or in a frame. This valuable esculent requires a long period of growth to attain perfection, and those who sow late rarely see such buttons as the plant is capable of producing.

CABBAGE *Brassica oleracea* Capitata group
Sow main-season crops of all the kinds required, and plant in the ground as fast as possible from early seedbeds and frames. The rankest manure may be used in preparing ground for cabbage; this will allow the use of the well-rotted manure for seedbeds and other purposes for which it will be required.

CARROT *Daucus carrota*
Sow Early Horn, Paris Market, or any other of the early types at the first opportunity, but wait for signs of settled spring weather to sow the main-season crops of large kinds, and then put them on deeply dug ground without manure.

CAULIFLOWER *Brassica oleracea* Botrytis group
Plant outdoors as weather permits from frames, choosing the best ground you have. In preparing a plot for cauliflower, use plenty of manure; and if it is only half rotten, it will be better than if old and mellow. Sow on a good seedbed for a late supply.

CHIVE *Allium schoenoprasum*
To be divided and replanted on spots it has not before occupied.

FAVA BEAN *Vicia faba*
Plant out those raised in frames and sow full crops. Hill up soil around those from early sowings that are forward enough.

GARLIC *Allium sativum*
Bulbs may still be planted, but no time is to be lost.

HORSERADISH *Armoracia rusticana*

To be planted now if not done already.

LEEK *Allium porrum*

Sow the main-season crop in a rich piece of well-prepared soil. They may be sown tolerably thick, because they will have to be planted outdoors.

LETTUCE *Lactuca sativa*

Plant outdoors and sow again in quantity. All the kinds may be sown now but make sure of enough of the romain type Wheeler's Tom Thumb and other summer kinds. In hot, dry soil, where lettuce usually runs to seed early, try a few of the bronze-leaved kinds; though less delicate than the green and white, they will be useful in the event of a hot, dry summer. Lettuce requires a deep free soil with plenty of manure.

ONION *Allium cepa*

Sow the main-season crop in furrows 9 inches (23cm) apart, and tread or beat the ground firm. The crop requires a rich soil in a thoroughly clean and mellow condition, and it makes a capital finish to the seedbed to give it a good coat of charred debris or smoother ash before sowing the seeds.

PARSLEY *Petroselinum crispum*

To be sown in plenty for summer and fall supply; thin as soon as it appears, to give each plant plenty of room; and in thinning, if requiring curly parsley, take out those plants that are the least curled.

PARSNIP *Pastinaca sativa*

Sow the main-season crop in furrows 1 foot (30cm) apart in good soil deeply dug; however, if the soil is extra rich and deep, allow 18 inches (45cm). The seeds should be covered about 1 inch (2.5cm) deep. Fresh seeds are indispensible.

PEA *Pisum sativum*

Sow now the finest kinds obtainable of tall-growing plants, and the large-pod bush kinds of the second early class. Be careful to put them on the best seedbed that can be made, and allow sufficient room between the taller kinds for half a dozen rows of cabbage or

Horseradish is a vegetable with a hot, mustard-like taste.

SPRING

"The gardener is bound to be vigilant now to assist nature in her endeavors to benefit him; he must promote the growth of his crops by all means in his power; by plying the hoe to keep down weeds, and open the soil to sunshine and showers; by thinning and regulating his plantations that air and light may have free access to the plants left to attain maturity; by continuing to shelter as may be needed; and by administering water during dry weather that vegetation may benefit to the utmost by the happy accession of increasing sunlight."
The Culture of Vegetables and Flowers from Seeds and Roots, Sutton & Sons, 1884.

American land cress is much easier to grow than watercress.

broccoli. A crowded quarter of peas is never properly productive, for they smother each other and the shaded parts of the haulm produce next to nothing.

SEA KALE *Crambe maritima*

To be sown in well-prepared beds; or plantations may be made by cuttings of the smaller roots of the thickness of a lead pencil, about 4 inches (10cm) in length. Plant them top end uppermost, and deep enough to be just covered.

SWISS CHARD *Beta vulgaris* ssp. *cicla*

Sow this in plenty. Swiss chard, the perennial spinach beet, is one of the most useful vegetables known because it endures heat and cold with impunity, and when common spinach (*Spinacia oleracea*) is running to seed, it remains green and succulent, and is fit not only to supply the table all the summer long, but in fact until the next spring, when it will run to seed and end its career.

TURNIP *Brassica rapa* ssp. *rapa*

To be sown in quantity, mid- to late spring.

SOME UNUSUAL & INTERESTING VARIETIES

With the main vegetable groups considered above, this section will turn the spotlight on some of the more unusual but nonetheless interesting varieties worthy of your consideration.

UPLAND CRESS *(Barbarea praecox)*

Also known as American land cress, Belle Isle cress, early winter cress, land cress, and scurvy cress. The seeds may be sown during the whole of spring, summer, and fall. An easy plant, it is not fussy about the type of garden soil it grows in, nor does it run to seed too soon. "The leaves of this plant have some resemblance to those of the Water-cress, but the plant itself always grows on the dry land. If sown in spring, it forms during the summer a tolerably full rosette of compound leaves of a dark and very glistening green color, which are used in seasoning and garnishing." *The Vegetable Garden*, Vilmorin-Andrieux, 1885.

GOOD KING HENRY *(Chenopodium bonus–henricus)*

This ancient venerable vegetable also answers to the sobriquets "fat hen plant" and "Lincolnshire spinach." According to this comment (when printers were wont to sometimes print the letter *s* as *f* in imitation of an elegant hand), it seems that Good King Henry was rarely seen in 1777: "The prefent plant, whofe excellence as a pot-herb feems not to be fo generally known as it deferves; at Bofton in Lincolnfire [England] and probably many other places in the kingdom, they are fensible of its value, yet ftrange to tell, this useful herb is unknown in the greatest Herb Market in the world, Covent Garden [London]." For best results sow the seeds in spring in a seedbed and transplant into rich deep soil in rows 18 inches (45cm) apart each way.

SCURVY GRASS *(Cochlearia officinalis)*

At least one brewery in North America produces a fine ale beer containing this most beneficial of plants. This writer in an 1807 edition of *The Medical and Physical Journal* seems well acquainted with its medicinal qualities: "It has long been considered as the most effectual of all the antiscorbutic plants; and its sensible qualities are sufficiently powerful to confirm this opinion. We have testimony of its great use in scurvy, not only from physicians, but navigators; such as Anson, Linschoten, Maartens, Egende, and others. And it has been justly noted that this plant grows plentifully in those high altitudes where the scurvy is most obnoxious. Forster found it in great abundance in the islands of the South Seas." To cultivate scurvy grass, sow the seeds where the plants are to grow, if possible in a cool, shady position. It is a plant that requires no special attention. The leaves are sometimes eaten in salads, but it is more usually grown for medicinal purposes, its antiscorbutic properties being well known.

The strangely named scurvy grass plant.

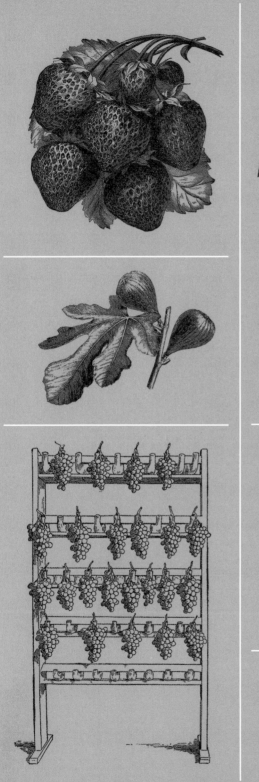

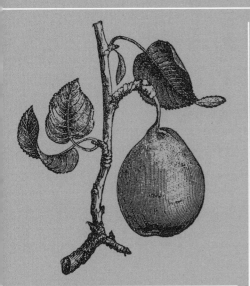

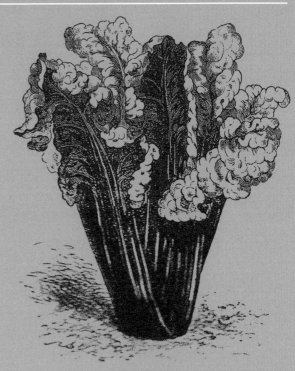

SECTION 2

THE FRUIT DIRECTORY

THOMAS ETTY ESQ

THE HERITAGE SEEDSMAN & BULB MERCHANT

STRAWBERRY
True Wild
(*Fragaria vesca*)

"...do grow upon hills and vallies, likewise in woods and other such places that ve somewhat shadowie: they prosper well in gardens. The ripe strawberrie quench thirst, and take away, if they be often used, the rednesse and heate of the face"

Average Seed Count ~ 100 seeds

CULTIVATION. Seed is best started into growth in a frame (at some 50- to 60- of the Fahrenheit) From January to April. The established (and hardened-off) seedlings being set out, apart some 10 inches.

Carefully Hand-packed by
www.thomasetty.co.uk ~ 01460 298249
Seedsmans Cottage, Puckfebridge, Somerset TA19 9EZ.
Packed Year Ending March 90th
Registered Seed Packer - FERA Ref No 2807

THE FRUIT DIRECTORY

THOMAS ETTY ESQ
THE HERITAGE SEEDSMAN & BULB MERCHANT

BLUEBERRY
(Vaccinium corymbosum)

"...have a sweet taste when mature, with variable acidity. The bushes typically bear fruit in the middle of the growing season: fruiting times are affected by local conditions such as altitude & latitude, so the peak of the crop can vary from May to August depending upon these conditions.
Average content 40 seeds

CULTIVATION: Sow late winter in a greenhouse, in a lime-free potting mix and only just cover the seed. The seeds might require a period of up to 3 months cold stratification before germinating. Once they are about 5cm tall, prick the seedlings out into individual pots and grow them on in a lightly shaded position in the greenhouse for at least their first winter. Plant them out into their permanent positions in late spring or early summer, after the last expected frosts.

Carefully Hand-packed by
www.thomasetty.co.uk • 01460 298249
Seedsmans Cottage, Puddlebridge, Somerset TA19 9RL
Packed Year Ending August 2016
Registered Seed Packer - DEFRA Ref No 2807

THOMAS ETTY ESQ
THE HERITAGE SEEDSMAN & BULB MERCHANT

RHUBARB
Mr Hawke's Champagne

A superior early variety, producing good-sized straight stalks of a bright crimson-colour.
First offered by Duncan Hairs of St Martin's Lane in London in 1854.
Having been bred by Mr Hawke at his nursery in Loampit Vale Lewisham

Average Content - 30 seeds

CULTIVATION: Sow the seeds in April, on rich light soil, in lines 1ft apart, the next spring transplant the roots to the spot they are to occupy permanently. Although Rhubarb will thrive on almost any soil, and certainly wherever a dock will grow, the finest produce may be expected from a deep, damp, heavy loam, abundantly manured.

Carefully Hand-packed by
www.thomasetty.co.uk • 01460 298249
Seedsmans Cottage, Puddlebridge, Somerset TA19 9RL
EU Rules & Standards - Standard Seed
Packed Year Ending November 2015
Registered Seed Packer - FERA Ref No 2807

THOMAS ETTY ESQ
THE HERITAGE SEEDSMAN & BULB MERCHANT

MELON
Early Black Rock or
Noire des Carmes.

Fruit spherical, but slightly flattened at the ⌐
with ribs clearly but not very deeply marke⌐
Flesh orange-coloured, thick, sweet, perfum⌐
of excellent quality. Noted in 1787.

CULTIVATION. For early crops sow the seed in J⌐
& pot off when the plants are large enough. They may
be shifted again, and may indeed be fruited in large pots,
but it is best to plant them out early in mounds of good turfy soil near the glass. Sow
again for succession as the requirements of the place suggest until the middle of May.
Unless a steady heat can be ensured, Melons are simply vexatious; therefore the
cultivator must have at command plenty of fermenting material or pits heated by hot
water. It is, however, a fact that with good management a crop of Melons may be
grown in summer in the same way as advised for Cucumbers, but a sunny lean-to

CUCUMIS

MELON

THE CANTALOUPE (also known as muskmelon or rock melon) is native to Africa and the warmer regions of southern Asia. It was imported into Europe by the ancient Greeks. Columbus took it to the New World on his second voyage in 1494, planting seeds on Haiti, but it did not reach Britain until the late sixteenth century, where the first melon seeds were germinated and cultivated using the heat from hotbeds. In 1597 John Gerard mistakenly referred to it as a gourd in his *Herball*. Old varieties of European-bred cantaloupes mostly have to be grown from seeds, because they are rarely available commercially. Almost certainly the watermelon originated in Africa, too, as archaeological evidence indicates it was cultivated in the Nile Valley about 200 BCE. It needs higher temperatures than the cantaloupe to grow successfully.

C. melo Reticulatus group
'ANANAS'
or 'Ananas d'Amérique à Chair Verte,' 'Jersey Lemon'

CULTIVATED BY 1794

Thomas Jefferson grew this small melon in 1794, and it was introduced commercially in the United States in 1824. Vilmorin-Andrieux also noted it in 1854, with the red variety Ananas d'Amérique à Chair Rouge, commenting that both "will readily carry and ripen from six to eight fruit on each plant." It is rare. The flesh is light green, firm, sweet, and perfumed.

C. melo Reticulatus group
'BLACK ROCK'
or 'Noir des Carmes'

CULTIVATED BY 1787

This French melon is said to have been preserved by Carmelite monks. It has a deeply ribbed, smooth skin and produces large and heavy fruits. A late variety, it requires a long growing season. The fruits are round with slightly flattened ends, and the skin ranges from grayish green to deep green, changing to yellow as the fruit matures. The flesh is reddish orange, soft, and sweet.

Black Rock melon.

C. melo Reticulatus group
'BLENHEIM ORANGE'

CULTIVATED BY 1880

This variety was raised from seeds brought from Afghanistan by Thomas Crump, head gardener to the English Duke of Marlborough, whose palace it is named after. In England it was introduced commercially by the seed company Carter's in 1882, who stated that "this Melon was sent out for the first time by us last year when we purchased the entire stock from the raiser." The R & J Farquhar Company of Boston, Massachusetts, listed it in 1925. This variety is known as a "netted" melon; the skin has the appearance of being covered by a net. The flesh is bright scarlet. Although raised for hothouse production, it is suited to short seasons and cool climates and is resistant to splitting if overwatered.

BEST IN SHOW

Blenheim Orange won first prize for the Best Melon at London's Royal Horticultural Society's show in July 1880. *The Times* newspaper later reported the event thus: "There is an idyll of Theocritus in which the competition for a prize given to the sweetest kiss is described, and the poet envies the judge his task of deciding. Whether the judges who had to taste the thirty-one Melons to award the Melon Prize are to be envied is a moot point. Ultimately they gave first honors to 'Blenheim Orange,' which was very properly grown by the Duke of Marlborough."

Queen Anne's Pocket Melon (see panel, right).

C. melo Reticulatus group
'CANTALOUPE DE CHARENTAIS'

CULTIVATION DATE UNKNOWN

This is a true cantaloupe, because the fruits have a smooth skin with light green stripes that mature to a creamy yellow. The delightfully scented, creamy orange flesh is filled with unsurpassed flavor. Too fragile to ship, Cantaloupe de Charentais *must* be homegrown. To help protect it from damage when harvesting, cut it from the vine instead of pulling or twisting it.

Citrullus lanatus
'MOON & STARS'

CULTIVATED BY 1926

This watermelon was called Sun, Moon and Stars when it was introduced in the United States in 1926 by Peter Henderson and Company, who described it as "an extraordinary variation … it has such a delicious taste." It later disappeared from commercial

LOST, RARE, OR SIMPLY FORGOTTEN?

The tennis ball-sized Queen Anne's Pocket Melon is a very old French variety and is said to have been used by ladies as a fragrant pomander. "The perfume, which resembles that of other melons without being so strong is rather agreeable as the fruit ripens, but the taste is not equally pleasant, and the plant is consequently only grown as a curiosity." *The Vegetable Garden*, Vilmorin-Andrieux, 1885. Also known as Melon Dudaim, in the American South it was often called Vegetable Pomegranate or Plum Granny, and the attractively striped orange-and-yellow balls were used to perfume rooms and wardrobes.

Unusual melon varieties are mostly raised from seeds.

catalogs and was thought extinct until 1981, when Kent Whealy, cofounder of Seed Savers Exchange, was contacted by Merle Van Doren of Macon, Montana, who had been growing the melon and donated some of his precious seeds. In 1987 the Southern Exposure Seed Exchange reintroduced the variety under the name of Amish Moon and Stars and Mr. Etty now offers it for sale in the United Kingdom and Europe. Oblong in shape with dark green skin spotted yellow, it is said that this melon can weigh 40 pounds (18kg).

C. melo Reticulatus group

'PETIT GRIS DE RENNES'

CULTIVATED BY C. 1600

A rare French melon that was first noted in the garden of the Bishop of Rennes several centuries ago. The gray-green rind ripens to a mustard-green color while the flesh

is orange, sweet, and perfumed. This is an early season variety adapted to cool climates, although it does especially well in a greenhouse.

C. melo Cantalupensis group

'PRESCOTT FOND BLANC'

or 'White Prescott'.

CULTIVATED BY 1809

A true French cantaloupe, this melon featured in *Nouveau Cours Complet d'Agriculture Theorique et Practique* (1809): "Fruits are 4 to 9 pounds (1.8–4kg), with deeply ribbed and warted gray-green skin that turns straw colored when ripening. Flesh salmon orange, incredibly sweet, and fragrant." It was introduced into the United States in 1850, has good resistance to drought, and excellent thick and perfumed flesh. Vilmorin-Andrieux noted that in French cultivation "a plant is generally allowed to carry only one fruit, or, in rare cases, two."

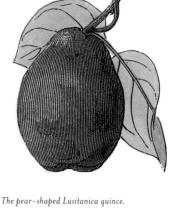

The pear-shaped Lusitanica quince.

LOST, RARE, OR SIMPLY FORGOTTEN?

The quince arrived in North America with the first English settlers, and seeds of quince are mentioned in the records of the Massachusetts Company as early as 1629. Over the centuries, competition from the more versatile apple and pear marginalized the quince and, by 1922, U.P. Hedrick wrote, "the quince, the 'golden apple' of the ancients, once dedicated to deities, and looked upon as the emblem of love and happiness, for centuries the favorite pome, is now neglected and the least esteemed of commonly cultivated fruit trees." Today, in the United States only a couple of hundred acres of quince are in commercial cultivation, thus its preservation and popularity rest entirely in the hands of gardeners. I suggest you order a tree today.

Prescott Fond Blanc melon.

CYDONIA

QUINCE

THE QUINCE ORIGINATES FROM THE FOOTHILLS of the Caucasus Mountains in southern Daghestan and Azerbaijan. It spread throughout Asia and the Mediterranean region, became established in northern Europe, and was then introduced into the Americas by early colonists. The fruit was cultivated by the ancient Greeks, and it is thought that many classical myths that feature apples actually refer to the quince. One of the first recorded references to the quince in the British Isles dates back to 1275, when Edward I planted four trees at the Tower of London. More than a century ago, it was still a common sight in gardens and orchards both in the British Isles and North America but is now, unfortunately, something of a rarity. In 1847 Thomas Bridgeman in *The Young Gardener's Assistant* noted of the quince, "It is used as a marmalade for flavoring apple pies, and makes an excellent sweetmeat; and it has the advantage over many other fruits for keeping, if properly managed." The quince is an ornamental tree with relatively good fall color and likes warmth and a good soil. The hard yellow fruits are pear shaped and in warm climates can be used straight from the tree, but in cooler regions they will need to ripen indoors. It must be cooked and can be used in sweet or savory dishes, being particularly favored for jellies and pastes.

C. oblonga
'LUSITANICA'
or 'Portugal'

CULTIVATION DATE UNKNOWN

The English naturalist John Tradescant (the Elder) brought this variety to the British Isles from Europe in 1611. The pear-shaped fruit is large with woolly skin, and the flesh turns a bright crimson when cooked. It is a vigorous tree, although it may take several years to establish before fruiting.

C. oblonga
'MEECH'S PROLIFIC'

CULTIVATED BY C. 1850

This is an American-bred quince from Connecticut that was named after the Reverend William W. Meech, who originally introduced it as the Pear-Shaped Orange Quince in an article in 1883. Meech was the author of a tome called *Quince Culture*, published in 1888, by which time the variety had assumed its present name. With large, golden-yellow fruits, the trees often begin to bear fruit when very young. Although available in Britain, this variety is much rarer in its homeland and is listed on Slow Food USA's Ark of Taste.

C. oblonga
'SMYRNA'

CULTIVATED BY 1887

Originally from Turkey, this quince has very showy blossoms followed by bright yellow fruits. It is hardier than most quinces and the fruit stores longer than other varieties. As with all quinces, a few placed in a bowl will perfume a whole room.

FICUS

FIG

FIGS MAY BE ONE OF THE VERY FIRST FRUITS domesticated by man. Carbonized evidence of figs has been found in a Neolithic village on the shores of the Jordan River, suggesting they were in cultivation about 9000 BCE. The Egyptians used the wood of the sycamore fig *(Ficus sycomorus)* to make coffins, hence its name of Pharoah's Fig. Centuries later, in the late 1500s, Spanish colonists introduced the fig into the Americas, and they were introduced into California in 1769 by Franciscan friars. This is when the cultivar known as Black Mission is said to have been planted by Friar Junipero Serra at the San Diego Mission. As well as producing delicious fruit, figs make a handsome and distinguished garden tree.

F. carica

'BLACK JACK'

CULTIVATION DATE UNKNOWN

This is a small variety suitable for growing in containers, which affords the advantage of being able to move it indoors for winter protection in cold climates. It crops heavily, with the fruit turning to purple immediately before they are ripe.

FIGS IN CONTAINERS

Figs fruit more prolifically if their roots are restricted. Note that in the wild they are often found growing in rocky habitats. Old gardening manuals often suggest creating an open-bottom boxlike structure in the ground with slabs and planting the fig within this. Figs also do well in plant containers; make sure water can drain freely, water well, feed regularly with seaweed in the growing season, and repot every two years. Position against a south-facing wall if at all possible, where the ripening figs will benefit from the extra light and warmth.

F. carica

'BROWN TURKEY'

or 'English Brown Turkey,' 'Texas Everbearing'

CULTIVATION DATE UNKNOWN

This fig was imported from mainland Europe into the British Isles by the seventeenth century, but it is certainly much older. It is one of the most popular figs for growing due to the excellence of its fruit and its hardiness. Although suitable for outdoor culture, it thrives best with the protection of a warm wall in cooler regions. It is long lived and very prolific, as described in the 1913 manual *Commercial Gardening*: "In Mr. E. H. Ogier's nursery at Duvaux, St. Sampson's, Guernsey, (Channel Islands), there is a Brown Turkey Fig tree about sixty years of age, which covers about 180 square yards (150 sq m) of ground. The shoots are kept up near the light by means of a framework made of battens nailed together at right angles, and leaving spaces about 4 feet (1.2m) square. Through these the grower can push his body, and attend to tying, pruning, picking fruits, etc., without damaging the plants. A large tree such as described will yield 300 to 400 dozen Figs twice, and even three times a year …The variety most favored is 'Brown Turkey', but several others are grown and treated in precisely the same way."

F. carica
'LONGUE D'AOÛT
or 'Banana,' 'Jerusalem'

CULTIVATION DATE UNKNOWN

Originally from Turkey, this has long been grown in France and was planted at the Palace of Versailles, near Paris, in the seventeenth century. The first crop of fruits are unusually long, hence its alternative name Banana, but strangely the second crop is less elongated. It is hardy and tolerates drought better than many other figs.

F. carica
'VIOLETTE DE BORDEAUX'

CULTIVATION DATE UNKNOWN

This is a hardy variety that hails from Spain. "Skin, quite black, covered with a fine blue bloom, and when dead ripe cracks in white longitudinal lines … Flesh, pale

coppery-colored, very tender and juicy, sugary and sweet. Excellent."
The Fruit Manual, Robert Hogg, 1884.

F. carica
'WHITE MARSEILLES'

CULTIVATION DATE UNKNOWN

This is one of the best flavored of figs. The fruits have lime green skin and sweet, translucent white flesh. Aged trees still grow at Lambeth Palace, London, which may be the original figs planted by Cardinal Pole in the early decades of the sixteenth century. It is mentioned in *The French Gardener,* translated by John Evelyn in 1669. Of White Marseilles Thomas Jefferson wrote to his friend William Thornton in 1809, "I will take some occasion of sending you some cuttings of the Marseille fig, which I brought from France with me, and is

Overwintering fig shoots.

unquestionably superior to any fig I have ever seen." At Monticello, in Virginia, Jefferson had been growing figs since the 1760s and planted them in what he termed "submeral beds," sited at the base of the kitchen garden wall, and he also took care to protect the tops of the trees from the vagaries of the Virginian climate.

The popular Brown Turkey fig.

FRAGARIA

STRAWBERRY

THE WILD, ALPINE, or woodland strawberry, *Fragaria vesca*, is highly prized for its small, sweet, and fragrant fruits. Vilmorin-Andrieux noted that "the Wood Strawberry possesses a quite peculiar perfume and delicacy of flavor. In low-lying districts its season lasts hardly a month, but in the mountains, on account of the difference in the time of ripening at different altitudes, Wood Strawberries may be gathered from June to September." Fruiting over a long period, it is best grown from seeds, because it does not produce sufficient runners from which to root new runners. The much larger garden strawberry was developed from crossing two larger wild strawberries from the New World in the eighteenth century, namely *F. virginiana* from North America and *F. chileonsis* from Chile, thus creating *F.* × *ananassa*, known as the "pineapple" strawberry.

"There are few in the vegetable kingdom that can equal the Strawberry in wholesomeness and excellence. The fruit is supposed to receive its name from the ancient practice of laying straw between the rows, which keeps the ground moist and the fruit clean."

The Young Gardener's Assistant,
Thomas Bridgeman, 1847.

F .vesca
'ALEXANDRIA'
or 'Alexandra'

CULTIVATION DATE UNKNOWN

With bright red, sweet, aromatic, and flavorsome fruits, Alexandria makes a vigorous and productive plant, sending out few runners and having a compact habit. The fruits are larger than many other alpine strawberries. "Flesh, rosy, of a sweet, high flavor. A very good variety, and very distinct." *The Fruit Manual*, Robert Hogg, 1884.

F. vesca
'BARON SOLEMACHER'

CULTIVATED BY 1935

Originally from Germany, this alpine strawberry grows in neat clumps, and this, coupled with the fact that it does not produce runners, makes it an excellent edging plant in the vegetable garden. It bears dark crimson berries with an intense taste.

Wooden strawberry baskets.

F. moschata
'CAPRON'
or 'Le Chapiron'

CULTIVATED BY 1576

From Central Europe and Scandinavia, this very old wild strawberry, known as Musk or Hautboy, was the first from which a named variety was developed. It has deep red, almost violet fruits and a musky smell, hence its name. The taste is said to resemble raspberries.

F. vesca
'MIGNONETTE'

CULTIVATION DATE UNKNOWN

This is a French strawberry with dainty fruits that are perfumed

and have a very sweet taste. Grow it as a perennial in the vegetable plot or as an annual in containers; the plant is especially attractive in hanging baskets.

F. virginiana
'VIRGINIA'
or 'Old Scarlet,' 'Scarlet'

CULTIVATION DATE UNKNOWN

Of this strawberry, Vilmorin-Andrieux commented that "This variety represents the botanical type of the species scarcely modified by cultivation." Native to North America, the fruits are sweet and tender. Traditionally the dried leaves are used to make tea.

F. vesca
'YELLOW WONDER'

CULTIVATION DATE UNKNOWN

Originally from Germany, this strawberry has creamy yellow fruits of wonderful taste and aroma, much admired by gourmets. It also has the advantage of seeming to be less attractive to birds than the red varieties. It too makes a good edging plant.

An alpine strawberry.

LOST, RARE, OR SIMPLY FORGOTTEN?

Time and again when reading through old seed catalogs and gardening manuals, one comes across a description of a plant which, for no obvious reason, is not now commercially available. The strawberry General Chanzy is one such, named after a nineteenth-century French general who fought in the Franco-Prussian War. Read what Vilmorin-Andrieux had to say about it in *The Vegetable Garden* and wonder at its extinction: "Plant very vigorous growing; leaves large and tall, and of a dark green color; leaf stalks covered with an abundance of long hairs; flower stems stout, erect, taller than the leaves, or partly so; fruit generally large and long, narrowed at both ends, sometimes hollow at the center, and of an exceedingly dark red color, which becomes nearly black when the fruit is fully ripe; flesh blood red throughout, sugary, vinous, and sometimes perfumed to a surprising degree. This variety ripens rather late and continues bearing for a considerable time."

The General Chanzy strawberry.

MALUS

APPLE

APPLES HAVE BEEN THE FRUIT OF CHOICE of many for a very long time. The Egyptian pharaoh Rameses II ordered that several varieties should be grown in the Nile Delta in 13 BCE. Later, the Roman author Pliny the Elder listed well over twenty varieties as well as explaining advanced cultivation techniques, such as patching a bud from one apple tree onto that of another. They were certainly eaten in Roman Britain, and eventually English varieties of apples were enriched and improved by imports from France and Flanders. The early colonists took the "eating" apple to North America and found the climate of the northeastern seaboard particularly suited to their growing. John Endicott, the governor of Massachusetts, is said to have planted the first apple tree in North America in the early 1600s. Today, the number of apple cultivars is numbered in the many thousands, yet only a few are readily available in stores. Certain qualities, such as a long shelf life and the ability to travel undamaged, have triumphed over those of taste and choice, thus many varieties are, unfortunately, facing an uncertain future.

M. domestica
'ASHMEAD'S KERNEL'

CULTIVATED BY 1700

This is an old apple with very pretty blossoms. Originally from Gloucestershire, England, it was introduced into North America in the 1950s, where it grows well (not all English apples do). It has an aromatic flavor, reminiscent of pear drops, and is a good keeper.

M. domestica
'BLENHEIM ORANGE'

CULTIVATED BY C. 1740

This fine apple was first found at Old Woodstock, near Blenheim in Oxfordshire, England. Spencer

Ambrose Beach wrote of it in *Apples of New York,* 1905, "Fruit large to very large, yellow, more or less washed and striped with red, attractive in appearance of excellent quality." Suitable for eating or cooking, it has crisp white flesh and a distinctive, nutty flavor.

M. domestica
'CALVILLE BLANC D'HIVER'

CULTIVATED BY 1598

This is a very ancient French apple, known originally as Blanche de

Zurich. Although a good eating apple, cooks seek it out, because it keeps its shape and flavor when cooked, and it is a favorite for making *tarte aux pommes*. The flavor develops with keeping, and the apple is high in vitamin C.

M. domestica 'COX'S ORANGE PIPPIN'

CULTIVATED BY 1830

Robert Hogg wrote in *The Fruit Manual*, 1884: "This excellent variety was raised at Colnbrook Lawn, near Slough, Buckinghamshire [England], by a Mr. Cox, who was formerly a brewer at Bermondsey, and who retired to Colnbrook Lawn, where he devoted the remaining years of his life to gardening pursuits. The apple originated in 1830, and is said to have been a pippin of Ribston Pippin." This is one of the very best dessert apples; it is medium size with an aromatic, crisp, and juicy flesh, and red and yellow skin.

M. domestica 'DABINETT'

CULTIVATED BY C. 1910

With its green and yellow skin and bittersweet taste, this is a cider apple and, therefore, not suitable for eating raw. It was found growing in a hedge in Somerset, England, in the early years of the twentieth century by William Dabinett and was named in his honor.

M. domestica 'ESOPUS SPITZENBURG'

CULTIVATED BY 1790

Another favorite fruit of Thomas Jefferson at Monticello in Virginia, this North American apple is said to have been discovered by a Dutch settler named Spitzenburg along the Hudson River near Esopus, New York. It has firm red skin and juicy yellow flesh, and it is the perfect choice for making apple pie.

M. domestica 'GRAVENSTEIN'

CULTIVATED BY C. 1600

A very old apple from Germany that was noted in Denmark in 1797. "It is one of the favorite apples of Germany, particularly around Hamburgh, and in Holstein, where it is said to have originated in the garden of the Duke of Augustenberg, at the Castle of Grafenstein." *The Fruit Manual*, Robert Hogg, 1884. Russian fur trappers took it to North America in the early years of the nineteenth century. The variety was well suited to the climate of Sebastopol, Sonora County, California, where it was used to establish new orchards. Due to competition from commercial vine growing, what was once 11,000 acres of Gravensteins

now, unfortnuately, only numbers a few hundred. A crisp and juicy apple that is excellent for eating and cooking, it ripens over a long period, making it the perfect choice for the home grower.

M. domestica 'IRISH PEACH'

CULTIVATION DATE UNKNOWN

This is a very old variety from Langford House, County Sligo, Ireland. It was popular in the British Isles by the turn of the nineteenth century and was introduced into North America about 1820. A good eating apple, it has pale yellow and green skin that is striped with dark red, and juicy and fragrant flesh. This apple does

not travel or store well, so should be eaten as quickly as possible after picking, preferably straight from the tree.

M. domestica
'JONATHAN'

CULTIVATED BY C. 1826

Thought to be a seedling of Esopus Spitzenburg, this apple was found on Mr. Rick's farm at Woodstock, Ulster County, New York, and was first described in 1826. Judge Buel, of the Albany Horticultural Society, named it after the man who discovered it, Jonathan Hasbrouck. By 1864 it had been exhibited at the Royal Horticultural Society in London. It is a medium-sized apple with red skin and crisp, juicy, and sweet flesh. It crops well.

M. domestica
'KING DAVID'

CULTIVATED BY 1893

A man called Ben Frost discovered this apple growing alongside a fence in Durham, Washington County, Arkansas. Despite these humble beginnings, today many

An apple parer and slicer.

proclaim this to be the very best apple in the world. A late-season dark red apple, it has firm and juicy yellow flesh and a good resistance to disease. It was introduced commercially by the Stark Brothers nursery in 1902 and in 1924 their catalog proudly boasted the following: "Bore all over the United States when all the old standby apples were killed by frost. Late bloomer—sure bearer ... Full of spicy, winelike juice—flesh, rich creamy color ... A fruiting King David tree is a glorious sight ... we found this marvelous apple tree many years ago on a trip over a rough Ozark Mountain road—still loaded with gloriously colored apples, October 25th, five weeks after Jonathan had fallen. After careful investigation we bought it."

M. domestica
'LAXTON'S FORTUNE'

CULTIVATED BY 1904

A cross between Cox's Orange Pippin and Wealthy, this sweet and aromatic dessert apple was bred by Laxton Brothers Nursery, Bedford, England. Although crisp when picked, it softens as it matures, so is not a good keeper.
It was introduced into North America in 1931. Holder of the Royal Horticultural Society's Award of Garden Merit.

M. domestica
'McINTOSH'

CULTIVATED BY 1811

The Apple Macintosh computer is said to have been named in honor

of this old North American cultivar, because it was the apple of choice of computer designer Jef Raskin. It was a New Yorker called John McIntosh, however, who discovered this sweet red apple as a seedling on his farm in Ontario, Canada. He cultivated it, and it became a great commercial success, reaching its apogee in the 1960s, since when its popularity has, unfortunately, been in decline.

M. domestica
'MÉDAILLE D'OR'

CULTIVATED BY C. 1865

A French russet cider apple bred by M. Goddard of Boisguillaume, Rouen, Médaille d'Or was introduced into England in 1884 before it traveled to the United States. It is a vigorous grower with golden yellow skin and tender yellow flesh. The fruit is also high in tannins.

M. domestica
'NEWTOWN PIPPIN'
or 'Albermarle Pippin,' 'Green Newtown Pippin'

CULTIVATED BY 1730

Probably the oldest commercially bred apple in North America, Newtown Pippin originated on the farm of Gresham Moore in Newtown, Queens County, New York, in 1730. This dessert apple with green skin is a heavy cropper and was a favorite of both George Washington and Benjamin Franklin. Thomas Jefferson planted two rows of grafted Newtown Pippin at Monticello, Virginia, in 1769. He

was such a fan that while in Paris he wrote,"They have no apple here to compare with our Newtown Pippin." It had been introduced into England by 1768, where it went under the name of "Newtown Pippin from New York." It now appears on the Slow Food USA Ark of Taste as an endangered variety.

M. domestica
'RED ASTRACHAN'

CULTIVATED BY 1780

A favorite with gardeners, this Russian apple arrived in the United Kingdom from Sweden in 1816. It was subsequently given to the Massachusetts Horticultural

Society by London's Royal Horticultural Society in 1835 along with the apples Alexander, Duchess of Oldenburg, and Tetofsky. In *The Young Gardener's Assistant,* 1947, Thomas Bridgeman noted, "This beautiful apple is of medium size, and roundish; the skin is dark red, covered with thick bloom like a plum; the flesh is white, tender, and somewhat acid. At perfection in early August."

M. domestica
'ROXBURY RUSSET'
or 'Boston Russet,' 'Putman's Russet,' 'Shippen's Russet'

CULTIVATED BY C. 1600

Originating in Roxbury, Massachusetts, this very old American apple is thought to be a seedling of a European variety introduced by colonists in the early years of the seventeenth century. It is sweet and medium size and good for eating, juicing, and making cider. "The tree is not large, but healthy, very hardy, and an immense bearer, and, when grafted on the paradise stock,

is well suited for being grown either as a dwarf or an espalier." *The Fruit Manual,* Robert Hogg, 1884.

M. domestica
'WINTER BANANA'

CULTIVATED BY 1876

This large and sweet eating apple was bred by David Flory of Indiana, and it won an award from the Royal Horticultural Society of London in 1912. The skin is yellow, flushed with orange and red, and the flesh is white.

M. sylvestris var. *domestica*
'WOLF RIVER'

CULTIVATED BY 1875

Found along the Wolf River, near Fremart, Wisconsin, this is a good dessert apple and cooks well, retaining its shape and flavor. Very hardy, it is large with red skin and pale yellow flesh.

THE APPLE STORE

In *Practical Fruit-Growing,* 1893, Joseph Cheal advises how to build an apple store. "Mark out the ground for the building 10 feet (3m) wide, and length according to requirements. Excavate the soil to a depth of 18 inches (45cm) to 2 feet (60cm), according to the means of thorough drainage. Next build a wall 4½ inches (11cm) thick and 4 feet (1.2m) high from the excavated level on each side, and use the surplus soil to form a solid bank at the outsides to the top of the wall as shown. Then form the roof of rafters, which may be made simply of rough poles, and cover the whole with a thick coat of thatch, at least 15 or 18 inches (38–45cm) through, and coming down well over the banks at each side. It then only remains to fit up the inside with four shelves on each side . . . A double door should be fitted at one end, and a double window at the other, which should also have a shutter to exclude the light. Leave the earthen floor, which ensures sufficient moisture to keep the fruit plump. The apples may be placed in layers four or five fruits thick."

TRAINING FRUIT TREE GROWTH

Many fruit trees, including apple, pear, plum, cherry, peach, apricot, and nectarine, can be trained into a variety of shapes, variously known as cordons, espaliers, and fans. In the cordon system, the stems are trained vertically, obliquely, or sometimes horizontally, either against a wall or along a series of wires stretched between upright posts. The shapes can vary from a simple single vertical stem to elaborate and complex creations. Such training is an efficient method for growing a number of fruit trees where space is restricted. It can also increase the fruit-producing power of a tree.

This shows the complex oblique cordon system used to grow a number of trees along a long wall. Note how the first and last trees are shaped to begin and terminate the row.

Strong and efficient hardware is needed to successfully train strong growing trees against brick walls. Illustrations A and B show traditional galvanized iron holdfasts; the pointed end is driven into mortar between bricks. Illustration C shows a driving eye; numbers of these are positioned at regular intervals along the wall to hold the wires in place. Illustration D shows a holdfast and nut and screw arrangement, which both holds the wire and allows for it to be tightened.

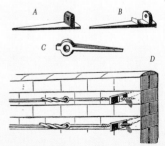

Apple trees trained into a low horizontal cordon, also known as stepovers, between posts. This is a useful shape to use for edging a path through vegetable beds.

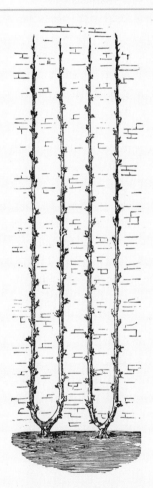

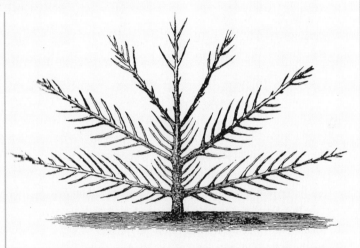

A peach tree trained in the fan system. This makes a very attractive display against a wall.

Pear trees planted as a double vertical cordon against a wall. Gardeners who are lucky enough to have tall garden walls can adopt this method of training.

Fruit blossoms can be blighted by late spring frosts. French fruit growers in the nineteenth century developed this system for protecting fruit trees trained against walls. The specially constructed walls are topped with tile copings to which straw protectors are attached. A canvas covering is then placed as shown, which allows light, air, and warmth to circulate around the trees while protecting the tender fruit buds from harsh frosts.

MESPILUS

MEDLAR

CULTIVATED BY THE GREEKS AND ROMANS, today the medlar is a rare sight. Given that the medlar and the rose are close relatives, it is perhaps unsurprising that the fruit resembles a large rose hip, and it ripens from tan to brown. In several Elizabethan and Jacobean plays, the medlar fruit is the subject of much innuendo, because of its appearance, and among its common names are "open-arse" and, in France, *cul de chien* (which translates as "dog's ass").

Depending on local climate, the fruit is either left to ripen on the tree or picked and brought indoors and kept in a cool, light place to mature. When ripe, the appearance of the fruit is dark brown, wrinkled, and soft; in fact, the fermentation process must begin before they can be consumed, turning the bitter-tasting flavor into sweetness. In 1848 the English botanist John Lindley used the term "bletting" to describe this process. The taste is of spiced apples and pears, and the fragrant fruits can be eaten fresh or cooked. Cultivated by the Assyrians, the medlar was also grown by the Greeks and Romans, and it may be the latter who introduced it into the British Isles. The earliest mention of it there is 1270 in the Westminster Abbey Customary. French Jesuits probably took it to North America in the sixteenth century. In the British Isles, the fruit was traditionally eaten with cheese and port wine at the end of a meal.

M. germanica
'BREDA GIANT'
or 'Dutch Giant'

CULTIVATION DATE UNKNOWN

Robert Hogg wrote in *The Fruit Manual*, 1884, that this old Dutch cultivar was "the largest and most generally grown of the cultivated medlars. The fruit is frequently 2½ inches (6cm) in diameter, and very much flattened. The eye is very open, wide, and unequally rent, extending in some instances even to the margin of the outline of the fruit. It is of

good flavor, but, in some respect, inferior to the Nottingham. The young shoots are smooth."

A medlar tree.

M. germanica
'ROYAL'

CULTIVATION DATE UNKNOWN

A medlar that may have originally hailed from Russia, it was introduced into England from France by nurseryman Thomas Rivers in 1860. The fruit is of good quality, and the tree is a heavy cropper that can start to bear fruit at an early age. Like all medlars, it is an extremely hardy and undemanding plant, and it bears large white blossoms in spring that change to pink.

PRUNUS

CHERRY

THE SWEET CHERRY *Prunus avium* and the sour cherry *P. cerasus* are both native to the temperate regions of the northern hemisphere, including Europe and North America. They make attractive garden trees, having showy blossoms in spring and good fall color. However, they are vigorous growers and make very big trees; if space is an issue they can be fan trained against a wall. Competition from birds for the ripe fruit is always a problem; indeed, the 1913 UK publication *Commercial Gardening* commented, "The Cherry, which in this country is nearly always grown as a standard is essentially an orchard tree. It is but rarely seen in gardens, for the reason that it is practically impossible to keep the birds away from the fruit on a few isolated trees, unless these are growing against a wall and can be netted."

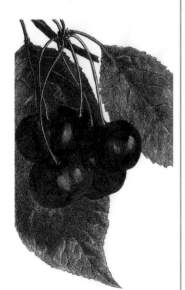

Black Tartarian cherry (see page 138).

P. avium

'BIGARREAU NAPOLÉON'

or 'Napoléon,' 'Napoléon Wax,' 'Queen Anne,' 'Royal Anne'

CULTIVATION DATE UNKNOWN

Thomas Bridgeman described this tree as being "remarkable for the vigor and beauty of its growth." A sweet and juicy, heart-shaped cherry, it crops well and has a pale yellow skin, red cheek, and firm white flesh once ripe. Robert Hogg noted in 1884: "The origin of this excellent cherry is unknown. Its present name is not that by which it was first known, for Truchsess received it from Herr Baars, of Herenausen, in 1791 under that of Grosse Lauermann's Kirsche, which is, in all probability, the original and correct one. That of Napoleon is of more recent origin, having first been given by Messrs. Baumann, of Bolwyller [Alsace, France]." *The Fruit Manual,* 1884. It should be noted, however, that it must have arrived in the English fruit-growing county of Kent quite early on, because it was known there at the time as Kent Nap.

Double copper preserving pans with water space.

P. avium
'BLACK TARTARIAN'

CULTIVATED BY C. 1794

This vigorous and productive tree is also very ornamental for the garden. Of its origins and arrival in England, the botanist John Lindley wrote: "This cherry is generally considered to have been brought by the late Mr. John Frasier, from Russia. It is stated to have been introduced from Circassia, by Mr. Hugh Ronalds, of Brentford, in

1794. It is a tree of great excellence …its branches usually loaded with a profusion of rich and handsome fruit. Fruit: heart-shaped, with an uneven surface, and of a shining purplish black color. Flesh: purplish, juicy and rich." *Pomologia Britannica*, 1841. It was introduced into North America at the end of the eighteenth century.

P. avium
'GOVERNOR WOOD'

CULTIVATED BY 1842

Raised as a seedling by Dr. Jared Kirtland, of Cleveland, Ohio, this heavy cropping tree bears juicy dark red fruits that are flushed with yellow.

P. cerasus
'MONTMORENCY'

CULTIVATION DATE UNKNOWN

This large tart cherry is widely grown today and is the popular choice in North America for traditional cherry pies. However, it is a very old variety, originating in the Montmorency Valley, France, probably before the seventeenth century. The fruit has light red skin and flavorsome yellow flesh. U. P. Hedrick described it in *The Cherries of New York* (1915) as having "abundant light pink juice, tender and melting, sprightly, tart, of very good quality."

U. P. Hedrick thought cherries "the most popular of all fruits."

GARDEN GHOSTS

Mr. Ulysses Prentiss Hedrick, more usually referred to as U. P. Hedrick, was an American botanist and horticulturist. Hedrick (1870–1951) had a particular interest in fruit trees and wrote prolifically on this and many other horticultural subjects. In 1915 he published *The Cherries of New York,* in which he noted of the cherry: "Probably it is the most popular of all fruits for the garden, dooryard, roadside, and small orchard. All in all, while adorning a somewhat humbler place in pomology, it is more generally useful than the showier and more delicate plum and peach." He produced many monographs devoted to the fruits of New York, including works on grapes, peaches, pears, and plums, along with books on small fruit and vegetables.

BIRD KNOW-HOW

"With birds, as with human beings, is found that too much familiarity breeds contempt, and that however cleverly scarecrows may be constructed, their want of motion begets suspicion in the birds that they are intended to alarm; and finding eventually that the supposed guardian of the seeds or fruit remains silent and motionless, they draw nearer and nearer, and ultimately hop around it and about it, treating it with the contempt it fully deserves. Motion, noise, and glitter are the things which birds mostly dislike. Figures of soldiers and sailors, whose arms end in fans that are turned by the action of the wind, formed in the semblance of broadswords, are disliked by the birds on account of the whirling and twirling that they keep up in every direction, according to the way of the wind."

Beeton's Dictionary of Every-Day Gardening, 1910.

PRUNUS

APRICOT, NECTARINE & PEACH

THE MAIN DIFFERENCE BETWEEN the peach and the nectarine lies in the skin; the former has a downy skin and the latter a smooth one. "That they are intimately related is shown by the fact that sometimes fruits, part Peach and part Nectarine will be born on the same plant. Instances are also recorded of a Peach arising from the seed of a Nectarine and vice versa." *Commercial Gardening*, 1913. As Ulysses Prentiss Hedrick comments, "The established history of the nectarine goes back 2,000 years and then merges into that of the peach." *The Peaches of New York*, 1917. Nectarines appear in the literature in England in the sixteenth century; a little later Parkinson described six varieties in 1629, noting "they have been with us not many years." Its first mention in the United States was in 1722 in Robert Beverly's *History of Virginia*. Apricots were cultivated in China more than three thousand years ago and were introduced into Europe by the Romans in 70–60 BCE. They are hardier than peaches, but to ripen properly they need the protection of a south-facing wall or to be cultivated under glass in cool climates. It is thought that English settlers took them to the east coast of North America, while Spanish missionaries introduced them to California, a state in which they are still grown commercially today in very large numbers.

P. persica var. *nectarine*
'JOHN RIVERS'

CULTIVATED BY C. 1850

Named by English nurseryman Thomas Rivers in honor of his grandfather, this nectarine has green skin with white and tender, juicy flesh. John Rivers founded the family nursery in 1725, and among the many cultivars developed by his grandson are the Czar plum, the apple Rivers Early Peach, and the Conference pear. John Rivers was introduced into the United States in the mid-1920s.

Apricot blossom.

P. persica var. *nectarine*
'LORD NAPIER'

CULTIVATED BY 1860

This is another nectarine raised by the Rivers Nursery of Sawbridgeworth, Hertfordshire, England, from a seed of a peach called Early Albert. A good heavy cropper producing large fruits and large blossoms. It ripens early and has white, aromatic flavorful flesh that is very juicy. The Royal Horticultural Society of London have given this plant their Award of Garden Merit.

P. armeniaca
'MOORPARK'

CULTIVATED BY 1760

Although 1760 is the date that Lord Anson's head gardener brought the first apricot to England, this variety is much older, probably dating back to the sixteenth century. Named after Anson's family seat, Moor Park, this is a reliable apricot with firm and juicy flesh that is rich and aromatic. "The tree is of vigorous growth, and

A half-standard peach in a plant container.

extraordinarily productive; the fruit is very large; of a bright gold color, or orange, with dark spots next the sun; flesh orange colour, melting, and excellent: ripens in August." *The Young Gardener's Assistant*, Thomas Bridgeman, 1847. It is still the most commonly grown apricot in Britain, and it even makes an appearance in Jane Austen's 1814 novel *Mansfield Park*.

"Let the tree, after the blossoms fall, be frequently shaken by a cord connected with a swinging door, or with a working pump-handle, etc.; or let the bugs be jarred from the tree and killed. Or keep geese enough in the fruit garden to devour all the damaged fruit as it falls. We know this last method is infallible."

The American nineteenth-century horticulturist and pomologist David Thomas gave this advice on preventing the depredations of the weevil on apricot, nectarine, and peach trees.

FRUIT GATHERERS

These fruit gatherers were attached to long poles and used to harvest fruit without the need of ladders. A: A funnel for gathering peaches. B: A funnel for pears. C: A Spanish orange gatherer. D: A Swiss fruit gatherer.

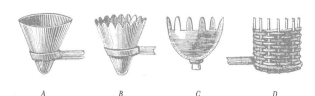

A   B   C   D

Few fruits are as delicious as a ripe peach.

P. persica
'PEREGRINE'

CULTIVATED BY 1906

This is a hardy variety of peach from England, yet it still needs some protection in cold regions. A reliable and high yielding

A pyramid peach in a plant container.

garden tree, it produces lovely pink blossoms. The fruits are large, with white skin and white juicy flesh flushed red. Bestowed with an Award of Garden Merit from the Royal Horticultural Society of London.

P. persica
'REDHAVEN'
or 'Red Haven'

CULTIVATED BY THE 1940S

An American peach developed by Dr. Stanley Johnston at the Michigan State Experiment Station, South Haven, Michigan, this variety has large fruits with orange skin flushed with deep red. The juicy flesh is pale yellow, firm, and sweet. It is a heavy cropper.

P. persica
'SUNCREST'

CULTIVATED BY 1959

This is one of the very best peaches: large, sweet, fragrant, with a yellow skin blushed with red. It appears on the Slow Food USA Ark of Taste and is the subject of the elegiac book *Epitaph for a Peach* by David

LOST, RARE, OR SIMPLY FORGOTTEN?

The British king George IV was crowned in 1821. In the same year, a peach selection was made in New York and named in the honor of the new king. The George IV peach enjoyed great success, described by the horticulturist A. J. Downing in 1845 as "the most popular peach for garden culture in the United States." Unfortunately, a hundred years later this peach was virtually forgotten due to competition from the vast number of new varieties that had been introduced. Today, it is scarce in North America, appearing on the Slow Food USA Ark of Taste, although it is being conserved at Monticello, Virginia. It has faired even less well in the United Kingdom; indeed, as far back as 1844 Richard Hogg wrote that "it was introduced from America several years ago, but is not now much in cultivation."

Mas Masumoto. Bred in Fresno, California, its fragility makes it difficult to ship, so it is now under threat, which is all the more reason to grow it in the home patch.

PRUNUS

PLUM

THE SPECIES *Prunus domestica* includes the plum, damson, bullace, greengage, and mirabelle. Plums are eaten fresh, cooked, or dried. The purple and oval-shaped damson is tart so must be cooked, as must the bullace. The chief distinction between the damson and bullace is the shape of the fruit; the latter is much rounder, and it can sometimes be white. The greengage is mostly eaten fresh and is considered to be the finest (green) dessert plum. The smaller yellow mirabelle is also eaten fresh.

P. domestica
'BURBANK'

CULTIVATED BY 1929

Luther Burbank bred an astonishing 113 varieties of plums, including the eponymous Burbank. He imported many Japanese plums into North America, which were then interbred with native stock. The skin of the Burbank plum is red and gold, and the firm and sweet flesh is orange. It is a hardy and prolific tree.

P. domestica
'GREEN GAGE'

CULTIVATED BY 1724

Green Gage is the most famous of plums. A very superior fruit, it has a round shape and green skin that ripens to yellow golden. In the early sixteenth century, the French king Francis I named the plum Grosse Reine Claude in honor of his wife Claudia. History tells us that an English priest named John Gage sent a consignment of Grosse Reine Claude fruit trees to his brother, Sir William Gage, at Hengrave Hall, Suffolk, England. The labels are said to have gone astray in transit, so Gage's gardener then conflated his employer's name with the color of the fruit, and thus was born the Green Gage. However, it is thought that the fruit was cultivated much

The Green Gage plum.

A damson.

earlier in England under its Italian name of Verdochia (or Verdoch). It was grown in North America as early as 1755 and gave rise to many varieties of gage plums. H. V. Taylor proclaimed it, "For all purposes unsurpassed." *The Plums of England*, 1949.

P. domestica
'JEFFERSON'
or 'Jefferson Gage'

CULTIVATED BY 1783

In *The Fruit Manual*, 1884, Robert Hogg tells us that "this remarkably fine plum" was "raised by Judge Buel [of the Albany Horticultural Society], and named in honor of President Jefferson." Jefferson certainly planted twenty-one budded trees of this variety in the South Orchard at Monticello, Virginia, in 1783. When discussing American plum varieties, *The Gardener's Assistant*, 1937, maintained that "Jefferson holds the first rank." It is a form that is much loved by gardeners today for its sweet and juicy, golden-yellow flesh.

P. saliciana
'METHLEY'

CULTIVATED BY 1926

This plum is said to have been a chance seedling found by Willoughby Methley of Balgowan, Natal, South Africa. It has large round fruits with purple and red skin and sweet amber flesh. It is a heavy cropper, best suited to warm climates.

P. salicina
'SANTA ROSA'

CULTIVATED BY 1906

Developed from imported Asian stock, this is a beautiful plum that has purple and red skin flushed with a blue bloom. The juicy flesh is amber and has a tangy taste. This is another Burbank introduction and was named after his research center at Santa Rosa in California.

GARDEN GHOSTS

Despite having little or no education beyond that provided by his high school, Luther Burbank (1849–1926) bred more than eight hundred new varieties of plants, including vegetables, fruits, nuts, grains, and flowers. Very early in his career, he developed the famous Burbank potato, still very much in production today. Many of the results of his plant-breeding experiments appeared in his 1893 catalog *New Creations in Plants and Flowers*, and his publication *Luther Burbank: His Methods and Discoveries and Their Practical Application*, ran to twelve volumes (1914–15). Influenced by the writings of Charles Darwin, Burbank's experiments helped turn plant breeding into a branch of modern science.

"How is it that we see so few Plums in America, when the markets are supplied with cartloads in such a chilly, shady, and blighty country as England?"

American Gardener,
William Cobbett, 1821.

A SELECTION OF CUTTING TOOLS TO BE FOUND OF USE IN EVERY GARDEN

KEY
A: Hedge Shears
B: Lopping Shears
C: Pruning Shears
D: French Secateur
E: Pruning Shears
F: Pruning Shears
G: Flower Gatherer
H: Grass-Edging Shears
I: Hook Tree Pruner
J: Billhook
K: Billhook
L: Shears
M: Asparagus Knife
N: Aerial Pruning Saw
O: Saw

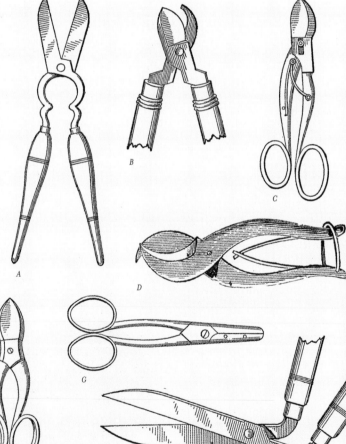

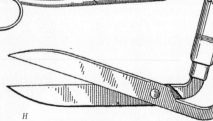

A

B

C

D

E

F

G

H

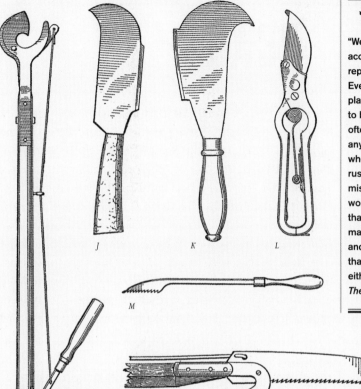

J

K

L

M

N

O

I

TOOL MAINTENANCE

"Wet days may be turned to good account by oiling, sharpening, and repairing any tools that require it. Even in small gardens a suitable place for the storage of tools ought to be found, instead of, as is too often the case, throwing them into any corner or out-of-the-way place, where they either get spoiled with rust or damp or are mysteriously missing when next required. Men work better when in good health than when in bad, and in like manner with good clean tools more and better work is accomplished than is possible when they are either rusty or blunt or rickety."
The Gardener's Assistant, 1936.

GARDEN LINE AND REEL
"A garden line should be of good material, wound on a reel, which not only permits the line to dry more speedily than when closely rolled up, but also facilitates its being readily extended and recoiled. When stretched and supported between two points, with the intention of indicating a straight line between them, the line should combine strength with lightness, as, for instance, small whipcord. A stout iron pin, 2 feet (60cm) long, with a loop after the pattern of a skewer, is a useful fastener for a garden line."
The Gardener's Assistant, 1936.

PYRUS

PEAR

PEARS ARE NATIVE to the Northern Hemisphere and date back to prehistoric times. There are many mentions of them in the agricultural literature of the Romans, including the writings of Pliny and Cato. In *The Odyssey,* Homer proclaimed that the pear was one of the "splendid gifts of the gods." It is possible they were introduced into Britain by the Romans; certainly there are many mentions of the fruit throughout the following centuries. In 1597 John Gerard wrote in his *Herball* that to list the many varieties of pear would require a dedicated volume. More varieties were introduced from the European continent from the sixteenth to the nineteenth centuries, particularly from France. The early colonists took the pear to the east coast of North America, from where it traveled west with the pioneers. Today, there are about three thousand varieties of pear in cultivation throughout the world, many of which are old

---

P. communis
'BEURRÉ BOSC'
or 'Kaiser'

CULTIVATED BY C. 1800

This is an old Belgian variety that was discovered by Monsieur Bosc, director of the Jardin des Plantes, Paris. It was introduced to North America in the 1830s. Well known as a dessert pear of first-rate quality, its flesh is firm and white with a sweet, buttery taste. The skin is golden, and it also cooks well. This makes a reliable and prolific garden tree.

P. communis
'BEURRÉ D'ANJOU'
or 'D'Anjou'

CULTIVATED BY 1800

This large pear with green skin and sweet white flesh was introduced into England in the early nineteenth century from the Angers region of France. So popular did it prove there that a Colonel Marshall Wilder from Boston introduced it to the United States in 1842.

P. communis
'CITRON DES CARMES'
or 'Madeleine'

CULTIVATED BY 1628

This early-season small pear has a rich, sweet taste and juicy flesh. It is far more suited to home growers than to commercial production, because it is too delicate to travel

A long-handled pruning tool.

well. In France it was named after Saint Madeleine by Carmelite monks, because it was said to ripen for her feast day on May 25. In North America, however, it is ready by mid- to late July.

P. communis

'DOYENNÉ DU COMICE'
or 'Comice'

CULTIVATED BY 1849

One of the very best dessert pears: large, sweet, aromatic, and juicy with pale green skin that turns pale yellow as it ripens. It was raised at the Comice Horticole Garden, Angers, France, first fruiting in 1849. This late-nineteenth-century report of the Comice pear comes from a Mr. R.D. Blackmore of Teddington, England: "This is, to my mind, the best of all pears; very healthy, a certain cropper, of beautiful growth, and surpassing flavor. I have grown it to the weight of 14 ounces (400g) on heavily cropped trees. But on a wall it is far inferior."

P. communis

'ROUSSELET DE REIMS'

CULTIVATION DATE UNKNOWN

A very ancient pear, claims have been made that it was the favorite pear of the French king Louis XIV, although it is certainly much older. Also known as the musk or spice pear, the fruits are small with yellow-green skin flushed with red. It was introduced into the British Isles in the seventeenth century where it is now rare, but it is more widely available in the United States.

P. communis

'SECKEL'
or 'Sugar Pear'

CULTIVATED BY C. 1800

Richard Hogg in *The Fruit Manual*, 1884, writes the following of this sweet and aromatic American pear: "The original tree is still in existence, and is growing in a meadow in Passyunk township, about a quarter of a mile from Delaware, opposite League Island, and about three miles and a half from Philadelphia. It is nearly a hundred years old, and about 30 feet (9m) high…The property on which the tree stands belonged in 1817 to Mr. Seckle (not Seckel) of Philadelphia, and hence the origin of the name." This is a hardy tree; the fruits are small, with skin flushed crimson and yellow juicy flesh. It was introduced from the United States into the United Kingdom in 1819.

P. communis

'WILLIAMS'
BON CHRÉTIEN'
or 'Bartlett,' 'Williams'

CULTIVATED BY 1770

One of the oldest and finest English dessert pears. A schoolmaster called Mr. Stair bred it at Aldermaston, Berkshire, England, and nurseryman Richard Williams introduced it commercially and gave it his name. James Carter of Boston took it to North America in 1797 for a Mr. Thomas Brewer, who planted it at his estate at Roxbury, Massachusetts. A later resident, Enoch Bartlett, found what was

---

LOST, RARE, OR SIMPLY FORGOTTEN?

Perry is a traditional drink made from fermented pear juice. Just as cider comes from special cider apples, perry can only be made from perry pears, which are not suitable for eating. Indeed the seventeenth-century English botanist John Evelyn wrote of the Barland perry pear that it had "such insufferable taste, that hungry swine will not smell to it, or if hunger tempts them to taste, they shake it out of their mouths." The Barland pear is still grown today and makes a large and long-lived tree. Although many old perry varieties exist still, they are under threat, so if you have the room, do consider planting one; among the best are Blakeney Red and Yellow Huffcap.

---

to him an unidentified pear and began to distribute it under his own name. It is thought that Gold Rush prospectors took it west to California, where it thrives still and is one of North America's most popular pears.

RHEUM

RHUBARB

ALTHOUGH BOTANICALLY A VEGETABLE, rhubarb is often regarded as a fruit and is cooked and served as such. For the sake of regulation in 1947, a court in New York ruled that it was indeed a fruit. Long known in Asia, rhubarb did not reach the West until the eighteenth century: "The first importation of the root into this country [England] was 1735, which was from China. Its first culture was in 1763." *On the Cultivation of Rhubarb,* Richardus, 1833. Beware—the leaves are toxic, although the stems are safe to eat once cooked. To produce long and tender stems early in the season, the plant should be covered with a large terra-cotta flowerpot used for forcing. It does not fare well in hot summers and is better not moved once it is established.

Rheum × hybridum
'GLASKIN'S PERPETUAL'
or 'Mr. Glaskin's Perpetual'

CULTIVATED BY THE 1920S

This variety is named after the amateur English gardener John Jessie Glaskin of Brighton, Sussex, England, who developed the variety at his orchard. Unlike other types of rhubarb, this can be cut in its first year without weakening the plant. It crops early and has long green stems that are less tart and more tender than most other varieties.

Rheum × hybridum
'VICTORIA'
or 'Myatt's Victoria'

CULTIVATED BY 1837

This is one of the very best rhubarb cultivars and was raised by the company of Joseph Myatt of New Cross, London, in 1837 in honor of Queen Victoria's accession to the throne. Myatt also raised excellent varieties of strawberries, potatoes, and peas. It has large, bright red stems that can reach up to 4 feet (1.2m) in height, so do plan carefully before planting it!

BLUEBERRY

or HIGH BUSH BLUEBERRY

GROWING BY CANDLELIGHT

In 1877 the first special forcing sheds were constructed in the English county of Yorkshire to produce very early and very sweet rhubarb. After being raised outside for two years, the rhubarb crowns are lifted and replanted inside the dark and heated forcing sheds. Under these conditions the rhubarb grows quickly, searching for light. The stalks are harvested by hand using only candlelight, and the resulting stems are vivid red in color with white, tender, and sweet flesh. Once this area of Yorkshire, known as the Rhubarb Triangle, produced 90 percent of the world's winter-forced rhubarb but, unfortunately, production has dwindled to just a dozen or so growers. Yorkshire Forced Rhubarb now appears on the Slow Food UK Ark of Taste as a threatened fruit.

THE BLUEBERRY IS A NATIVE PLANT of North America. It features in the mythology of Native Americans who knew them as "starberries," due to their star-shaped flowers. Claims for their health-promoting powers in recent years have boosted their popularity both commercially and among home growers. The blueberry did not reach the United Kingdom until 1949, when *The Gardeners' Chronicle* printed an article stating that a parson from Lulu Island, British Columbia, Canada, would send one hundred blueberry plants free to anyone in the United Kingdom who wanted to grow them. A Mr. Trehane from Dorset took up his offer, and it proved the beginning of a successful nursery business that still thrives today.

Beware: the leaves of rhubarb are toxic.

V. corymbosum 'BLUERAY'

CULTIVATED BY 1939

Bred by the US Department of Agriculture and introduced in the late 1930s, this is a dependable blueberry. It has large, light blue fruits with a sweet flavor.

V. corymbosum 'JERSEY'

CULTIVATION DATE UNKNOWN

This is an old variety with deep blue fruits that have a sweet and complex flavor. Producing high yields, it is also a tough and hardy plant. Like all blueberries, to thrive, Jersey needs a well-drained, acidic soil.

V. corymbosum 'PATRIOT'

CULTIVATION DATE UNKNOWN

This is a vigorous ornamental bush as well as being productive in fruit. It has large, mid-blue berries and is especially suited to growing in the home patch, because the fruits ripen over a long period.

V. corymbosum
'PIONEER'

CULTIVATED BY 1912

Dr. Frederick Coville made this selection from a cross of two blueberries found in the wild. The medium-sized, light blue fruits are sweet and produce a good harvest. Pioneer is not good for storing or shipping, but it is beloved by home gardeners for its superior taste and fine quality.

V. corymbosum
'RUBEL'

CULTIVATED BY 1916

Elizabeth White was the daughter of a New Jersey cranberry farmer, and worked closely with botanist Dr. Frederick Coville to develop the first cultivated highbush blueberries in Whitebog Village, New Jersey, in the early decades of the twentieth century. She employed local people, called "pineys," to search in the pines within a twenty-mile (32km) radius of Whitebog Village. It was her practice to name the selections collected from the wild after the people who foraged for them, so alongside Rubel there are Adams, Donphy, Grover, Harding, and Sam. The eponymous Rubel has an excellent flavor and is very vigorous.

VITUS
GRAPE

THE GRAPE IS ONE OF THE EARLIEST KNOWN fruit crops—its cultivation dates back to 6000–6500 BCE. The Egyptians were the first to ferment grapes to make wine, and the practice then spread throughout Europe during the expansion of the Roman Empire. Following on from the Romans, viticulture was continued by many monastic institutions. Spanish missionaries planted the first grapes in southwestern North America in about 1700, and their cultivation spread to central California, where most commercial grape growing takes place today. In the wild, grape vines are naturally vigorous climbers, which has meant gardeners have had to develop sophisticated methods of pruning to keep the plants productive at a manageable size. It is said that there are as many as ten thousand grape varieties, yet a mere 20 percent of these are grown widely.

V. labrusca
'DIAMOND'
or 'Moore's Diamond'

CULTIVATED BY C. 1860

This very sweet white grape—a cross of Concord and Iona—was developed in New York. It is now rare in the United Kingdom. It resembles the variety Niagara but has smaller fruits. The skin may split in damp summers.

V. vinifera
'MUSCAT OF ALEXANDRIA'

CULTIVATION DATE UNKNOWN

Some say this grape dates back to ancient Egypt; it is certainly one of the oldest in existence. In 1910, *Beeton's Dictionary of Every-Day Gardening* hailed it as "Rich amber, bunch immensely large, with a

V. vinifera
'SCHIAVA GROSSA'
or 'Black Hamburgh,'
'Muscat of Hamburg'

CULTIVATION DATE UNKNOWN

An old variety of table grape with juicy and sweet, dark purple fruits. In cool climates the fruit sets best when cultivated indoors. The Great Vine at Hampton Court Palace, London, is this variety and was planted by the famous landscape gardener Lancelot "Capability" Brown in 1768. It is still fruiting today, a testament to its vigor. "The Vine lives to a great age under favorable circumstances. Pliny mentions one 600 years old; vines 100 years old are accounted young in the vineyards of Italy; and Bosc states there are some in Burgundy upwards of 400 years old." *The Gardener's Assistant*, 1936.

A grape rack with specially made bottles.

deliciously rich Muscat flavor; requires a warm vinery." With an excellent taste, this white-seed variety needs a warm climate or indoor cultivation. In *The Fruit Manual*, 1884, Robert Hogg advises: "The vine is an abundant bearer, but the bunches set badly. To remedy this defect, a very good plan is to draw the hand down the bunches when they are in bloom, so as to distribute the pollen, and thereby aid fertilization."

V. labrusca
'NIAGARA'
or 'White Concord'

CULTIVATED BY 1868

Although an old variety, the 'Niagara' grape is still grown widely in North America, although it can be hard to find elsewhere. A cross of 'Concord' and 'Cassady', it is a green seedless grape from Niagara County, New York, and was introduced commercially in 1882.

HISTORICAL NOTE

Traditional wisdom has it that a dead sheep should be buried in the ground alongside a new grapevine. A healthy application of homemade compost may do just as well, although in the past, several experts have counseled against using animal manure, among them Thomas Bridgeman. "It has been proved by repeated experiments that the best manure for vines is the branches pruned from the vines themselves, cut into small pieces, and mixed with the soil by means of a garden hoe. Dr. Liebig, in his 'Organic Chemistry,' mentions several instances of vines being kept in a thriving condition for from ten to thirty years by the trimmings of vines alone. The discovery was made by poor peasants, who could not afford to buy the ordinary kinds of manure." *The Young Gardener's Assistant*, 1847.

NOTES ON THE CULTIVATION OF ESCULENT VEGETABLES

to be undertaken during the summer months.

In a considerable measure, the crops now take care of themselves and we may consider the chief anxieties and activities of the season over. Watering and weeding are the principal labors of early summer, and both must be pursued with diligence. Ordinary watering, where every drip has to be dipped and carried, is often injurious rather than beneficial, for the simple reason that it is only half done. I advise to abstain from giving water as long as possible, and then to give it in abundance, watering only a small plot every day in order to saturate the soil.

Throughout the summer months it may either be hot, with frequent heavy rains and vegetation in the most luxuriant growth, or the soil may be iron and the heavens brass, with scarce a green blade to be seen. The light flying showers that can occur now do not render watering unnecessary; in fact, a heavy soaking of a crop after a moderate rainfall is a valuable aid to its growth, for it requires a long-continued heavy downpour to penetrate to the roots.

SOME VEGETABLES IN NEED OF THE GARDENER'S ATTENTION AT THIS MOST PRODUCTIVE TIME OF YEAR

ASPARAGUS *Asparagus officinalis*

Stop cutting by early summer, when emerging spears are small and the tips open. Liquid manure will do great things for asparagus now, and a dressing of salt may be given with great advantage.

Sow cabbage seeds in summer.

BROCCOLI *Brassica oleracea* Italica group

To be planted outdoor at every opportunity from earlier sowings. In early summer, sow for cutting late spring next year. Plant outdoors in late summer far enough apart, or if crowded where they are already planted for the winter, take out every alternate plant and make another plantation.

CABBAGE *Brassica oleracea* Capitata group

In cool regions, sow a good breadth of small cabbages early summer; they will be valuable to plant as the summer crops are cleared away. In warm climates, sow in late summer for a fall harvest.

CAULIFLOWER *Brassica oleracea* Botrytis group

In the North, to be sown early summer where they are to remain, and of course to be thinned to a proper distance in due time. Any that are planted out now from seedbeds in Zones 8 and 9 must have water, and be shaded during midday for a week. Come late summer they can be sown to stand the winter in Zones 8b to 10, and there is no better place for them than a bed in a frame, in an open, sunny spot, but they may be wintered in open quarters under temporary glass. It is important to have the plants as hardy as possible by free exposure, and, therefore, they must not be sheltered or shaded until frost threatens them, and then the glass must be put on, but they must have air at every opportunity.

Sow suitable cauliflower varieties in late summer for overwintering.

CELERY *Apium graveolens*

Plant outdoors in late summer without loss of time, in showery weather if possible, but if the weather is hot and dry, shade the plants and give water. Twigs laid across the trenches will also give shade enough with very little trouble.

CHICORY *Cichorium endivia*

These plants prefer cool weather, and depending on the type and your climate, you may be able to sow midsummer for a late crop. It will be well to make two sowings, say four weeks apart. Select, if possible, a dry, sloping bank for the purpose.

CUCUMBER *Cucumis sativus*

For pickling, cucumbers may be sown on ridges in early summer. On ridges, they generally do well without water, but they must not be exposed to drought. If watering must be done, make sure the first is of soft water well warmed by exposure to the sun, and water them liberally three or four evenings in succession, and then give no more for a week or two.

ONION *Allium cepa*

Can be sown early summer for scallions. Beds of large kinds to be thinned in good time. The best onions for keeping are those of moderate size, perfectly ripened. In late summer sow those to stay outdoors the winter for a spring crop. Two small sowings—a month apart—will be better than one large sowing. Take up onions for storing; and if any are as yet unripe, spread them out in the sun in a dry place where they can be covered quickly in case of rain. In wet, cold seasons it is sometimes necessary to finish the store onions by putting them in a nearly cold oven for some hours before they are put away.

PARSLEY *Petroselinum crispum*

Sow midsummer for winter use. This is a most important matter even in the smallest garden. In hot regions, provide partial shade.

Store onions for winter use.

PEA *Pisum sativum*

In late summer peas may still be sown for a fall harvest. Crops coming forward for late bearing should have attention, more especially to make them safe against storms by a sufficiency of support, and in case of drought to give abundance of water.

POTATO *Solanum tuberosum*

To be taken up midsummer, a couple of weeks after the haulm (tops) begins to wither, and stored, as the act of lifting will promote complete ripening of the roots. Quick-growing kinds may be planted to dig as new potatoes in fall.

RADISH *Rhaphanus sativus*

In hot-summer areas, sow long-season cultivars for winter use. Radishes can be sown through the summer in other areas.

SPINACH *Spinacia oleracea*

To avoid heat and long days, you can sow spinach seeds in late summer for a fall harvest, selecting ground lying high and dry for the seedbed. Sow every four weeks until four to six weeks before the first frost, leaving the last sowing to overwinter for a spring harvest. In mild winter areas, you may be able to continue harvesting through the winter.

TOMATO *Solanum lycopersicum*

To be gathered as soon as ripe, which for those in the South may be as eary as May, but those farther north may need to wait until midsummer. If bad weather interferes with the finishing of the crop, cut the full-grown fruit with a length of stem attached and hang it up in a warm kitchen or in a sunny greenhouse.

TURNIP *Brassica rapa* Rapifera group

May be sown in variety and quantity from mid- to late summer for a fall harvest.

Tomatoes are one of the most welcome of summer crops.

A bicolor variety of radish.

The hardy Swiss chard.

SOME ESCULENT PLANTS SUITABLE FOR LATE SUMMER SOWINGS

SWISS CHARD *Beta vulgaris* ssp. *cicla*

Often referred to as leaf beets, Swiss chard is especially suited for late sowing because it is extremely hardy but may also be used as a "cut-and-come-again" vegetable at all stages of growth. In hot climates, sew in partial shade. If they dye back in the most extreme weather, they will begin growing anew in spring, when they may be cropped until they run to seed. At which point, the prudent gardener, having sown another crop in early spring, will find a crop that may be appreciated (almost) continuously.

Sow from midspring to late summer, 1 inch (2.5cm) deep in rows 1 foot (30cm) apart and gradually thin to 6 inches (15cm) apart in the rows. The thinnings may be eaten as they are taken. Think not to crop the whole plant. Instead remove only enough leaves as are required, for the plant will continue to produce new leaves from the center throughout the growing season. Swiss chard will grow in any reasonable soil in sun or light shade.

CORN SALAD *Valerianella locusta*

Also known as lamb's lettuce and mache, corn salad is raised from seeds, which should be sown in a bed or border of light rich soil (although it will succeed in many locations). It may either be sown broadcast, and lightly raked in, or in shallow furrows 5 to 6 inches (12–15cm) apart. All the culture that is then required is confined to watering the seedbed and the young plants in dry weather and protecting them, where possible, during severe frost. The plants will be sufficiently thinned by removing the most advanced for consumption, leaving the youngest to come in for use in succession.

Sow in furrows 6–8 inches (15–20cm) apart; be mindful to keep the hoe well at work, and when ready thin the plants out to 4 inches (10cm) apart. They should be eaten young. In the summer months the whole plant is edible, but in the winter or spring the outer leaves only should be used.

A selection of pruning and budding knives.

MINER'S LETTUCE *Claytonia perfoliata*

This favorite of winter greens, also known as winter purslane, may be expected to yield a continuous supply of leaves from midfall to late spring, though it may need protection of a cold frame in the North. Four or five cuts during this period may reasonably be expected. As well as the leaves, which are rich in vitamin C, miner's lettuce produces tiny white edible flowers; unusually these grow through the center of the leaves.

The seeds are sown in shallow furrows, where the plants will grow. Gradually thin the seedlings to 6 inches (15cm) apart and use the thinnings in salads.

The leaves of miner's lettuce are eaten as a salad. They can also be cooked and used like spinach.

A useful tool for pruning tall trees and shrubs.

"July is like January in one respect for gardeners, for everything depends on the weather."

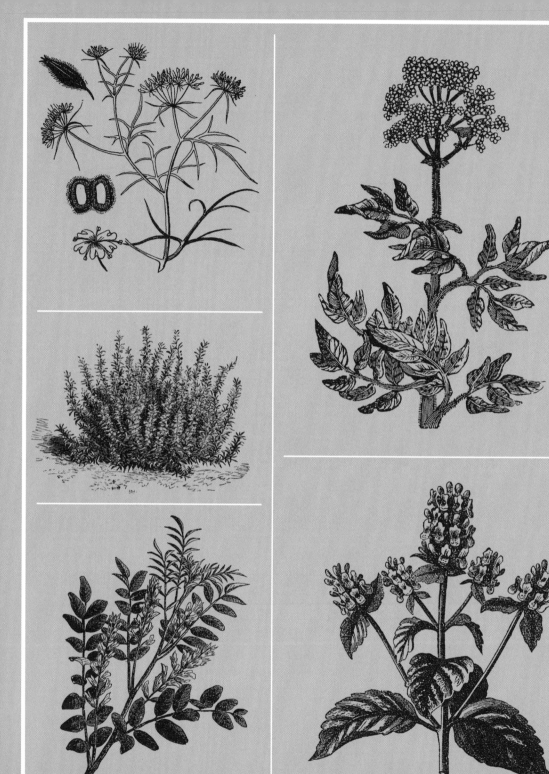

THE HERB DIRECTORY

THE HERB DIRECTORY

A SPECIAL SELECTION OF CULINARY, ECONOMIC & PHYSICAL HERBS

LADY'S MANTLE
Alchemilla mollis

CULTIVATED BY 1548

This is a beautiful garden plant with dainty yellow flowers and velvety green leaves that were so aptly described by John Parkinson: "The hollow crumplings and the edges also of the leaves, will containe the dew in droppes like pearles, that falleth in the night." *Theatrum Botanicum*, 1640. It has long been associated with alleviating gynecological and skin problems. The young leaves have a bitter taste and can be used in salads.

Allium schoenoprasum
CHIVE

CULTIVATION DATE UNKNOWN

A useful culinary herb, the narrow leaves of chives are mildly pungent, with hollow insides, and the

Chive.

flowers are pink or violet. The plants make small, tight clumps 4 to 6 inches (10–15cm) tall that are best divided every three years. "The plants are usually grown as an edging, and appear to do better that way than when grown in a bed … The leaves, when wanted for table use, are cut with a knife, and seem to grow more vigorously the oftener they are cut." *The Vegetable Garden*, Vilmorin-Andrieux, 1885. Concerning chives, Culpeper gave this medicinal warning: "They send up very hurtful vapors to the brain, causing troublesome sleep, and spoiling the eye sight." *Complete Herbal*, 1653.

Althaea officinalis
MARSHMALLOW
or White Mallow

CULTIVATION DATE UNKNOWN

Growing to 6 feet (1.8m) tall, with pink or white flowers. Herbalists have long exploited the seeds, leaves, flowers, and roots of this hardy herbaceous perennial. Its association with the pink confectionary comes from a sweet paste created by mixing with water a mucilage from the powdered root and heating it with sugar. Culpeper quotes the ambitious claims made by Pliny for the humble mallow: "Pliny saith, that whosoever shall take a spoonful of any of the mallows shall that day be free from all diseases that may come unto him, and that it is special good for the falling sickness." *Complete Herbal*, 1653.

Marshmallow.

> ☠ We do not want to alarm, but consider it our proper duty to advise that seeds marked thus may be injurious or hazardous to health; we advise proper caution when handling them. We further caution against using any of the herbal cures noted in these pages without reference to more recent publications or discussion with a qualified medical practitioner. We use these charming historical snippets only for descriptive purposes.

Anethum graveolens
DILL

CULTIVATION DATE UNKNOWN

In use since the time of the ancient Egyptians, dill has long been cultivated for both its medicinal and culinary properties. It arrived in North America with the early settlers in the seventeenth century, where it is said to have gained the name "meetin' seed," because it was given to children at church so they could chew their way through long sermons. A tall, elegant, and stately plant, it has fernlike leaves and yellow umbelliferous flowers. "The plants are pulled up or cut off low when some of the seeds are ripe. The rest of the seeds will develop and can be separated from the umbels after a few days 'drying off' or in the frame. It is most important to get these flaky seeds absolutely 'husky' before storing them away, and they should be dried by sunshine or slow warmth for several days after they have been separated from the umbels." *Garden Herbs*, George E. Whitehead, 1944.

Angelica archangelica
ANGELICA
or Archangel

CULTIVATION DATE UNKNOWN

According to Culpeper, angelica "makes the heart merry, drives away melancholy, quickens the spirits." In the Middle Ages, it was known as "the herb of the fairies," because it was believed to offer protection against plague. Being a native of damp habitats, it can grow to an impressive 8 feet

Angelica.

(2.4m) tall, and the roots, seeds, leaves, and stems are all used for culinary and medicinal purposes. In *The Vegetable Garden*, 1885, Vilmorin-Andrieux describes how "the stems and leaf stalks are eaten preserved in sugar. The leaves are also used as a vegetable in some parts of Europe. The root, which is spindle-shaped, is employed in medicine; it is sometimes called 'The Root of the Holy Ghost.' The seeds enter into the composition of various liqueurs." A biennial plant, it flowers in its second year of growth from early to midsummer.

Anthemis tinctoria
GOLDEN CHAMOMILE
or Dyer's Chamomile

CULTIVATED BY 1561

This plant can grow up to 2½ feet (75cm) tall and the golden yellow flowers are used as an herbal dye. The resulting color will depend upon what mordant is used, which fixes the color. Bright yellow is achieved by using alum and cream of tartar, while an olive green results from using either copper or acetic acid. When *tinctoria* is the species name of a plant it indicates it can be used as a dye.

Anthriscus cerefolium
CHERVIL

CULTIVATION DATE UNKNOWN

In the nineteenth century Vilmorin-Andrieux asserted that chervil "is much in demand in English gardens," understandable when one considers its fine and delicate foliage and pretty white flowers. For maximum flavor, plant in light shade and harvest the leaves before the plant flowers. John Gerard wrote of chervil that it "is pleasant to the stomache and taste ... It is used very much among the Dutch people in a kinde of hotchpot which they do eate, called Warmus. The leaves of sweet Chervill are exceeding

---

GARDEN GHOSTS

John Gerard (1545–1612) was a much-respected English botanist, herbalist, and advisor to Queen Elizabeth I. In 1597 he published *Herball, Generall Histoire of Plants*, much of which was based on a translation of an earlier Dutch work. However, his innovation was to incorporate novel plants from the New World into the *Herball*, because a large number of native American species were introduced into Europe by Spanish colonists during this period.

Chervil.

good, wholesome, and pleasant, among other salad herbs, giving the taste of anise seed unto the rest." Tradition has it that chervil should be consumed on Maundy Thursday as it is said to restore the digestive system following on from the privations of Lent.

Arnica montana
MOUNTAIN ARNICA ☠
or Arnica

CULTIVATION DATE UNKNOWN

This is a hardy plant with oval leaves and large yellow flowers that grow to 2 feet (60cm) in height. The topical application of arnica preparations to heal bruises, strains, and sprains has been practiced for centuries and is still popular today, although contact with the plant can also cause skin irritation. It should never be taken internally.

Borago officinalis
BORAGE

CULTIVATION DATE UNKNOWN

This hardy annual plant has small, starlike blue flowers born on prickly stems and reaches 1–2 feet (30–60cm) in height. The flowers, which are much loved by bees, can be added to salads and the young leaves have a cooling, cucumber flavor. Vilmorin-Andrieux noted, "This plant can be grown without trouble, by sowing the seeds in any corner of the garden at any time from spring to the end of fall ...It is one of the pretty true blue flowers, and almost worth growing in certain places for its beauty ...It is sold chiefly to hotel keepers for making claret cup. The flowers are used to garnish salads, but the plant is grown for the manufacture of cordials."
The Vegetable Garden, 1885.

Arnica.

Borage.

GARDEN GHOSTS

Culpeper's *Complete Herbal and English Physician*, usually referred to as the *Complete Herbal*, was rarely out of print since it was first published in 1653. Written by the maverick English apothecary and physician Nicolas Culpeper (1616–54) it is a mix of herbal medicine, astrology, and the theoretical treatise known as the *Doctrine of Signatures*. Practiced since the Middle Ages, the doctrine is based on the premise that like cures like; so a plant that resembles a particular part of the human body can be used in its treatment. For instance, the plant eyebright (*Euphrasia*) was believed to cure a sickness of the eye, because its flower looks like a bright blue eye. Similarly, brainlike walnuts were used to treat psychiatric disorders.

Carum carvi
CARAWAY

CULTIVATION DATE UNKNOWN

Caraway has been in cultivation since ancient times, and the seeds have been found in Egyptians' tombs. The seeds, leaves, and roots all have a number of culinary uses. Culpeper makes much of its beneficial qualities for those experiencing an excess of gas and, in addition, explains, "The powder of the seeds put into a poultice, taketh away black and blue spots of blows and bruises." Caraway is an undemanding, hardy biennial that thrives best in full sun; Vilmorin-Andrieux tells us that in the nineteenth century the custom was to gather the seeds in meadows "where the plant grows spontaneously."

Caraway.

Roman chamomile.

Chamaemelum nobile
ROMAN CHAMOMILE

CULTIVATION DATE UNKNOWN

Growing to only 2 inches (5cm) high, or a little more where the footfall is light, *C. nobile* makes an excellent alternative to the usual grass lawn. It was very popular in Elizabethan England and was used for garden seats as well as lawns, mainly because when brushed against, its leaves release an attractive fragrance. "Camomile flowers are highly esteemed for their agreeable tonic properties. They are mainly relaxant, and only moderately stimulant; expend their influence somewhat promptly; manifest a decided action upon the circulation, nerves, and stomach." *The Physiomedical Dispensatory,* William Cook, 1869.

Cnicus benedictus
BLESSED THISTLE
or Holy Thistle, St. Benedict's Thistle

CULTIVATION DATE UNKNOWN

This thistle-like annual plant is native to the Mediterranean region and grows to 2 feet (60cm) tall. It has large, prickly leaves and bright yellow flowers. Culpeper tells us that the planet Mars rules the blessed thistle and it is "good for all sorts of malignant and pestilential fevers, and for agues of all kinds. It destroys worms in the stomach, and is good against all sorts of poison."

Conopodium majus
PIGNUT
or Earth Nut, Earth Chestnut

CULTIVATION DATE UNKNOWN

The tuber of this hardy perennial plant resembles a chestnut, hence one of its common names. They are edible, can be eaten raw or cooked, and have a delicious nutty taste. The seeds are also used for flavoring and as a substitute for cumin, and the leaves as a garnish and flavoring, in much the same way as parsley. Growing to 2 feet (60cm) tall, it bears small pretty white flowers.

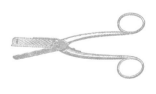

Scissors.

Coriander.

Coriandrum sativum
CORIANDER
or Cilantro

CULTIVATION DATE UNKNOWN

Coriander has been cultivated for culinary and medicinal use for at least three thousand years and continues to be popular with home growers today. It is best sown in its growing position in spring in full sun and needs a fertile, well-drained soil. A hardy annual, it grows to 2 feet (60cm) tall and bears dainty white or pink flowers above feathery foliage, both of which exude a heady aroma. Coriander seeds are used as a spice; the leaves are the herb known as cilantro.

Cuminum cyminum
CUMIN

CULTIVATION DATE UNKNOWN

Hailing from Upper Egypt, this hot and aromatic spice is low growing, with thin leaves and small lilac flowers. In ancient Egypt it was used to mummify pharaohs, and it was also cultivated by the Greeks and Romans. The latter introduced it throughout Europe, where its popularity continues to the present day. It has a nutty, peppery flavor, and many claims are made for its nutritional benefits. An easy plant to grow, in *The Vegetable Garden* Vilmorin-Andrieux notes that "no attention is necessary, except the occasional use of the hoe."

Cumin.

Dipsacus sativus
INDIAN TEASEL
or Card's Thistle, Fuller's Teasel

CULTIVATION DATE UNKNOWN

This biennial plant is a close relative of the common teasel (*D. fullonum*), growing up to 6 feet (1.8m) tall, and has prickly comblike flowers colored lavender to purple, much visited by birds and bees. It is believed to be a cultivated form of the common teasel, but its European origins are obscure. It was introduced into North America in the nineteenth century. The curved spines found on the seed heads of Indian teasel are very strong and were traditionally used to raise the nap on woollen cloth; some purists still claim their results are superior to those achieved by modern mechanized techniques. Medieval herbalists believed that rainwater collected in the cuplike form at the base of the leaves held special properties. Teasels are prolific self-seeders and can become invasive if not controlled.

STREWING HERBS

Strewing is the practice of spreading sweet-smelling and aromatic herbs and flowers on the floors of houses to mask unpleasant odors and repel insects and vermin. Popular throughout Europe from the late medieval to early Renaissance periods, herbs and flowers were mixed with rushes and straws and strewn around indoors. As the floors were walked over, the plants' natural oils were released along with pleasant fragrances. Meadowsweet, rosemary, yarrow, and sweet woodruff were among the most popular plants used, along with strong-smelling herbs, such as lavender, mint, hyssop, and sage. In 1660 the first Royal Herb-Strewer was appointed, whose job it was to keep the English royal palaces smelling sweet.

Echinacea pallida

PALE PURPLE CONEFLOWER
or Echnihacea

CULTIVATED BY 1699

This perennial plant is native to the grasslands of North America. The Reverend John Banister, an English naturalist studying American flora, sent samples of the plant to England from Virginia in 1699. Growing to a height of 3 to 4 feet (1–1.2m), it produces fragrant deep purple to pink flowers and needs a sunny spot. The Native American tribes of the Great Plains used this coneflower for a wide range of medicinal purposes, including flesh wounds and snake bites. It is thought to be beneficial in stimulating the immune system and is particularly popular in German herbal preparations. The plant is closely related to eastern purple coneflower (*E. purpurea*), which has large, reddish purple flowers with slim petals.

Eryngium maritimum

SEA ERYNGO
or Sea Holly

CULTIVATION DATE UNKNOWN

As early as the Tudor period in the sixteenth century, the roots of this hardy perennial were considered to have aphrodisiac properties and were candied and eaten as sweetmeats. In Shakespeare's *The Merry Wives of Windsor*, Falstaff refers to them as "snow eryngoes." The leaves are also edible, along with the young flowering shoots that can be boiled and used as a substitute for asparagus. Culpeper advised, "The Distilled Water of the Herb when young, helpeth the melancholy of the Heart, as also for them that have their Necks drawn awry, and cannot turn them, without turning their whole Body." The plants grow to 3 feet (1m) tall with small blue, thistle-like flowers.

Filipendula ulmaria

QUEEN OF THE MEADOW
or Meadowsweet, Bridewort

CULTIVATION DATE UNKNOWN

This is a very pretty plant with small clusters of sweet-smelling, creamy white flowers. Reaching 2 to 4 feet (0.6–1.2m), it thrives in moist, fertile soil in sun or partial shade. In *Herball, Generall Histoire of Plants*, 1597, John Gerard wrote: "It is reported, that the floures boiled in wine and drunke, do make the heart merrie. The leaves and floures far excel all other strowing herbes, [see panel, left] for to decke up houses, to straw in chambers, halls, and banqueting houses in the Summer time; for the smell thereof makes the heart merrie, and delighteth the senses." Today, it is used in potpourri and for natural dyes; the leaves and stems produce a blue dye, the flowers a greenish yellow dye, and the roots a black dye.

Foeniculum vulgare

SWEET FENNEL

CULTIVATION DATE UNKNOWN

A most beautiful herb, at home equally in the flower garden, physic garden, or vegetable plot. It can grow as high as 7 feet (2.1m) and is topped with clusters of small yellow flowers. As well as the common green variety, there is also a bronze form, though both have the same medicinal properties. Culpeper noted, "The seed boiled in wine, and drank, is good for those that are with serpents, or have eat poisonous herbs, or mushrooms." *Complete Herbal,* 1653. Beeton's *Dictionary of Every-Day Gardening,* 1910, gives the following advice on this hardy herbaceous perennial, "A good bed of fennel will last for years; but to ensure fine leaves, the flower stalks should always be cut off as soon as they appear, so as to never ripen the seeds."

Fennel.

Galium verum
YELLOW BEDSTRAW
or Lady's Bedstraw

CULTIVATION DATE UNKNOWN

This hardy perennial is often found growing in well-drained meadows. Many legends link it to the Virgin Mary, and traditionally it was dried, then used to stuff mattresses. In *Botanologia*, 1664, Robert Turner helpfully advised that "the decoction of the herb and flowers used warm is excellent to bathe the surbated Feet of Footmen and Lackies in hot weather." Cheese makers boil the whole plant to curdle milk and also use the golden flowers to color cheese. Cheese rennet and cheese-running are among its English regional names. The stems, leaves, and flowering tips produce a yellow hair dye; for a red dye, use the roots.

Genista tinctoria
DYER'S GREENWEED
or Dyer's Broom

CULTIVATION DATE UNKNOWN

When young, this hardy subshrub produces a very good quality yellow dye, especially from the flowers and young shoots. It is sometimes mixed with woad to make a solid green dye. Alum, cream of tartar, and sulfate of lime are used to fix the color. Growing to just 2 feet (60cm) tall, it has yellow pealike flowers.

Meadow geranium.

Geranium pratense
MEADOW GERANIUM
or Meadow Cranesbill

CULTIVATION DATE UNKNOWN

A tallish grassland perennial reaching 2 to 4 feet (0.6–1.2m), it has deeply cut leaves and long, red-tinted stems. It flowers throughout the summer months, more freely in the early part of summer. The violet-blue flowers make an attractive addition to salads.

Glycyrrhiza glabra
LICORICE

CULTIVATION DATE UNKNOWN

It is the roots of this tall plant with pale purple, pealike flowers that are used. A sweet flavoring is extracted from the root and used in a variety of candies. In his *Complete Herbal*, 1653, Nicholas Culpeper notes the

effects of licorice on afflictions of the chest: "Boiled in fair water, with some maiden hair and figs, maketh a good drink for those that have a dry cough or hoarseness, wheezing or shortness of breath and for the griefs of the breast and lungs."

Licorice.

Hypericum perforatum
ST. JOHNSWORT

CULTIVATION DATE UNKNOWN

An undemanding hardy plant, it grows to 3 feet (90cm) tall and has yellow flowers with a lemon fragrance. Nicholas Culpeper praised its healing properties thus: "[it] is as singular a wound herb as any other, either for inward wounds, hurts, or bruises, to be boyled in wine and drunk, or prepared into oyl or ointment, bath or lotion outwardly. It opens obstructions, dissolve swellings, and closes up the lips of wound."

Hyssopus officinalis
HYSSOP

CULTIVATION DATE UNKNOWN

Writing in the seventeenth century, Culpeper commented that hyssop "is so universally known, that I consider it altogether needless to write any description of it." Less grown today, its blue, white, or pink flowers are much visited by pollen-gathering bees. It thrives in a warm, dry site and is quite hardy, making it an attractive, if spreading, edging plant. Culpeper listed many medicinal uses while Vilmorin-Andrieux noted that "all the parts of this plant, especially the leaves, have a very aromatic odor and a rather hot and bitter taste … The leaves and the ends of the branches are used as a condiment, especially in the countries of the North." *The Vegetable Garden*, 1885.

Hyssop.

Inula helenium
ELECAMPANE INULA

CULTIVATION DATE UNKNOWN

In his *Complete Gardener's Practice*, 1664, Stephen Blake wrote, "To be revenged on a person who steals your tulips, sprinkle dry powdered elecampane root on clove gillyflowers, give to the party who will delight to smell it, and when they draw the powder into their nostrils they will fall sneezing until tears run down their thighs." The roots of elecampane inula can be cooked and eaten as a root vegetable, and as far back as ancient Rome, they were candied and sold as sweetmeats. However, by the nineteenth century, Vilmorin-Andrieux wrote: "We mention this plant merely to give some account of it, as its cultivation in the kitchen garden is now almost

GARDEN GHOSTS

The herb bee balm (*Monarda didyma*) is just one of the hundreds of plants that the self-taught botanist John Bartram (1699–1777) introduced into Europe from his native North America. Despite having little formal education, the impressive garden that Bartram established on his farm at Kingsessing, near Philadelphia, is considered to be America's first botanical garden, and it is still in existence today. A Quaker, Bartram undertook many botanizing trips throughout the southeastern states, discovering, collecting, and recording plants. Carl Linnaeus called him "the greatest botanist in the world." King George III appointed him as "Botanizer Royal for America" in 1765. His son William was also a noted botanist and naturalist who continued to expand the family's botanic garden and export North American plants around the world.

entirely abandoned. Formerly its thick fleshy roots were used in the same way as the roots of Salsify and Scorzonera are at present, but nowadays they are only used for medicinal purposes." It is a large and hardy perennial with large yellow flowers, and it reaches 3 to 5 feet (1–1.5m) tall.

Lavandula augustifolia
ENGLISH LAVENDER

CULTIVATION DATE UNKNOWN

Lavender has been cultivated for centuries and has a wide range of culinary, medicinal, and cosmetic uses. "A decoction made with the flowers of lavender, horehound, fennel, asparagus root, and a little cinnamon is very profitably used to help the falling sickness, and the giddiness or turning of the brain, to gargle the mouth with the decoction thereof is good against a toothache." *Complete Herbal,* Nicholas Culpeper, 1653. Lavender is a hardy, evergreen shrub that thrives in a dry and sunny site, growing to a height of 3 feet (90cm), depending on how it is clipped. It is grown for its blue, purple, or white fragrant flowers. French lavender (*L. stoechas*) is

less hardy in damper climates and has long purple bracts, shaped like little rabbit's ears born on tall stems of short, gray-green foliage. Even more than English lavender, it needs a hot, very well-drained and sheltered position to thrive, withstanding drought well.

Levisticum officinale
LOVAGE
or Sea Parsley

CULTIVATION DATE UNKNOWN

Growing to 6 feet (1.8m) tall, with clusters of small, greenish yellow flowers and large, deeply divided leaves, it is the seeds and leaves of this hardy herbaceous perennial plant that are used. In the past, the leaves were placed inside shoes to revive tired feet, and the Scots are said to have harvested it at the seashore and eaten it to protect against scurvy. It also makes an excellent soup, and the leaf stalks and stems can be steamed and served with white sauce. When *officinale* or *officinalis* is the species epithet of a plant, it indicates that it is useful, that it has medicinal or culinary uses, and that it was, or still is, often sold in stores. Lovage is said to restore the appetite and revive the love life!

Marrubium vulgare
HOREHOUND

CULTIVATION DATE UNKNOWN

The medicinal use of horehound dates back to the ancient

Lovage.

Egyptians. Pliny praised it, and John Gerard noted that "sirupe made of the greene fresh leaves and sugar, is a most singular remedie against the cough, and wheezing of the lungs." Growing to 18 inches (45cm), the plant has wrinkled leaves with a woolly texture, and the white flowers are small and insignificant. "The plants are perfectly hardy and require no attention while growing. The leaves are used for seasoning,

Lavender.

Horehound.

or as a popular cough remedy."
The Vegetable Garden, Vilmorin-
Andrieux, 1885.

Melissa officinalis
LEMON BALM

CULTIVATION DATE UNKNOWN

Culpeper praised the restorative
properties of lemon balm, writing,
"It is a herb of Jupiter, and under
Cancer, and strengthens nature
much in all its actions." *Complete
Herbal,* 1653. *The London
Dispensary* in 1696 advised that
"balm, given every morning, will
renew youth, strengthen the brain,
and relieve languishing nature."
Hardy, growing to a height of 3 feet
(90cm), lemon balm has small, pale
yellow flowers and lemon-scented
leaves. It grows best in a sunny site.

Mentha
MINT

CULTIVATION DATE UNKNOWN

Native to the Mediterranean,
the Romans introduced mint

Mint.

throughout Europe, and later it was
taken to the Americas by the early
colonists. Its popularity is due to its
many culinary and medicinal uses.
In his *Herball,* John Gerard noted,
"It is good against watering eies
and all manner of breakings out
on the head and sores. It is applied
with salt to the bitings of mad dogs
…They lay it on the stinging of
wasps and bees with good success."

FOOL'S PARSLEY

Vilmorin-Andrieux warns that common, or flat-leaf, parsley may
be "easily confounded with Fool's Parsley (*Aethusa cynapium* L.),
a native and virulently poisonous plant." Pliny is said to have successfully
treated sick fish by sprinkling fool's parsley on his pond. To avoid the
accidental use of the latter when preparing sauces, it is advised the
gardener should make "it a rule never to grow any kind except the
Curled-leaved or Fern-leaved varieties, which are quite as good for
flavoring as the Common Parsley, and much better for garnishing."
Of course, raising plants from the seeds of a reputable seed merchant
should render this advice unnecessary.

M. × piperita
PEPPERMINT

CULTIVATION DATE UNKNOWN

This hardy perennial herb, growing
1 to 2 feet (30–60cm) in height, is
the source of peppermint oil. Of
peppermint, Culpeper wrote, "A
safe medicine for the biting of a
Mad Dog, being bruised with salt
and laid thereon. The Pouder of it
being dried and taken after Meat
helpeth digestion, and those that
are Splenetick."

M. pulegium
PENNYROYAL ☠
or Churchwort

CULTIVATION DATE UNKNOWN

Pennyroyal grows to 6 inches
(15cm) tall with bright green,
strongly peppermint-scented
leaves. Vilmorin-Andrieux
commented, "The whole plant
gives out a very agreeable odor,
which is somewhat more powerful
than that of any other kind of
Mint." Along with its culinary and
medicinal uses, its essential oil
is used in aromatherapy.

M. suaveolens
APPLE MINT
or Round-Leaved Mint

CULTIVATION DATE UNKNOWN

An aromatic herb with a fruity,
spearmint flavor. The leaves are
hairy with an apple fragrance, and
the plant reaches 2 feet (60cm) in
height. It is cultivated as a culinary
herb and used in the production of
sauces and jellies.

THE SHAKERS & THEIR SEEDS

Today, the Shakers are most often associated with the beauty and simplicity of their furniture; somewhat less is known about their activities as one of America's first large-scale producers of commercial seeds. Originally a small band of English religious dissenters who had followed the young and charismatic Ann Lee across the Atlantic in 1774, the Shakers were more formally known as the United Society of Believers in the First and Second Appearance of Christ. While imprisoned for her beliefs in her home country, Lee had a vision urging her to found a Utopian society, a "heaven on Earth" in the New World. After many trials and tribulations, the first Shaker settlement was established in Albany, New York, in the late eighteenth century.

"BEAUTY RESTS IN UTILITY"
In the early days, Shaker gardeners were forbidden to grow flowers simply for their beauty or scent; they believed that crops must have a utilitarian use. Nasturtiums such as these would have been grown not for their flowers but for their berries, which are similar to capers when pickled in vinegar. Gradually, this rule was relaxed, and the community at Canterbury, Connecticut, began to sell ornamental flower seeds of old garden favorites, such as hollyhocks, sweet peas, and zinnias.

PURE & GENUINE

Although they lived in strict and close religious communities, the Shakers were adroit at interacting commercially with outsiders, those whom they considered to live in "the World." Their greatest business success was the production, processing, and distribution of vegetable, herb, and flower seeds. In the year 1853 alone, the New Lebanon community in Columbia County made an impressive $10,000 from the sale of seeds. The Shakers sold seeds of exceptional quality; farmers were supplied with bulk quantities packaged in cloth sacks, while kitchen gardeners were offered seeds in small paper envelopes, the forerunner of today's seed packets.

Introducing the selection of seed varieties offered, the Shaker catalog states that they have been chosen "with a view to obtain those that are most useful from the numerous varieties cultivated in the country . . . we can therefore recommend them to be pure and genuine." Particularly popular were their medicinal herbs and preparations, which were sold as far afield as Europe. At one time the combined Shaker settlements were cultivating more than two hundred acres of physic gardens.

Shaker elder Frederick Evans wrote that "Shakerism combines science, religion, and inspiration. It is a practical religion." A strong thread of practicality and sound horticultural advice certainly runs through the pages of their seed catalog *The Gardener's Manual*. In a prepesticide world, their methods for controlling "the ravages of insects" were organic and included salt water, wood ash, sand, grit, and sawdust. A concoction of rye flour, ashes, and plaster, along with water soaked in cow dung was said to see off yellow bugs. The Shakers were also early proponents of the theory of planting the right plant in the right place for maximum success, and were strongly aware of factors dictated by site, soil, and prevailing conditions. One of their "Millennial Laws" (a set of rules that aimed to standardize the behavior of Believers) states, "Believers may not spend their time cultivating fruits and plants not adapted to the climate in which they live." Sound advice indeed.

> *"If you would have a lovely garden, you should live a lovely life."*
>
> Shaker saying

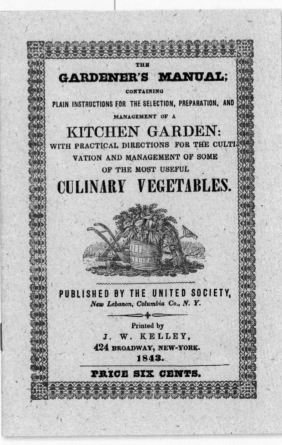

THE GARDENER'S MANUAL;

CONTAINING

PLAIN INSTRUCTIONS FOR THE SELECTION, PREPARATION, AND MANAGEMENT OF A

KITCHEN GARDEN:

WITH PRACTICAL DIRECTIONS FOR THE CULTIVATION AND MANAGEMENT OF SOME OF THE MOST USEFUL

CULINARY VEGETABLES.

PUBLISHED BY THE UNITED SOCIETY, *New Lebanon, Columbia Co., N. Y.*

Printed by
J. W. KELLEY,
424 BROADWAY, NEW-YORK.
1843.

PRICE SIX CENTS.

THE GARDENER'S MANUAL

The Shaker's seed catalog, *The Gardener's Manual*, first appeared in 1836. It proved so successful that this revised and enlarged edition was published in 1843. Distributed by seed merchants, it combined sound cultivation advice with a detailed list of seeds, as well as notes on the preserving and cooking of homegrown produce.

Monarda didyma

BEE BALM

or Beebalm, Bergamot, Golden Melissa, Indian Nettle

CULTIVATION DATE UNKNOWN

A native of North America, bee balm has been cultivated by Native Americans for centuries. The dried leaves make a pleasant and medicinally beneficial tea. The American botanist John Bartram introduced seeds of bee balm into Europe in the eighteenth century, and when imported tea was difficult to obtain in New England after the Boston Tea Party (1773), it was to bee balm that colonial settlers turned for a restorative beverage. This hardy herbaceous perennial plant grows to 3 feet (90cm) tall and has fragrant, bright red blooms with shaggy petals.

Myrrhis odorata

SWEET CICELY

or Anise, Myrrh

CULTIVATION DATE UNKNOWN

Of sweet cicely, Vilmorin-Andrieux noted in the nineteenth century that "the plant is not much cultivated, but it is interesting and graceful, and will grow in any corner or on a hedgebank." It is an attractive, hardy plant with ferny leaves and delicate umbelliferous white flowers that can reach a stately 3 feet (90cm). John Gerard described the leaves as, "exceeding good, holsom, and pleasant among other sallade herbs, giving the taste of anise seed." The roots are used raw in salads or cooked as a root vegetable; the leaves are good added to omelets, soups, and stews; and the nutty-tasting seeds can be eaten raw. It is also useful for reducing the acidity of tart fruit, for instance, when making jam or stewing rhubarb. Always sow fresh seeds; their viability is short-lived.

Nepeta × faassenii

CATMINT

or Catnip

CULTIVATION DATE UNKNOWN

Concerning this herb, all cat owners will doubtless concur with Nicholas Culpeper, who wrote, "It has a strong scent between mint and pennyroyal. It is called Catmint because the cats are very fond of it, especially when a little flaccid and withered, for they will roll themselves on it, and chew it in their mouths with great pleasure." He goes on to advise that it also "promotes the birth and cleansing; and by some authors it is recommended against barrenness." The white or lavender flowers also

Catmint.

act as a magnet for bees. Hardy and sun loving, it grows in well-drained soil. The leaves and young shoots can be used for seasoning food, while infusions are said to relieve colds and fevers, and a poultice made from the leaves can be placed on bruises.

Ocimum basilicum

BASIL

CULTIVATION DATE UNKNOWN

Over time, basil has featured in the mythologies of many cultures. For the ancient Greeks it was a symbol of hatred and misfortune; for Hindus placing a basil leaf on the chest ensures their passage to paradise; while on the Italian island of Sicily, if a young woman removes a pot of basil from her window, she sends a signal to her lover to enter her house. Of basil, John Gerard wrote in his *Herball*, 1597, "The seed drunke is a remedy for melancholy people; for those that are short-winded, and them that can hardly make water." This is a plant that is best suited to warm climates. In cool regions, never sow into cold soil and be sure the small plants are hardened off before planting outdoors in midsummer. Alternately, grow under cover in a greenhouse. Here is a selection of the many varieties available.

'BUSH'

This is a small, compact, and more branching version of the common basil. It is highly aromatic.

Basil.

'LETTUCE LEAVED LARGE'

An old ornamental variety "with broad, crimped, undulating leaves, from 2 to 4 inches (5–10cm) long, and of a low-growing thick-set habit …The leaves of this Basil, which are much larger than of any other kind, are also much fewer in number." *The Vegetable Garden*, Vilmorin-Andrieux, 1885. It remains true today that it has the largest leaves of any basil variety.

'RED RUBIN'

With reddish purple leaves, this makes a decorative plant for the warm-climate flower border, as well as a useful addition to many dishes, including salads.

'SWEET GENOVESE'

This is the variety that is most used in traditional Italian dishes. It is possibly the most commonly grown and said to make the most authentic pesto.

Oenothera
EVENING PRIMROSE

CULTIVATION DATE UNKNOWN

A hardy biennial, with some of the taller variants reaching up to 6 feet (1.8m) tall, with stems topped with highly scented yellow flowers. The buds seem to open at twilight, giving a very fine display, staying open during the daytime thereafter. The leaf and stem were a traditional food and medicine for Native Americans, and its medicinal properties have long been known and continue to interest research scientists today. In France it was cultivated traditionally for the root, which was prepared and eaten like salsify.

Origanum majorana
SWEET MARJORAM
or Annual Marjoram

CULTIVATION DATE UNKNOWN

Although a perennial plant, sweet marjoram is often grown as an annual in cold and wet climates, where it has trouble overwintering. Vilmorin-Andrieux advised that "the seeds may be sown in the end of March or early in April. The plant springs up rapidly, so that the leaves may commence to be gathered in the course of May." It has many medicinal as well as culinary uses, about which Culpeper waxed enthusiastically, "Our common Sweet Marjerom is warming and comfortable in cold diseases of the Head, Stomach, Sinews, and other parts, taken inwardly, or outwardly applied. The Decoction thereof being

HISTORICAL NOTE

Old gardening manuals and catalogs often refer to herbs by a range of terms that can be confusing to the modern gardener. Aromatic herbs are naturally those with the sweetest smell. Pot herbs relate to plants with culinary uses that are bound for the cooking pot, although herbs used for flavoring are also sometimes called sweet herbs. Salet, or salad, herbs bear tender young leaves suitable for eating raw, while medicinal herbs were often known as simples.

drunk help all the Diseases of the Chest which hinder the freeness of breathing."

Sweet marjoram.

Oregano.

Origanum vulgare

OREGANO

or Perennial Marjoram, Pot Marjoram

CULTIVATION DATE UNKNOWN

Very hardy, this herb needs little attention, forming a neat clump covered in red or lilac flowers and growing to a height of 2 feet (60cm). Like all oregano and marjoram varieties, it is highly fragrant, as Culpeper noted: "Marjoram is much used in all odoriferous waters, powders, etc., that are for ornament or delight."

Petroselinum crispum

PARSLEY

CULTIVATION DATE UNKNOWN

As popular an herb in ancient times as it is today, one of the earliest mentions of parsley occurs in Greek mythology, where it symbolizes Herculean strength. Most probably, parsley was spread throughout Europe by the Romans, and numerous superstitions have become attached to it over time. It can be very slow and erratic to germinate and is adversely affected by hot and dry weather.

Common parsley.

Parsley.

Thomas Bridgeman, in *The Young Gardener's Assistant*, 1847, advises that "a few grains of Long radish seeds, sown about an inch apart in each drill [furrow], are well adapted to promote the growth of Parsley; because Radish seeds being quick in germinating, will open up the pores of the earth; and the plants, as they progress in growth, will create a shade, sufficient to protect the Parsley from the full rays of the sun." Several varieties are available, of which the following types are some of the most interesting.

'ITALIAN GIANT' or 'Gigante d'Italia'

CULTIVATED BY 1800

With a strong and spicy flavor, and flat, dark green leaves, this variety resembles celery. Its relatively thick stems can even be blanched and eaten like celery.

'MOSS CURLED'

CULTIVATED BY 1838

This vigorous and large variety with finely curled leaves is as ornamental as it is palatable. There are a number of moss

---

HISTORICAL NOTE

For their medicinal needs, the early English settlers in North America were dependent on the seeds and rootstocks of plants they had brought from the old country, along with the information provided in herbals by Parkinson and Gerard. Colonists also began to exploit the local knowledge of Native Americans and cultivate native plants for their own uses. Following his exploration of the region, the seventeenth-century English traveler John Josselyn published *New England's Rarities Discovered* in 1672. This included several medicinal compounds used by Native Americans and helped encourage a trade in American plants back to England and beyond.

curled variants, including Moss Curled 4–Afro, which has even more finely curled foliage.

P. crispum var. tuberosum

PARSLEY ROOT
or Hamburg Parsley

CULTIVATION BY C. 1600

A variety grown for its thick edible roots instead of its leaves. In *The Gardeners Dictionary* of 1787 Philip Miller wrote of this variety, "This is now pretty commonly sold in London Markets, the roots being six times as large as the common parsley. I brought the seeds of it from thence in 1727; but they refused to accept it, so that I cultivated it several years before it was known in the markets."

Peucedanum ostruthium

MASTERWORT 🏵
or Imperatoria Ostruthium

CULTIVATION DATE UNKNOWN

This is a graceful perennial herb that grows to 2 feet (60cm) tall and has large white, umbelliferous flowers. It resembles angelica. Native to Central Europe, it naturally occurs in damp fields and woodlands. As an herb, its uses are mostly culinary; the aromatic roots are said to taste hotter than pepper. In the past its medicinal uses included the treatment of hysteria and the tremors, and it was chewed to ease toothaches. Care should be taken when tending, because the sap can cause irritation to the skin.

Pimpinella anisum

ANISE
or Anise Burnet Saxifrage, Aniseed

CULTIVATION DATE UNKNOWN

First cultivated for medicinal and culinary use by the ancient Greeks and Romans, the roots, leaves, flowers, and seeds of anise have all been exploited throughout the centuries. In 1810, Robert John Thornton wrote in his publication *A New Family Herbal* that anise "…is a seed which has an aromatic smell and a pleasant warm, sweetish taste; it has been used as a carminative, a cordial, and stomachic, and for strengthening the viscera, the essential oil is among the mildest of the kind we have." Vilmorin-Andrieux noted, "It is of very ancient use in England, and was known to the ancients, being indeed among the oldest of medicines and spices. It is one of the spices which the Grocers' Company of London had

Anise.

the weighing and oversight of from 1453. According to the wardrobe accounts of Edward IV, it appears the royal linen was perfumed by means of 'lytill bagges of fustian stuffed with Ireos and anneys.'" *The Vegetable Garden*, 1885. Anise was taken to the United States by the early colonists and is one of the herbs grown and traded by the Shakers. Growing to 12 to 18 inches (30–45cm) in height, this half-hardy annual bears clusters of small white flowers and needs a sunny and sheltered site.

Reseda luteola

WELD
or Dyer's Rocket, Dyer's Weed, Dyer's Weld

CULTIVATION DATE UNKNOWN

Weld has been used by dyers since ancient times and yields an especially pure and fast yellow dye. Curiously, Culpeper makes no mention of this, concentrating instead on its medicinal properties: "Some do highly commend it against the biting of venomous creatures, to be taken inwardly, and applied outwardly to the hurt place; as also for the plague or pestilence."

Clippers.

Rosmarinus officinalis
ROSEMARY

CULTIVATION DATE UNKNOWN

A hardy and long-lived shrub in warm climates, growing to 3 to 6 feet (1–1.8m) in height, depending on how it is clipped. Vilmorin-Andrieux wrote, "The rosemary does not require any culture, so to say. Tufts of it planted in a good well-drained soil, and, if possible, at the foot of a south wall, or on a slope with a southern aspect, will continue productive for many years without requiring any attention." *The Vegetable Garden*, 1885. Grown for its culinary and medicinal properties since earliest times, rosemary is a handsome plant with blue, mauve, or white flowers born on fragrant leaves, which Vilmorin-Andrieux described as a "lively green color on the upper surface and silvery gray underneath." It makes an attractive loose hedge.

Rosemary.

Rue.

Ruta graveolens
RUE ☠

CULTIVATION DATE UNKNOWN

Hardy and evergreen, growing to 2 feet (60cm) tall, rue has yellow flowers and striking glaucous leaves with a strong smell and a milky sap, which can act as an irritant to the skin. The seeds have been used in cooking since Roman times, but it is the leaves that are used either as an infusion or added to compresses; when dried, they make an effective insecticide. Culpeper knew it as "Wild Meadow Rue" and advised boiling the root with water for treating "the places of the body most troubled with vermin and lice washed therewith while it is warm, destroys them utterly."

Salvia officinalis
SAGE

CULTIVATION DATE UNKNOWN

Since it is a native of southern Europe, it is only to be expected that sage likes a hot and sunny spot in well-drained soil. The hairy leaves are highly fragrant and the purple-blue flowers are much loved by bees. Leaf color is a soft green, but purple and variegated forms are also grown; they are hardy in all but the harshest winters, although the variegated type needs some protection. Prune in spring instead of fall. In *Garden Herbs*, 1944, Mr. Whitehead advised that although sage is a long-lived plant, "It pays to vanquish the aged and renew stock every four or five years. Old plants grow straggly and tired." Long associated with longevity, its reputed health benefits include an aid to digestion, a tonic for the nerves and blood, soothing coughs and colds as well as having antiseptic and antifungal properties. It also has many culinary uses.

Sage.

Saponaria officinalis
BOUNCINGBET
or Soapwort

CULTIVATION DATE UNKNOWN

As one of its common names suggests, the plant is used for washing delicate fabrics; the leaves produce a soapy sap. Many textile conservationists use it for cleaning precious fabrics, including the Bayeux tapestry. It is a hardy perennial with a spreading habit, reaching a 1½ to 3 feet (45–90cm) tall, and the pale pink flowers attract pollinating insects. The Shakers grew bouncingbet on their herb farms in the nineteenth century.

Satureja hortensis
SUMMER SAVORY

CULTIVATION DATE UNKNOWN

A hardy evergreen that is native to southern Europe, summer savory is a soft-leaved aromatic herb that bears

Summer savory.

Winter savory.

small pink or white flowers. It is the spicy leaves and young shoots that are most often used in cooking, and Vilmorin-Andrieux advised that they be boiled with beans. The roots can be used raw in salads or cooked as a root vegetable.

Satureja montana
WINTER SAVORY

CULTIVATION DATE UNKNOWN

Winter savory is, like summer savory, a native of southern Europe, In *The Vegetable Garden*, 1885, Vilmorin-Andrieux wrote of winter savory: "The plant is sufficiently hardy to withstand ordinary winters in the climate of Paris, provided it is grown in well-drained soil free from stagnant moisture. It requires no attention; but if the stems are cut down every spring to about 4 inches (10cm) from the ground, a much more abundant supply of vigorous young shoots will be produced. The leaves and young shoots are used for flavoring, like those of Summer Savory." However, it should be noted that the taste of winter savory is stronger and spicier than that of its summer counterpart.

Symphytum officinale
COMFREY

CULTIVATION DATE UNKNOWN

Great claims have been made for the medicinal properties of comfrey. In his *Complete Herbal*, 1653, Culpeper wrote, "This is a herb of Saturn, and I suppose under the sign of Capricorn, cold, dry, and earthy in quality." He goes on to discuss its benefits for treating various complaints including phlegm, "inward griefs and hurts," sores, cuts, broken bones, hemorrhoids, ulcers, gangrenes, and "mortifications." This hardy herbaceous perennial prefers full sun, where it will display mauve to pink flowers and grow to 3 to 4 feet (1–1.2m) in height with large, oval leaves.

Comfrey.

Tagetes lucida
SWEET MARIGOLD
or Mexican Marigold, Mexican Tarragon

CULTIVATION DATE UNKNOWN

A native of South America, the Mexican marigold can be hit badly by harsh winters but will rejuvenate in the spring. The leaves make a good substitute for French tarragon, while a yellow dye can be obtained from the flowers. Secretions from the roots are produced three or four months after sowing and have an insecticidal effect on the soil. They can be effective against nematodes and are also said to deter persistent weeds such as couch grass. The growing plant also has a repellent effect on various insect pests, such as the asparagus beetle and bean weevils. For South American people, this plant is considered a "sacred weed"; they interplant it between their potato crops to discourage eelworms.

Tagetes patula
FRENCH MARIGOLD

CULTIVATION DATE UNKNOWN

The French marigold is a popular plant frequently grown for annual summer displays, but it is also often used as a companion plant because the strong aroma of the leaves is said to lure the cabbage white butterfly away from brassicas. It is also said to be effective

French marigold.

planted alongside tomatoes, because it attracts hoverflies and other beneficial creatures. French marigold is a half-hardy annual herb with bright orange, yellow, or red flowers born over a long period. It grows to 12 inches (30cm) tall, but is often lower.

Tanacetum parthenium
FEVERFEW

CULTIVATION DATE UNKNOWN

Long associated with relieving problems associated with childbirth and headaches, it has also been written that feverfew leaves "dried and made into pouder, and two drams of it taken with honey or sweet wine, purgeth melancholy and flegme; wherefore it is very good for them that are giddie of the head, or which have vertigo." *Herball, Generall Histoire of Plants*, John Gerard, 1597. Feverfew is a hardy perennial, 2 feet (60cm)

tall, with small white and yellow daisy-like flowers. It thrives in a sunny position.

Tanacetum vulgare
TANSY ☠

CULTIVATION DATE UNKNOWN

Of tansy, Vilmorin-Andrieux commented that it "demands no cultural care, and a plant or two growing in a corner of the garden is usually sufficient for all requirements." A tall plant that can reach up to 4 feet (1.2m), the small bright yellow flowers grow in clusters above aromatic fernlike leaves. Culpeper advised, "The herb fried with eggs (as it is accustomed in the spring time), which is called a tansy, helps to digest and carry downward those bad humors that trouble the stomach." A staple of monastic physic gardens in the Middle Ages, tansy was also used as a disinfectant and a strewing herb. Be careful if using topically, because it can irritate the skin.

Thymus vulgaris
THYME

CULTIVATION DATE UNKNOWN

Cultivated since the time of the ancient Greeks, thyme is the quintessential Mediterranean herb scenting the air above sun-baked fields and hillsides. Common thyme (*T. vulgaris*) is a small, woody perennial; growing to 15 inches (38cm), it makes a good edging plant. Wild thyme (*T. praecox*), also known as creeping thyme or mother of thyme, has a tight, low, creeping

Thyme.

Valeriana officinalis

VALERIAN

CULTIVATION DATE UNKNOWN

A tall and stately hardy herbaceous perennial, this bears clusters of pale pink flowers and grows best in a rich, moist soil. It is a well-known and frequently used medicinal herb that has a proven history of efficacy, noted especially for its effect as a tranquilizer, particularly for those people experiencing nervous overstrain. It was used to treat shell shock during World War I. Valerian has been shown to encourage and improve sleep quality and reduce blood pressure.

Valerian.

habit, particularly suited to growing in paving, with pink or violet flowers, 3 inches (7.5cm) tall. Interestingly, Culpeper stated that "a strong infusion of it, drank in the manner of tea, is pleasant, and a very effective remedy for headaches, giddiness, and other discords of that kind; and it is a certain remedy for that troublesome complaint, the nightmare." It is not known when this native of the Mediterranean became more widely spread throughout Europe. It was certainly in cultivation in England by the mid-1500s. Of the named varieties, Provence is a woody variety with blue-gray foliage and pale pink flowers, and its flavor and aroma is of lavender and lemon mixed with thyme.

THOMAS ETTY ESQ
THE HERITAGE SEEDSMAN & BULB MERCHANT

CORIANDER

" The seed prepared and covered with sugar, as comfits, taken after meat closeth up the mouth of the stomacke, staieth vomiting, and helpeth digestion. "

Average content 300 seeds

CULTIVATION. Sow from April to August where the plants are to stand, it a ... in any kind of well drained soil

Carefully
www.thomasett
Seedsman Cottage, Pu
Packed Yea
Registered Seed P

THOMAS ETTY ESQ
THE HERITAGE SEEDSMAN & BULB MERCHANT

HYSSOP

(Hyssopus officinalis)

"Being bruised and Salt, Honey, and Cummin Seed put to it, it helpeth those that are stung by Serpents. The Oyl thereof being anoynted killeth Lice, and taketh away itching of the Head. It helpeth those that have the Falling-sickness which way soever it be applied."

CULTIVATION. Seed is best sown thinly, out of doors in April or May in rows some 18 inches asunder, thin establishing seedlings until they are placed some 15 inches apart in all directions.

Carefully Handpacked by
www.thomasetty.co.uk – 01480 099049
Seedsman Cottage, Puddlebridge, Somerset TA19 9DL
Packed Year Ending January 2016
Registered Seed Packer - PESA Ref No. 2607

NOTES ON THE CULTIVATION OF ESCULENT VEGETABLES

to be undertaken during the fall months.

At this time of the year, the weeds will be a plague to the overworked and the idle gardener alike, while the best-kept land will be full of seeds blown upon it from the sluggard's garden. The first shower of rain will bring them up in terrific force. All that I have to say about them is that *they must be kept down*, for they will not only choke the rising crops in seedbeds and spoil the look of everything, but they very much tend to keep the ground damp and cold, when, if they were away, it would get dry and warm for the benefit of all the proper and rightful crops that grow upon it. As there are now many used-up crops that may be cleared away, depending on your climate, cabbage, chicory, lettuce, and even thinnings of spinach may be planted out in their place for the winter.

SOME VEGETABLES IN NEED OF THE GARDENER'S ATTENTION AS THE YEAR APPROACHES ITS END

Globe Artichoke.

ARTICHOKES *Cynara cardunculus*

Globe artichokes must be protected before frost attacks them. In the first place, cut off the leaves to 1 foot (30cm) off the ground, and then pile up along each side of the rows a lot of dry litter consisting of straw or dead leaves, being careful in so doing to leave the hearts of the plants free to the light and air.

ASPARAGUS *Asparagus officinalis*

Beds of asparagus are to be cleared up now by removal of the ferny foliage, clearing away of weeds and laying on a coat of manure or seaweed. It matters not how rank the manure is that is used for a mulch.

BEANS *Phaseolus*

It is customary on dry warm soil to sow beans now for a first crop, and I consider the practice to be commendable. On cold damp soil, and on clay lands everywhere, it is a waste of seeds and labor to sow now, but every district has its peculiar capabilities, and every cultivator must judge for him- or herself their own particular conditions. Beans sown now should be put on well-drained land in a sheltered spot.

CABBAGE *Brassica oleracea* Capitata group

I advocate crowding the land in early fall with cabbage plants, for growth will be slow and the demands of the kitchen constant. "Crowding," however, is not quite the same thing as overcrowding, and it is only a waste of labor, land, and crop to put the plants so close together that they have not full space for development. The usual rule in planting out the larger kinds of cabbage at this time of year is to allow a distance every way of 2 feet (60cm) between the plants. But I carry the crowding principle so far as to put the small-growing coleworts and other miniature cabbages in the interspaces.

CARDOON *Cynara cardunculus*

These should now be tied round and hilled up. Gradually build up soil, little by little, around the stems. Always do this when the ground is dry. This will protect the leaves from frost throughout the winter months.

CARROT *Daucus carota*

To be taken up and stored in boxes in moist sharp sand. Late-sown crops to be thinned and weeded.

CAULIFLOWER *Brassica oleracea* Botrytis group

In early fall, plant out cauliflowers for winter and sow another small pinch of seeds in a frame or in a tray in the greenhouse. As fall turns

Cardoon and carrots.

FALL

Weeds and falling leaves are the plagues of the season. It may seem that they do no harm, but assuredly they are directly injurious to every crop upon the ground, for they encourage damp and dirt, prevent a free circulation of air among the crops, prevent the access of sunshine to the ground, and in the case of weeds, steal nutrients. Keep the ground clean and tidy, even to the removal of the lower leaves of all cabbages where they lie half decayed upon the ground.

into winter, cauliflowers will be turning in, and possibly those coming forward will be all the better off for being covered with a leaf to protect the heads from frost. If the barometer rises steadily and the wind goes around to north or northeast, cut all the best cauliflowers and put them in a shed or any out-of-the-way place, where they will be safe for use.

CELERY *Apium graveolens*

Now is the time for celery to be hilled up, and protecting material got ready to assure its safety during frost. Hard frost coming after heavy rain may prove destructive to celery. It is well, if there is a crop worth saving, to cut a trench around the plantation to favor the escape of surplus water.

CHICORY *Cichorium endivia*

Belgian endive is now to be blanched for use as it acquires its full size. Blanching before now is counterproductive, because the blanching makes an end of growth.

HORSERADISH *Armoracia rusticana*

To be taken up and stored ready for use, and new plantations to be made as opportunity offers, once the ground can be spared.

LETTUCE *Lactuca sativa*

The latest sown crop will require thinning, but this must not be too strictly carried out, for between now and spring, depending on the climate, there may be opportunities. It may for the present, therefore, be left somewhat thick. If no late sowing was made, or if it was made and has since failed, cut down to the ground the strongest plants, so that a new growth may be secured quickly.

POTATOES *Solanum tuberosum*

Main-season types to be taken up as soon as they are ripe as fall begins, or, indeed, before they are fully ripe if there is any prospect of cold, wet weather. In midfall, they must be taken up with all possible speed. In times when the work is slack, the seed potatoes for next season's planting may be got ready, and put in baskets and boxes, preparatory to being spread out in the daylight in lofts and sheds when the New Year has turned.

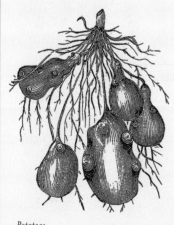

Potatoes.

SEA KALE *Crambe maritima*

To be prepared now for forcing into early growth. Those to be forced in frames should be taken up and exposed some time before they are in heat to create for the roots an artificial winter. Those to be forced on the ground should be divested of their leaves and the crowns sprinkled with sulfur to prevent rot. Cover with a large terra-cotta flowerpot and pile up manure around the pot to provide heat. This encourages the sea kale to grow.

SPINACH *Spinacia oleracea*

In favorable seasons and mild localities, winter spinach sown in early fall will make a good plant before the winter. Thin to 6 inches (15cm) apart plants that are already up, and plant out the thinnings if another plantation is required.

Now we are in the dull days before winter, the affairs of the garden may be best reviewed in detail, and the seed list for the next sowing season may be made out. This is also the best season for a review; kinds that have done well or ill, wants that have been felt, and mistakes that have been made are now fresh in one's memory, and in ordering seeds, roots, and plants for next season's work, we can much better now bring experience and observation to bear upon our procedure, with an increased view to future benefit.

🍂 Consistent with the pleasant revision of garden plans by the fireside, we should not neglect to revise the work outdoors. Begin even now to prepare for next year's crops by trenching, manuring, planting, and collecting material to stack up in the compost pile.

🍂 Land got ready now for spring seeds and roots, and kept quite coarse, will only require to be leveled down and raked over at a day or two's notice when spring comes. Such land will produce better crops than if got ready in a hurry.

🍂 Be ready with protecting material, remembering that a few nights of hard frost may destroy entire crops of lettuce, chicory, celery, and cauliflowers. Yet with a little labor and litter, and covering when required, such crops can be saved completely.

FALL JOBS

If you are in want of work, ply the hoe among all kinds of crops, being careful not to break or bruise healthy leaves, or loosen the roots of anything. Dig vacant plots, and lay the land up in ridges in the coarsest manner possible. Heavy land may be manured now, but it is well not to put manure on light soil until spring.

Leaf beet.

——— ✏ ———

Let not the weather surprise you; the prudent gardener is armed at all times, knowing not what an hour may bring forth!

——— ✏ ———

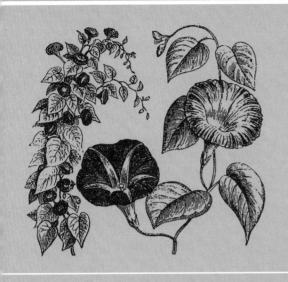

SECTION 4

THE FLOWER DIRECTORY

THE FLOWER DIRECTORY

A SPECIAL SELECTION OF OLD-FASHIONED & ANTIQUE BLOOMS TO GRACE YOUR GARDEN

Agrostemma githago
CORNCOCKLE

CULTIVATION DATE UNKNOWN

The lovely corncockle was once common in cornfields but is now rare. Modern agricultural methods are too efficient at separating wheat seeds from weed seeds for it to survive in the field and ruin the bread, as it did in years past. It is noted thus in a sixteenth-century farmer's manual: "The Cuckole hath a longe small cockle, lafe, and wyl beare fyue or vi floures of purple colour, as brode as a grote, and the sede is rounde and blacke, and maye well be suffred

> We do not want to alarm, but consider it our proper duty to advise that seeds marked thus may be injurious or hazardous to health; we advise proper caution when handling them. We further caution against using any of the herbal cures noted in these pages without reference to more recent publications or discussion with a qualified medical practitioner. We use these charming historical snippets only for descriptive purposes.

in a breade-corne." *The Boke of Husbandrie*, Fitzherbert, 1523.

Alcea rosea
HOLLYHOCK

CULTIVATION DATE UNKNOWN

No cottage garden is complete without its hollyhocks—tall and stately plants that can reach 6 feet (2m) in height. The flowers are large and colorful, sprouting from thick round stalks and set amid round hairy leaves. A biennial or short-lived perennial, it enjoys full sun.

A. rosea
'NIGRA'
or 'Black,' 'Jet Black'

CULTIVATION DATE UNKNOWN

As early as 1629, John Parkinson described a hollyhock "of a dark red like black blood." In his catalog of 1827, the nurseryman John B.

Russe, of Boston, Massachusetts, listed a "Black Antwerp hollyhock: Althea nigra." A unique and impressive variety.

A. rosea
CHATER'S DOUBLE GROUP
or 'Chater's Double Mixed'

CULTIVATED BY 1840

This variety has old-fashioned, ruffled double flowers ranging in color from white through to pink, red, and yellow. Double flowers have a proliferation of petals, giving each one the appearance of a pom-pom.

Antirrhinum majus
SNAPDRAGON
or Antirrhinum

CULTIVATED BY 1597

John Gerard proffered this explanation for this flower, which is a children's favorite everywhere it grows: "The floures grow at the top of the stalkes of a purple or yet a white color, fashioned like a frogs mouth, or rather a dragons mouth, from whence we have taken the name Snapdragon." *The Herball or Generall Histoire of Plantes*, 1597. Originally a native of southern Europe, snapdragons were taken to North America by the early colonists, where they quickly became a popular and much-grown garden flower. Thomas Jefferson grew them at Monticello. The catalog of the Boston-based firm Washburn and Company listed 14 varieties of antirrhinum in 1897.

Aquilegia
COLUMBINE
or American Bluebell, American Snapdragon, Granny's Bonnet, Lady's Shoes, Pigeon Foot

CULTIVATION DATE UNKNOWN

The wild and cultivated forms of this old-time cottage garden favorite are clump-forming herbaceous perennial plants that can grow to 3 feet (1m). The flowers are bell shaped with long spurs and come in a wide range of colors. Beware: Columbines are promiscuous interbreeders; to keep the strain growing true, remove their seed heads before they have a chance to self-sow, and always raise new plants from seeds each year.

A. x *hybrida*
'McKANA GROUP'
or 'McKana Hybrids'

CULTIVATED BY C. 1945

Bearing a wealth of long-spurred flowers that range in color from pastel rose to blue, yellow, white, and crimson, this is a variety to

Aubretia.

turn heads. Thrives in sun or shade.

A. vulgaris

CULTIVATION DATE UNKNOWN

The wild European columbine usually has blue flowers, although variants of white, purple, and pink can also occur. It was described by John Gerard thus: "The stalke is a cubit and a halfe high, slender, reddish and slightly haired, the slender whereof bring forth everie one; one floure with five little hollow hornes, as it were hanging forth, with small leaves standing upright, of the shape of little birds." *The Herball, or Generall Histoire of Plantes,* 1597. *A. canadensis* is the red-flowered North American counterpart, and among its common names are Canadian columbine and Turk's cap.

A. vulgaris **var.** *stellata*
'NORA BARLOW'

CULTIVATION DATE UNKNOWN

Originally a sixteenth-century variety called Rose Columbine, it was renamed after the granddaughter of Charles Darwin (see page 191). It is spurless and has double flowers with pink and green petals.

Armeria maritima
SEAPINK
or Thrift, Thrift Seapink

CULTIVATION DATE UNKNOWN

This mat-forming evergreen perennial with pink flowers grows to 15 inches (38cm) in height. It was described in the catalog of the

Columbine.

American seed producer Washburn and Company as, "adapted for rock-work, edging, or culture in pots." In his *Herball* of 1597, John Gerard advised that "their use in Physicke

---

GARDEN GHOSTS

Cottage gardeners everywhere who grow the lovely pink and green columbine *Aquilegia vulgaris* var. *stellata* Nora Barlow should honor its namesake, the long-lived scientist Emma Nora Barlow (1885–1989). Granddaughter of the famous Charles Darwin (1809–82), Nora worked at the UK's John Innes Institute studying plant genetics during the early years of the twentieth century. She based a number of papers on several of her grandfather's books, including *The Different Forms of Flowers on Plants of the Same Species* (1877).

as yet is not known. Neither do any seeke into the Nature thereof, but esteem them only for their beutie and pleasure. Used in the garden for the bordering up of beds and bankes, for the which it serveth very fitly."

Aubrieta
AUBRETIA
or Rock Cress

CULTIVATION DATE UNKNOWN

Named after the French botanical artist Claude Aubriet (ca. 1665–1742), this hardy perennial forms a spreading compact mat of flowers, ranging in color from white through to pale pink and rich purple. Needing full sun and well-drained soil, aubretias are perfect for growing on the tops of walls, in rock gardens, or for edging flower borders.

Calendula officinalis
POT MARIGOLD
or Ruddles, Scotch Marigold

CULTIVATION DATE UNKNOWN

Favored by cooks, herbalists, and dyers of cloth, the orange-flowered pot marigold has always been regarded as a useful plant. "The herbe and flowers are of great use with us among other pot herbes and the flowers eyther greene or dryed, are often used in possets, broths, and drinkes, as a comforter of the heart and spirits, and to expel any malignant or pestilential

quality, gathered neere thereunto." *The English Physitian Enlarged*, Nicolas Culpeper, 1669. It is an easy and reliable hardy annual with a long season of pretty flowers.

Campanula medium
CANTERBURY BELL
or Bell Flower, Cup-and-Saucer

CULTIVATION DATE UNKNOWN

This lovely bell-like flower was introduced into the British Isles from Spain in 1596 and is named after the English cathedral city, Canterbury. A half-hardy annual that grows well over 2 feet (60cm) tall, it forms a dense clump of leaves from which rise graceful stems bearing summer flowers colored blue, pink, or white. "There is a kinde of floure growing about Canterbury, which is called Canterbury Bells, because they grow there more plentifully than in any other country. These pleasant floures wee have here in our gardens especially for the beauty

Canterbury bell.

of their floure." *The Herball, or Generall Histoire of Plantes*, John Gerard, 1597.

Cardamine pratensis
CUCKOO FLOWER
or Lady's Smock, Spinks

CULTIVATION DATE UNKNOWN

Known as the cuckoo flower for its sprays of pale lilac flowers in spring, which appear along with the first cuckoo. It is a hardy perennial that grows in damp, shady places reaching a height of 12 to 20 inches (30–50cm). Folklorists claim it is sacred to the fairies and it is unlucky xto bring it indoors.

Centaurea cyanus
CORNFLOWER
or Bachelor's Buttons, Bluebottle, Blue Sailors, Break-Your-Spectacles, Cornbottle, Ragged Robin, Ragged Sailor

CULTIVATION DATE UNKNOWN

Once a common sight in cornfields and meadows, this native European plant is now scarcely seen growing in the wild. The wild form is blue, although pink, white, and purple varieties are available to the gardener. This annual is a cottage garden favorite, growing to over 2 feet (60cm) tall, and thrives in full sun. "The floures grow at the top of the stalkes, of a blew color, consisting of many small floures set in a scaly head; the seed is smooth, bright shining, and wrapped in a woolly or flocky matter." *The Herball, or Generall Histoire of Plantes*, John Gerard, 1597.

Cornflower.

Cobaea scandens
CUP AND SAUCER VINE
or Cathedral Bells, Mexican Ivy, Monastery Bells

CULTIVATED BY C. 1500

This half-hardy perennial from Mexico is usually grown as a half-hardy annual in cooler climates. It is a rampant climber and will quickly cover a vertical support, preferring a sunny, sheltered site. As its name suggests, the large flowers are shaped like a cup, and they range from pale violet to purple, with a honey-like fragrance.

Consolida ajacis
LARKSPUR
or Doubtful Knight's-Spur

CULTIVATION DATE UNKNOWN

A lovely cottage garden favorite, the larkspur is hardy and best suited to a sheltered site in sun, but provide a support in the form of a stake if growing in an exposed position. In his *Herball, or*

Generall Histoire of Plantes, 1597, John Gerard gave this delightful description of the larkspur: "The floures grow along the stalks toward the tops of the branches, of a blew color, consisting of five little leaves which grow together and make a hollow floure, having a taile or spur at the end."

Dianthus
CARNATION, PINK & SWEET WILLIAM
Of *Dianthus*, Washburn and Company, based in Boston, Massachusetts, proclaimed in their seed catalog of 1867, "A magnificent genus, which embraces some of the most popular flowers in cultivation. The Carnation, Picotee, Pink, and Sweet William, all 'household

Larkspur.

Sweet William.

words,' belong to this genus." All are quintessential antique flowers that are perfect for cottage garden plantings.

D. barbatus
'AURICULA-EYED MIXED'

CULTIVATED BY 1865

This Sweet William was bred by William Dean of Bradford Nursery, in Shipley, Yorkshire, England. At the time, it was hailed as being "most exquisite in form and color." With its large, many colored, fragrant single flowers, each with an attractive eye, it makes a hardy biennial that grows to 18 inches (45cm) tall, making them perfect for the cutting garden.

D. caryophyllus
'CLOVE PINK'
or 'Clove Gilliflower,' 'Jove's Flower'

CULTIVATION DATE UNKNOWN

This very old cottage garden favorite is everything an heirloom flower should be: simple, romantic, and extremely fragrant. It is also easy to grow, hardy, and useful. "The conserve made of the floures, and sugar is exceeding cordiall and wonderfully above measure doth comfort the heart." *The Herball, or Generall Histoire of Plantes*, John Gerard, 1597.

Carnation.

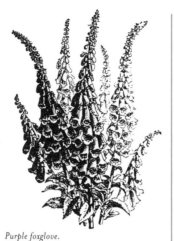

Purple foxglove.

While extracting the sweets which furnish our tables with honey and our manufacturers with wax." *Flora Londinensis*, William Curtis, 1777.

Helianthus annuus
SUNFLOWER
'Giant Yellow Single'

CULTIVATION DATE UNKNOWN

The cheerful sunflower was introduced into Europe from the Americas in the sixteenth century. This is one of the taller varieties, growing as high as 10 feet (3m), although this is not as high as the aptly named American Giant, which can reach a mammoth 15 feet (4.5m). Pinch off the side shoots if a single stem topped by one large single bloom is preferred.

D. caryophyllus
'ENFANT DE NICE'

CULTIVATED BY 1889

The blooms of this carnation range in color from white to red with large double flowers that emit a spicy scent. Although they grow to a stately 2 feet (60cm), the stems are strong and the plants generally vigorous.

D. caryophyllus
'GIANT CHAUBAUD'

CULTIVATED BY 1839

These fragrant, double, fringed carnation flowers come in an array of colors: orange, red, rose, violet, white, and yellow. Growing to 18 inches (45cm) high, they make very good cut flowers.

Digitalis purpurea
PURPLE FOXGLOVE ☠
or Dead Man's Bells, Dragon's Mouth, Fairy Thimbles, Fox Finger, Witches' Gloves

CULTIVATION DATE UNKNOWN

The purple-flowered common or wild foxglove grows to a stately 2 to 5 feet (0.6–1.5m) and is a biennial or short-lived perennial. Many of the flower's common names allude to the resemblance of the flower to the fingers of a glove, and the plant features in several old folktales; indeed its original name is said to have been "folksglove," because it was believed that woodland fairies made gloves from the flowers. Foxgloves are much loved by bees, as this quote illustrates: "How singularly and regularly do the blossoms hang one over the other; how delicate are the little spots which ornament the inside of the flower! Like the wings of small butterflies; how pleasing it is to behold the nestling bee hide itself in its pendulous blossoms!

Sunflower.

Globe candytuft.

Iberis umbellata
GLOBE CANDYTUFT

CULTIVATED BY 1596

This is a sweet-smelling hardy annual growing to 8 inches (20cm) high, covered by a mass of colored flowers all summer long. Originally from the Greek island of Crete, the globe candytuft was noted by both John Parkinson and John Gerard, although the latter only knew the white and purple variety.

Ipomoea purpurea
MORNING GLORY

CULTIVATION DATE UNKNOWN

A twining and fast-growing climber, this has large trumpet-shaped flowers in a range of red to purple. It is mostly grown as a half-hardy perennial, although it can be overly vigorous and potentially invasive in warm and frost-free climates, where it is fully hardy. The 1899 catalog of Ross Brothers of Worcester, Massachusetts, wrote, "Its great beauty entitles it to a place in every collection of flowering annuals, and no flower-lover should fail to plant it."

I. purpurea
'GRANDPA OTT'S'

CULTIVATION DATE UNKNOWN

This is one of the most popular heirloom varieties, producing huge displays of deep purple-blue blooms, each with a red star in its throat borne on very vigorous vines. Named after the Baptist John Ott who farmed at St. Lucas, in Iowa, who gave seeds of this variety to his daughter Diane Ott Whealey in the 1970s. She is the cofounder of the Seed Savers Exchange.

I. purpurea
'KNIOLA'S BLACK KNIGHT'

CULTIVATION DATE UNKNOWN

A stunning variety delivering dark purple, almost black flowers with a cerise throat and ivory eye. The flowering season is long, and plants can grow to 10 feet (3m) tall.

I. purpurea
'SCARLET O'HARA'

CULTIVATION DATE UNKNOWN

An attractive and vigorous climber with lush foliage and 3- to 4-inch (7.5–10cm)-diameter, wine red flowers. The plant itself grows to 6 to 12 feet (1.8–3.6m) in height.

I. tricolor
'HEAVENLY BLUE'
or 'Clark's Heavenly Blue'

CULTIVATED BEFORE 1922

This variety is excellent for covering walls or fences, because it can reach 10 feet (3m), with sky-blue flowers 4 inches (10cm) long. Overly rich soil may encourage leafy growth at the expense of flowers, so be restrained with the fertilizer.

Morning Glory.

THE VICTORY GARDEN & DIG FOR VICTORY CAMPAIGNS

During World War I and World War II North America and Britain faced serious threats to their food supply. Governments on both sides of the Atlantic rose to the challenge by inspiring their citizens to grow their own food; this homegrown food lessened each county's dependence on the imported produce that was so vulnerable to attack at sea. Just prior to entering World War I, the American National War Garden Commission introduced the Victory Gardens campaign in March 1917. Charles Lathrop Pack, their president, coined the slogan "Every garden a munitions plant," which appeared on propaganda material, such as posters and information leaflets. In Britain a similar campaign had the clarion call "Dig for Victory."

Both movements were revived in World War II with great success. During this period, Britain's food imports were halved and a quarter of all the country's eggs were produced by home-reared hens. The US Department of Agriculture estimated that twenty million Victory Gardens were planted in the early 1940s, and by 1944, these gardens were responsible for a staggering 40 percent of all vegetables grown in North America. In the United Kingdom, "allotments" (community gardens) and large yards were turned into family-run smallholdings rearing pigs, goats, rabbits, and chickens; prodigious quantities of fruits and vegetables were also grown. In the same spirit, grand public spaces were turned from ornamental gardens into productive plots. At London's Kensington Gardens, herbaceous borders were filled with cabbages and potatoes instead of flowers, and Hyde Park had its own piggery. Similarly, San Francisco's Golden Gate Park became a productive vegetable garden, along with numerous baseball fields across the breadth of the country. School gardens and community plots flourished while patriotic Americans without gardens grew edible plants in window boxes and on rooftops.

The American and British governments made substantial efforts to engage their citizens in the fight to produce enough food on the home front through a mixture of propaganda, education, and encouragement, while promoting related skills, such as canning and preserving vegetables. So successful was the Dig for Victory campaign that many believe that the wartime diet was one of the healthiest ever consumed by the British population, either before or since, because, despite the privations of rationing, most could enjoy a nutritious mix of home-reared meat, eggs, and plentiful vegetables.

Naturally, all the fruits and vegetables grown in these gardens would have been heirloom and heritage varieties (indeed in the debate concerning what exactly constitutes a heritage variety some cite 1945 as the cut-off date). Today's committed growers of old open-pollinated seed varieties are perhaps rekindling some of this wartime spirit on their own plots, displaying a degree of self-reliance and also showing some defiance in the face of the increasing dominance of commercial F1 hybrids.

Examples of World War II Dig for Victory posters

Lathyrus odoratus
SWEET PEA ☙

CULTIVATION DATE UNKNOWN

China, Malta, South America, and Sri Lanka have all laid claim to being the original home of the wild sweet pea. Indeed, in 1753 Linnaeus erroneously gave a pink and white sweet pea the name *Lathyrus zeylanicus*, meaning "from Ceylon" (now Sri Lanka). The earliest surviving documentation of the flower dates from 1695 on the island of Sicily (see Cupani, right). Whatever the true origin of the sweet pea, it was nineteenth-century British plant breeders who took this sweet-smelling climbing plant to ever more dazzling extremes of color, fragrance, and flower size.

Sweet Pea.

L. odoratus
'AMERICA'

CULTIVATED BY 1896

Bred by the sweet-pea breeder Morse-Vaughan, the eye-catching combination of bright red and white petals on this strongly scented late bloomer make it a great favorite.

L. odoratus
'BLACK KNIGHT'

CULTIVATED BY 1898

A deep claret and violet bicolor strongly scented Grandiflora sweet pea (see panel, below). It is one of 115 varieties that Henry Eckford exhibited at London's Crystal Palace Exhibition in 1900.

L. odoratus
'CAPTAIN OF THE BLUES'

CULTIVATED BY 1890

A Grandiflora variety with bright purple-blue flowers with paler wings and a strong scent. This was described as "Approaching Blue" in the 1899 catalog of the North American seed company Ross Brothers.

L. odoratus
'CUPANI'

CULTIVATION DATE UNKNOWN

With its beautiful maroon and violet coloring, this most ancient sweet pea deserves a place in every garden. Francisco Cupani first recorded it in 1695. He belonged to the Order of St. Francis and cared for the botanical garden at Palermo, Sicily. Robert Uvedale, an Enfield school master and contact of Francis Cupani, is generally credited with introducing this, the first sweet pea into England, in 1699. It is one of the strongest smelling varieties available.

L. odoratus
'DOROTHY ECKFORD'

CULTIVATED BY 1901

A fine, free-flowering pure white Grandiflora sweet pea, with its flowers carried in threes. In 1907 it was voted the best white variety by the Floral Committee of the National Sweet Pea Society.

GARDEN GHOSTS

Perhaps the most famous breeder of sweet peas is Henry Eckford (1823–1905), a Scottish gardener who introduced more than two hundred varieties into cultivation. Eckford is responsible for the Grandiflora varieties, which had much larger flowers than earlier forms. The 5th Earl of Spencer's gardener, Silas Cole, developed the famous Spencer sweet peas at the family seat of Althrop House, Northamptonshire (the subsequent home of Diana, Princess of Wales). Cole took a sport of Eckford's Prima Donna and from it bred lovely blooms characterized by large wavy petals. North American breeders then began to produce varieties that were more tolerant of the hotter American summers, and the first dwarf sweet pea was discovered in California in 1893. It is said that the Atlee Burpee Company paid $1,500 for the whole stock of just over a thousand seeds of this dwarf form, which they then introduced as Cupid in 1895.

L. odoratus
'HENRY ECKFORD'

CULTIVATION DATE UNKNOWN

This unusual heirloom Grandiflora is named after the "father of the sweet pea" and has orange-red fragrant flowers.

L. odoratus
'KING EDWARD VII'

CULTIVATED BY 1903

A rich crimson Grandiflora sweet pea that many consider to be the best of its color. Taller and stronger growing than most of Eckford's Grandifloras, with a strong scent.

L. odoratus
'LADY GRISEL HAMILTON'

CULTIVATED BY 1895

A pale lavender Eckford Grandiflora sweet pea with a hooded standard and strong scent. A reliable performer.

L. odoratus
'LORD NELSON'

CULTIVATED BY 1907

One of the best heirloom sweet peas of a rich dark blue. In North America, it was sold as Brilliant Blue by the Atlee Burpee Company.

Sweet pea.

L. odoratus
'MISS WILLMOTT'

CULTIVATED BY 1900

An Eckford Grandiflora variety with deep orange-pink blooms named after the horticulturist Ellen Willmott (see panel, right).

L. odoratus
'MRS. COLLIER'

CULTIVATED BY 1906

Bred by the Scottish company Dobbie & Co. of Edinburgh, Mrs. Collier bears a creamy white, sweet-smelling bloom.

L. odoratus
'PAINTED LADY'

CULTIVATED BY 1737

This was the first named sweet pea variety, and in 1889 the first named North American sweet pea variety, Blanche Ferry, was developed from it. Painted Lady bears large and lovely flowers that are colored pink and cream.

L. odoratus
'PRINCE EDWARD OF YORK'

CULTIVATED BY 1897

A stunning Eckford Grandiflora variety with cerise and magenta flowers. Named for the then Prince Edward, later King Edward VIII, who famously abdicated in 1936.

L. odoratus
'QUEEN ALEXANDRA'

CULTIVATED BY 1905

Mr. Etty considers this scarlet sweet pea to be one of Henry Eckford's finest strains, putting all other red varieties in the shade. It has

GARDEN GHOSTS

The sweet pea Miss Willmott is one of many plants named after the English horticulturist Ellen Willmott (1858–1934). Others include *Rosa willmottiae* and *Eryngium giganteum*, commonly known as Miss Willmott's Ghost. Willmott transformed the vast grounds at her family home Warley Place in Essex, England, into one of the most celebrated gardens of her day. Along with creating this garden, and others in France and Italy, she bred prize-winning daffodil hybrids and wrote several horticultural books. She and Gertrude Jekyll were among the very first recipients of the Royal Horticultural Society's Victoria Medal of Honour, introduced in 1897 to mark the year of Queen Victoria's Jubilee. (The other 58 recipients were all men.) At one time her gardening staff is said to have numbered one hundred; this doubtless contributed to her near bankruptcy in later life.

a beautiful scent. Queen Alexandra was the wife of King Edward VII.

Limnanthes douglasii
DOUGLAS' MEADOWFOAM
or Poached Eggplant

CULTIVATED BY 1842

A native flower of the western United States, it is named after David Douglas, who collected it in the nineteenth century (see panel on page 205). It is a tough and quick-growing annual with cheerful yellow, saucerlike flowers edged with white that resemble a poached egg. Good for attracting pollinators, such as bees, it makes a useful edging plant in the kitchen garden.

Lobularia maritima

SWEET ALYSSUM

or Healbite, Madwort, Sweet Alice, Sweet Alison

CULTIVATED BY 1710

A native of the Mediterranean region, it thrives in sunny, rocky sites. It grows as an annual or a perennial, depending on climate, and has a low, spreading habit and a sweet fragrance. It is available in a wide range of colors. Sweet alyssum is an effective companion plant among vegetables, because it attracts beneficial insects, although

HISTORICAL NOTE

Few growers of sweet peas would take issue with the view expressed in *The Gardener's Assistant* of 1936: "For cut-flower purposes, the Sweet Pea has scarcely a rival. For flowers that will scent a whole room grow old heirloom varieties as many newer hybrids have been bred for flower size only and have little or no fragrance. For long-lasting indoor flowers, cut sweet peas in the morning, after the dew has dried from them, then stand in water for four hours before arranging." Remove the old, dead flower heads as they appear to prolong the flowering season.

it is more usually used as an attractive edging for flower beds and borders. Madwort and healbite are among its common names, alluding to the old belief that it could cure rabies.

Lunaria annua

HONESTY

or Grandpa's Specs, Money Flower, Moon Seed, Silver Dollar

CULTIVATED BY 1548

Even more attractive than the purple flowers of honesty are the silvery paper seed cases that are left in their wake. It is a hardy annual or biennial that grows to 2½ feet (75cm) tall, preferring a spot in light shade. Legend has it that planting a patch of honesty by the side of gates and doorways wards off burglars. The Washburn and Company catalog (1867) gives its common name as the "satin-flower," and its description shows what a popular plant it was in the nineteenth century: "An old plant, but singularly interesting for the transparent, silvery-like tissue or coats of the seed-vessels in their dry, matured state, through which the fruit is conspicuously seen, and retaining the same picturesque effect for any length of time; well adapted, in a cut state, for grouping with everlasting flowers, etc."

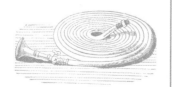

Garden hose with rose attachment.

Lupine.

Lupinus

LUPINE 'RUSSELL HYBRIDS'

CULTIVATED BY 1937

"A splendid genus of the most ornamental, beautiful, and free-flowering of garden plants, with long, graceful spikes of bloom; colors rich and varied." (Washburn and Company catalog, 1867, Boston, Massachusetts.) The lupine, or lupin, is a native of North America, but it took a Yorkshireman by the name of Mr. George Russell to realize their potential and famously develop his range of hybrid lupines with bold blooms. His 'Russell Hybrids' are available in a wide range of striking colors, born on tall spires growing to 3 feet (1m) or more tall. Today, lupines are reliable herbaceous perennials available in almost every color of the rainbow.

Matthiola incana
STOCK
or Gilliflower, Tenweek Stock

CULTIVATION DATE UNKNOWN

This is one of the most highly scented old-fashioned flowers for the cottage garden and for cutting. It is a half-hardy annual growing to 12 inches (30cm) tall. "Of these there are many highly ornamental varieties presenting various shades of purple, blue, lilac, red, brown, and white, and flowering according to the time of sowing from May till October, or later." *The Botanist's Companion*, 1816. Washburn and Company of Boston, Massachusetts, listed a "Ten-week Stock" in their 1867 catalog, noting that it was "the most universally cultivated, and usually blooms from ten to twelve weeks after being sown

Stock.

Forget-Me-Not.

…when cultivated in rich soil, and occasionally watered with weak guano water, throw out an immense quantity of lateral spikes of bloom, so that each plant forms a perfect bouquet … it would be difficult to surpass the grand effect produced in beds or ribbons by these exceptional gems." Today, stock is usually found masquerading under the name *M. incana* Annua.

Myosotis arvensis
FORGET-ME-NOT

CULTIVATION DATE UNKNOWN

This hardy annual, 6 to 12 inches (15–30cm) in height, grows best in moist soil in part sun or shade. The tiny, bright blue spring flowers have a yellow center. Its ability to self-seed freely makes it a cottage garden favorite; for this reason, it can be a little too persistent for some gardeners, but its seedlings are weeded out easily. The author, naturalist, and philosopher Henry David Thoreau (1817–62) much

admired this unpretentious little flower: "It is one of the most interesting minute flowers. It is the more beautiful for being small and unpretending; even flowers must be modest." Not surprisingly, in the Language of Flowers the forget-me-not denotes true love.

Nicotiana alata
TOBACCO PLANT

CULTIVATION DATE UNKNOWN

These half-hardy annuals have large, pale green, sticky leaves, and some varieties have flowers that open in the evening. Louise Beebe Wilder (1878–1938) was the Director of the New York Botanical Garden and a prolific writer of gardening books. Of the tobacco plant she wrote that it cut "a poor figure by day … but with the coming of night the long creamy tubes freshen and expand and give forth their rich perfume and we are then glad to have so much of it."

COMPANION PLANTING

The concept of planting mutually beneficial plants close to each other has long been practiced by traditional farmers, as well as by the gardener on his or her home patch. Evidence suggests that certain combinations of plants can deter (or distract) pests, as well as maintain the health of the soil, and even improve the flavor of crops. The pollination of many types of fruit is naturally helped if plants that attract pollinating insects, such as bees, butterflies, and hoverflies, are planted nearby. Brightly colored marigolds are known to deter pests, such as aphids, and are thus a useful container plant for the greenhouse. In the vegetable plot, it is advised to plant strong-smelling crops, such as onions and leeks, alongside carrots, because they repel damaging insects, such as the carrot fly. Many experienced gardeners swear that the flavor of tomatoes is greatly improved if a quantity of basil is grown close by.

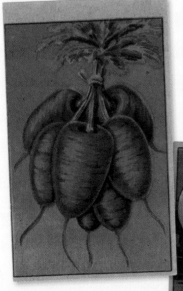

Strong-smelling onions deter pests, such as the carrot fly.

SOME EXAMPLES OF GOOD GARDEN COMPANIONS

🌿 Plant fava beans near broccoli, because they supply nutrients to the soil, promoting stronger growth and improving yields.

🌿 Sage, southernwood, sweet corn, and wormwood can all be planted alongside cabbages to both deter pests and provide some shelter against damage from the weather.

🌿 To deter pests and prevent disease in carrots and celery, try planting chives and garlic in the same bed.

🌿 Keep pests away from tender lettuce by planting them next to the herb sage. The bushy sage will also offer some protection against adverse weather.

🌿 Peaches, plums, and strawberries all benefit from growing in close proximity to the herbs chives, coriander, lavender, oregano, summer savory, winter savory, or thyme, because all attract pollinators and also deter unwanted insect visitors.

🌿 A novel way to grow tomatoes is to use sweet corn plants as a support, like the Native American method known as the Three Sisters (see page 83). A patch of nasturtiums growing nearby will also act as a trap to lure away damaging pests.

A careful choice of companion plants will not only deter pests but also attract pollinating insects, resulting in improved crops of fruits, such as strawberries and plums.

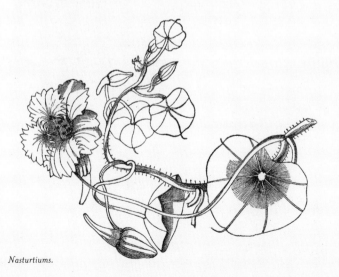

Nasturtiums.

Tabacco.

N. alata or *N. affinis*

CULTIVATED BY 1880

Growing to 3 feet (90cm) tall with fragrant, pure white, star-shaped flowers, this is a much-valued tobacco plant that blooms over a long summer period. Colorful by day, fragrant by night; many varieties in different colors are also available.

N. sylvestris

CULTIVATION DATE UNKNOWN

A native of woodlands, this variety thrives best in a semi-shaded spot. The white, scented flowers are long and tubular and carried in clusters atop the tall stems. The flowers remain open through the day and into the evening.

Nigella damascena
DEVIL IN THE BUSH
or Love-in-a-Mist

CULTIVATED BY 1659

A beautiful annual plant with delicate feathery leaves and bright blue flowers that transform into very attractive dried seedpods. Pink and white varieties are also available. Its medicinal properties were exploited in times gone by as this old text shows (when printers were wont to sometimes print the letter *s* as *f*, in imitation of an elegant hand): "Nigella muft be fowne in a ground that is fat or well tilled. The fune of the feed taketh doth ftay the rheume, drie the braine and causeth the fmelling that is loft to come againe; boyled with water and vinegar, and holden in the mouth it affuageth tooth-ache." The nineteenth-century Washburn and Company catalog, from Boston, Massachusetts, offers an interesting comment on the appellation devil in the bush: "From the extraordinary motion manifested by the stamens, this genus has received these singular names." Allow the plants to self-seed after flowering so they can be enjoyed again next year.

Papaver
POPPY

CULTIVATION DATE UNKNOWN

The poppy was cultivated in ancient Persia, Egypt, and Mesopotania, with the first written reference to the plant appearing in a Sumerian text dating back to 4000 BCE. All are hardy annuals and range in height from 2 to 4 feet (0.6–1.2m), depending on the variety and growing conditions. The attractive and prolific flowers are followed by seed heads that can also make a handsome addition to the garden border.

P. nudicaule
ICELANDIC POPPY

CULTIVATION DATE UNKNOWN

These are short-lived perennials native to the subpolar regions of North America and northern Europe, and they normally self-seed, coming back year after year, if conditions suit them. The plants form a low tuft of light green leaves and bear large, satiny, lightly fragrant flowers on hairy stems. The bowl-shaped flowers last for weeks on end, in a range of shades that include cream, orange, pink, red, salmon, and yellow. In one word: beautiful.

Poppy.

P. rhoeas
CORN POPPY
or Wild Poppy

CULTIVATION DATE UNKNOWN

Culpeper noted many medicinal uses for the corn poppy, which he also knew as the "corn-rose." "The empty shell, or poppy heads, are usually boiled in water, and given to procure rest and sleep; so do the leaves in the same manner; as also if the head and temples be bathed with the decoction warm, or with the oil of poppies, the green leaves or heads bruised, and applied with a little vinegar, or made into a poultice with barleymeal or hog's grease, cools and tempers all inflammation; as also the disease called St. Anthony's fire." *Complete Herbal*, 1653.

P. rhoeas Shirley group
SHIRLEY POPPY

CULTIVATED BY 1880

The Reverend William Wilks raised this poppy from a single scarlet flower edged with white that he found growing among wild field poppies. He named it after his parish of Shirley in Surrey, England. This is what he wrote of his beloved flower, "Let it be noticed that the true Shirley Poppies (1) are single, (2) always have a white base with (3) yellow or white stamens, anthers and pollen, (4) never have the smallest particle of black about them. Double Poppies and Poppies with black centers may be greatly admired by some, but they are not Shirley Poppies." The flowers range in color from white through to lilac, pink, and red.

Poppy.

P. somniferum
OPIUM POPPY

CULTIVATION DATE UNKNOWN

On the subject of this beautiful poppy, John Gerard quoted Claudius Galenus, in 1659, "This seed, is good to season bread with; but the white is better than the black. It is often used in comfits, served at the table with other junketing dishes." A hardy annual with large, open flowers in shades of pink and purple that must be allowed to self-seed so that it can reappear the following year.

Cross section of terra-cotta flowerpot.

GARDEN GHOSTS

Scotsman David Douglas (1799–1834) made several important botanical expeditions to North America in the 1820s and collected hundreds of trees, shrubs, ornamental plants, herbs, and mosses. Many bear his name, such as *Limnanthes douglasii*, although the most famous must surely be *Pseudotsuga menziesii*, known commonly as the stately Douglas fir. Unfortunately, he met a grisly and early end while botanizing on the Sandwich Islands (the Hawaiian Islands). Douglas's eyesight was poor, and he fell into a pit trap (a large hole dug to ambush animals), which is thought to have already held a captured bullock. When missionaries later found his gored body, his faithful dog was still in attendance at the pit's edge.

Polemonium caeruleum
CHARITY
or American Great Valerian, Jacob's Ladder, Ladder to Heaven

CULTIVATION DATE UNKNOWN

Cultivated in ancient Rome, this elegant and upright plant, growing up to 3 feet (1m) in height, bears masses of lavender-blue flowers with an open bell shape and orange stamens. White-flowered varieties are also available.

Primula auricula

AURICULA PRIMROSE

or Bear's Ears, Mountain Clowslip

CULTIVATED BY 1596

The original auricula was a wild flower native to the alpine meadows of northern Europe. It is a simple and beautiful plant, with fragrant yellow, white-throated flowers. Such is their fascination for gardeners that thousands of different varieties have been bred over the years, and there are societies dedicated to them, in all their varied forms, on both sides of the Atlantic. "This beautiful and brave plant hath thicke greene, and fat leaves, somewhat finely snipt about the edges; among which riseth up a stem a hand high,

Auricula.

bearing a tuft of floures at the top of divers colour." *The Herball, or Generall Histoire of Plantes*, John Gerard, 1597.

Primula elatior

OXLIP

or Great Cowslip

CULTIVATION DATE UNKNOWN

A rare and beautiful spring flower native to Europe that is larger than the cowslip and has a more subtle color than the primrose. It makes a semi-evergreen herbaceous perennial that can reach 12 inches (30cm) in height, but is usually lower. Butterflies love it.

Primula veris

COWSLIP PRIMROSE

or Cowslip, St. Peter's Keys

CULTIVATION DATE UNKNOWN

A hardy perennial growing to 6 inches (15cm) tall, this lovely wild flower bears clusters of yellow blooms with a sweet smell in spring. In the wild it is endangered, mainly due to unlawful harvesting. Its culinary uses include the

Cowslip.

making of jams, salads, and wine. The 1867 catalog of the North American seed supplier Washburn and Company advised that these "Favorite, early, free-flowering plants ...should be extensively grown for filling the beds and borders of spring flower-gardens."

Tropaeolum majus

NASTURTIUM

CULTIVATION DATE UNKNOWN

Nasturtiums have been grown as garden flowers for centuries. In 1597 John Gerard wrote in *The Herball, or Generall Histoire of Plantes:* "The flours are dispersed throughout the whole plant, of color yellow with a crossed star overthwart the inside of a deepe orange color, unto the backe part of the same doth hang a taile or spure, such as hath the larks-heel." Gardeners today will still find these cheerful hardy annuals easy

HISTORICAL NOTE

Thomas Jefferson grew auriculas at his garden at Monticello and wrote about them in his garden diary. They also feature in his letters. Bernard McMahon, author of *The American Gardener's Calendar: Adapted to the Climates and Seasons of the United States*, 1806, supplied Jefferson with auriculas, and in 1807 he wrote to Jefferson, "Of Auriculas we have none here worth a cent, but I expect some good ones from London this spring; if they come safe, you shall have a division next spring." They were duly sent.

to grow, and they come in a wide range of colors. Their versatility was prized in the nineteenth century: "In the greenhouse or conservatory they may be had in bloom the greater part of the year; and in favored situations in the open air for edgings, covering trelliswork, or handles of rustic baskets, or trailing from vases, their elegance of form and brilliancy of color render them peculiarly valuable." Washburn and Company catalog, 1867.

T. majus
'EMPRESS OF INDIA'

CULTIVATED 1881

Rich crimson flowers grow amid attractive deep green foliage on this nontrailing and compact variety, growing to just 12 to 16 inches (30–40cm) in height. It was named in honor of Queen Victoria.

Nasturtium.

T. majus
'TALL CLIMBING'

CULTIVATED BY 1686

This old variety has mixed colored flowers that can trail to an impressive 6 feet (1.8m). Useful as an annual covering for a fence or trellis.

T. majus
TOM THUMB SERIES

CULTIVATED BY 1838

This is another small, compact Victorian variety with flowers ranging in color from pale yellow to deep red. Bred by the English seed merchants Watkins and Simpson of Drury Lane, London, England, it was later listed by the North American Washburn and Company as King of Tom Thumbs—one of their "Novelties for 1865." Within their catalog, it was described as: "Magnificent. The lustrous, blue-green foliage contrasting vividly with the intense scarlet of the blossoms, produces an unequaled blaze of brilliance, and the plant must become a universal favouite."

Viola odorata
SWEET VIOLET
or English Violet, March Violet, Sweet Pansy

CULTIVATION DATE UNKNOWN

Sweet violets are winter- and spring-flowering hardy perennials tolerant of most soil types. They are best suited to part shade. Their low-growing habit makes them useful

cover under deciduous shrubs or trees, and as edging plants.

V. odorata
'KÖNIGIN CHARLOTTE'
or 'Queen Charlotte'

CULTIVATED BY 1900

This is the traditional sweetly scented violet, with deep purple-blue, upturned flowers, and heart-shaped leaves. Growing to 8 inches (20cm) tall with a dense and spreading habit, it makes pretty ground cover.

V. odorata
'REINE DES NEIGES'

CULTIVATION DATE UNKNOWN

Mr. Etty assumes that this is a sport of Königin Charlotte, because it has the same characteristic upward-looking flowers. With fragrant blooms of pure white, it is one of the longest-flowering violets.

Sweet violet.

NOTES ON THE CULTIVATION OF ESCULENT VEGETABLES

to be undertaken during the winter months.

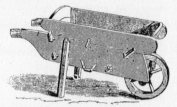

We are now at the mercy of the weather and must shape our course accordingly. Keep feet off the ground during heavy rains, but prepare to go on it the moment it is fit to bear your weight without poaching (see panel, right), and make ready for the busy spring ahead. During rainy weather, survey the stock of plant-supporting twigs, haul out all the debris from the yard, and make a "smother" (or small fire) of waste prunings and piles of twitch and other stuff for which you have no decided use. If properly done, the result will be black ash of the most fertilizing nature, such as a mere fire will not produce. If the weather is open and dry, trench spare plots, and make ready well-manured plots for sowing peas and beans.

Seaweed is beneficial to asparagus.

SOME VEGETABLES IN NEED OF THE GARDENER'S ATTENTION AT THIS TIME OF YEAR

ASPARAGUS *Asparagus officinalis*
Lightly fork in manure to beds of asparagus. In gardens near the coast, seaweed is the best manure for asparagus.

CABBAGE *Brassica oleracea* Capitata group
Cabbages may be planted outside at any time when the weather permits. Depending on your climate, in late winter, sow in plenty, although in cold districts it is still too early for the sowing of large kinds. Where plantations stand thick, draw from among them

every alternate plant to allow the rest ample space for hearting. It is well to remember that the smallest and loosest hearts of immature cabbages make a more delicate dish than those with complete hearts.

CELERY *Apium graveolens*

Hill up celery for the last time in early winter. In case of severe weather, have protecting material at hand in the shape of dry litter or mats. I find twigs a capital foundation on which to throw floating row cover for quickly covering celery, the protection then being as quickly removed when the frost is over.

On wet ground, farmers allow their grazing stock to trundle and knead the earth with their hooves, because it opens up the earth. This is known as "poaching." Over the winter months, the gardener must be careful not to poach his or her patch by working on ground that is too wet.

In fine weather, wheel out manure; and as long as the ground can be dug without waste of labor, proceed to open trenches, make drains, and mend walks, for these are the times for improving, and a garden must be very perfect indeed if it affords no work for winter weather!

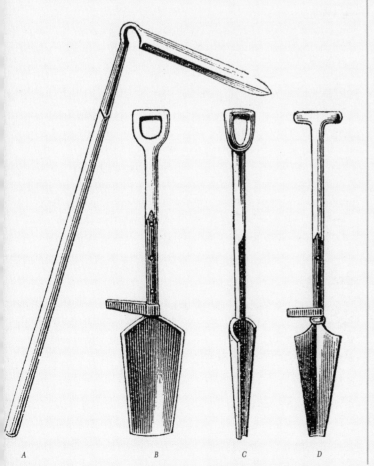

DRAINING TOOLS
A selection of draining tools including a wide spade for making the upper part of the trench (B) and narrower spades for working the lower part (C and D). The tall spade (A) is used for clearing loose soil from the bottom of the trench.

A   B   C   D

Chicory.

Moss Curled parsley.

Over winter,
fall-sown spinach
must be kept clear of weeds,
and in gathering (if it
happens to be fit to supply
a harvest), pick off the
leaves separately with
a little care.

CHICORY *Cichorium endivia*

It will be valued now and must be blanched as required. Plant a few in frames and other protected places in the North, or even the unused corners of sheds; they may be safer here than outdoors, and can be blanched as needed. (See How to Blanch Endive, page 61, but tie up the leaves of chicory.)

HERBS

Many kinds of herbs may be sown or divided now, and it will be well to look over the herb garden and see how things stand for the supplies that will be required. Soon there may be such an excess of work that this department may be injuriously neglected.

LETTUCE *Lactuca sativa*

Sow lettuce seeds in frames. Plant out in mild weather any that are fit from frames and hotbeds, making sure first that they are well hardened.

PARSLEY *Petroselinum crispum*

In all cold districts, it is a good plan to secure a bed of parsley in a frame or pit. If a few plants are transferred to flowerpots in fall, they may be wintered in any place where they can have light and air freely. For the kitchen gardener, it is so important to have parsley at command as wanted, that it may be worthwhile now to put a frame over a few rows where they stand in the open quarter instead of risk the loss of all in the event of severe weather. Sow seeds at the end of winter, because parsley foliage will soon be wanted in quantity.

POTATOES *Solanum tuberosum*

Potatoes are most prized when they come in early, and the early kind may be forwarded on beds of leaves and exhausted hotbeds by covering with light rich soil and employing old frames for protection, kept handy in case of frost.

RHUBARB *Rheum × cultorum*

To increase your rhubarb stock, crowns should be taken up now and divided and planted again in rich, moist soil. Do not gather from this new plantation until at least one year has passed. This method will guarantee rhubarb stalks to be proud of, not only for size, but for color and flavor.

WARM BORDER

In every garden there should be a sloping, sheltered spot for forwarding early crops. If your situation does not offer this advantage naturally, it is worth some trouble and expense to secure it by artificial arrangements. A clipped and dense hedge of beech, hornbeam, or holly, or a substantial wall, are capital sources of shelter for such a border, which may be further improved by placing reed hurdles against it to break the force of cutting winds. The soil should be light and rich, and the position well drained to prevent the slightest accumulation of water during heavy rains. Supposing you have such a border, sow upon it, as early as the weather permits, any of the smaller kinds of cabbage, lettuce, silverskin onion, radish, spinach, and carrot. All these crops may be grown in frames with greater safety, because in many exposed places the warm border is almost an impossibility.

WEEDS

In late winter, many weeds will come into flower, and if allowed to set seed, it will make enormous work to keep them down. It is well to remember that as long as they are not in flower, weeds are really useful as manure when dug into the soil. Therefore, a weedy patch is not of necessity going to ruin, but if the weeds are not stopped in time, they spread by their seeds and mar the order and decency of the garden. Dig them in, and their decay will help nourish the next crop.

Resist the temptation to pull rhubarb stalks until the plant has been established for a year or two.

———— ✒ ————

In greenhouses, sheds, and garages, many jobs may be found to keep the hands employed, such as making collections for outdoor use of the little paltry things commonly used, such as plant labels and balls of string. For they are invariably missing when wanted, from their liability to be trodden into the ground or kicked anywhere by a heedless foot.

———— ✒ ————

GLOSSARY

Annual
A plant that is sown, germinates, flowers, sets seed, and dies within a single year.

Bicolor
A plant that has two colors.

Biennial
A plant that is sown, germinates, flowers, sets seed, and dies over two years.

Blanch
The exclusion of light, by various methods, from the young shoots of a plant to produce a pale and tender crop.

Bush
Growing habit of a particular type of tomato or bean that forms a compact shape and requires no training. For tomatoes, also known as determinate.

Climber
Growing habit of plants that produce long stems that twine around tall supports.

Cold frame
An unheated structure that provides some degree of shelter to young and tender plants.

Cordon
Growing habit of a particular type of tomato that requires training by removing side shoots and providing a support. Also known as indeterminate or vine.

Cultivar
A cultivated variety of a plant that has distinct characteristics.

Deciduous
A plant that loses its leaves seasonally, most usually in fall.

Determinate
Growing habit of a particular type of tomato that forms a compact shape and requires no training. Also known as bush.

Dwarf
Growing habit of plants that are small or low growing. Sometimes referred to as bush.

Early, first early, second early
Refers to types of potatoes and when they are ready for harvesting.

Forcing
A method of forcing a plant to flower or bear fruit before its natural season.

Hand glass or light
A glass structure used to protect tender young plants.

Hardy
A plant that can withstand seasonal changes without protection.

Hotbed
Traditional method for forcing early crops using a wooden frame filled with soil and manure and topped with a removable glass cover.

Indeterminate
Growing habit of a particular type of tomato that requires training by removing side shoots and providing a support. Also known as cordon or vine.

Main season
Refers to a principal seasonal crop, also called maincrop.

Open pollinated
A natural method of pollinating plants, such as by insects or the wind.

Perennial
A plant that that lives longer than three years.

Runner
Also known as stolons, a runner is a stem that grows at the bottom of a plant, then roots and creates new plants.

Spit
The term used for the depth of a spade when digging.

Sport
A part of a plant that shows marked differences from the rest of the plant and is used to propagate new cultivars.

Variety
A cultivated variety of a plant that has distinct characteristics.

Vine
Growing habit of a particular type of tomato that requires training by removing side shoots and providing a support. Also known as cordon or indeterminate.

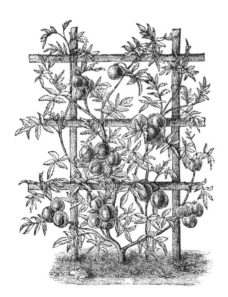

SEED SUPPLIERS & USEFUL ORGANIZATIONS

I n 1856, the Reverend Thomas Scott wrote to the English seed company Suttons & Sons (which is still trading today) from his Itchingfield Rectory in Sussex, "The seeds I have had from you have turned out so remarkably good, that I have determined always to send to you in the future." Another satisfied customer, a Mr. Charles Theobald, wrote, "Your seeds were excellent, and gave great satisfaction. Your Hangdown Beans certainly surpass all I ever saw; the Lettuce, I think, cannot be too widely known and cultivated as they are superior to all other sorts I ever grew." Here follows a list of suppliers of heirloom and heritage vegetable, herb, and flower seeds, along with some nurseries selling fruiting plants. If you find similar satisfaction growing plants from any of these companies, may I suggest you follow in the footsteps of the Reverend Scott and Mr. Theobald by sending these good people your compliments and thanks?

HEIRLOOM & HERITAGE SEED SUPPLIERS IN THE UNITED STATES & CANADA

A'bunadh Seeds
www.gardenofeden2010.wordpress.com

Amishland Heirloom Seeds
www.amishlandseeds.com

Annapolis Seeds
www.annapolisseeds.com

Annie's Annuals and Perennials
www.anniesannuals.com

Baker Creek Heirloom Seeds
www.rareseeds.com

Burpee Seeds and Plants
www.burpee.com

Cottage Gardener Heirloom Seed
www.cottagegardener.com

D. Landreth Seed Company
www.landrethseeds.com

Edible Antiques
www.edible-antiques.myshopify.com

Florabunda Seeds
www.florabundaseeds.com

Franchi Heirloom Seeds Canada
www.franchiheirloomseeds.ca

Gary Ibsen's Tomato Fest
www.tomatofest.com

Greenmantle Nursery
www.greenmantlenursery.com

Hardy Fruit Trees Nursery
www.hardyfruittrees.ca

Harvest Moon Farms and Seed Company
www.harvestmoon-farms.com

SEED SUPPLIERS & USEFUL ORGANIZATIONS

Heritage Harvest Seed
www.heritageharvestseed.com

Horizon Herbs
www.horizonherbs.com

Johnny's Selected Seeds
www.johnnyseeds.com

Mandy's Greenhouse
www.mandysgreenhouse.com

Matchbox Garden and Seed Company
www.matchboxgarden.ca

Naramata Seed Company
www.naramataseedco.ca

Nature and Nurture Seeds
www.natureandnurtureseeds.com

Pumpkin Moon Farm
www.pumpkinmoonherbals.com

Ravenhill Herb Seeds
www.ravenhillfarm.ca

Redwood City Seed Company
www.ecoseeds.com

Renee's Garden Seeds
www.reneesgarden.com

Restoration Seeds
www.restorationseeds.com

Rhora's Nut Farm and Nursery
www.nuttress.com

Richters
www.richters.com

St. Clare Heirloom Seeds
www.stclareseeds.com

Seeds From Italy
www.growitalian.com

Seeds of Change
www.seedsofchange.com

Siloam Orchards
www.siloamorchards.com

Silver Creek Nursery
www.silvercreeknursery.ca

Soggy Creek Seed Company
www.seeds.soggycreek.com

Stark Brothers
www.starkbros.com

Sustainable Seed Company
www.sustainableseedco.com

Swallowtail Garden Seeds
www.swallowtailgardenseeds.com

Territorial Seed Company
www.territorialseed.com

The Cook's Garden
www.cooksgarden.com

The Living Seed Company
www.livingseedcompany.com

Three Sisters Farm
www.threesistersfarm.com

Trade Winds Fruit
www.tradewindsfruit.com

Tree and Twig Heirloom Vegetable Farm
www.treeandtwig.ca

Trees of Antiquity
www.treesofantiquity.com

Upper Canada Seeds
www.uppercanadaseeds.ca

Urban Tomato
www.urbantomato.ca

Victory Heirloom Seeds
www.victoryseeds.com

ORGANIZATIONS PROMOTING THE PRESERVATION OF HEIRLOOM & HERITAGE VARIETIES IN THE UNITED STATES & CANADA

Kokopelli Seed Foundation
www.kokopelli-seed-foundation.com

Landis Valley Museum Heirloom Seed Project
www.landisvalleymuseum.org

Organic Seed Alliance
www.seedalliance.org

Saving Our Seeds Seed Bank
www.savingourseeds.org

Seed Savers Exchange
www.seedsavers.org

Seeds of Diversity Canada
www.seeds.ca

The Cherokee Nation
www.cherokee.org

Thomas Jefferson Center for Historic Plants
www.monticello.org

HEIRLOOM & HERITAGE SEED SUPPLIERS IN THE UNITED KINGDOM & EUROPE

Alsagarden
www.alsagarden.com

Association Kokopelli (formerly Terre de Semences Organic Seeds)
www.organicseedsonline.com

Beans and Herbs at the Herbary
www.beansandherbs.co.uk

Bernwode Fruit Trees
www.bernwodeplants.co.uk

Bingenheimer Saatgut AG
www.bingenheimersaatgut.de

Brogdale
www.brogdaleonline.co.uk

Chiltern Seeds
www.chilternseeds.co.uk

Ferme de Sainte Marthe
www.fermedesaintemarthe.com

Franchi Seeds of Italy
www.seedsofitaly.com

Habitat Aid
www.habitataid.co.uk

Heritage Fruit Tree Company
www.heritagefruittrees.co.uk

JBA Seed Potatoes
www.jbaseedpotatoes.co.uk

Keepers Nursery
www.keepers-nursery.co.uk

L'Atelier Vert (Everything French Gardening)
www.frenchgardening.com

Le Biau Germe
www.biaugerme.com

Magic Garden Seeds
www.magicgardenseeds.com

Orange Pippin Fruit Trees
www.orangepippintrees.co.uk

Pennard Plants
www.pennardplants.com

Plantes et Jardins
www.plantes-et-jardins.com

Simpson's Seeds and Plants
www.simpsonsseeds.co.uk

Suffolk Herbs
www.kingsseeds.com

Suttons Seeds
www.suttons.co.uk

Tamar Organics
www.tamarorganics.co.uk

The Real Seed Catalogue
www.realseeds.co.uk

Thomas Etty Esq.
www.thomasetty.co.uk

Thompson and Morgan
www.thompson-morgan.com

Tweed Valley Fruit Trees
www.tweedvalleyfruittrees.com

Vilmorin
www.vilmorin-jardin.fr

W Robinson and Sons Ltd
www.mammothonion.co.uk

Unwins
www.unwins.co.uk

Victoriana Nursery Gardens
www.victoriananursery.co.uk

ORGANIZATIONS PROMOTING THE PRESERVATION OF HEIRLOOM & HERITAGE VARIETIES IN THE UNITED KINGDOM & EUROPE

Arche Noah
www.arche-noah.at

Association Kokopelli (formerly Terre de Semences Organic Seeds)
www.organicseedsonline.com

Brogdale, Home of the National Fruit Collection
www.brogdaleonline.co.uk

Eco-PB (European Consortium for Organic Plant Breeding)
www.eco-pb.org

Garden Organic (keepers of the Heritage Seed Library)
www.gardenorganic.org.uk

Irish Seed Savers Association
www.irishseedsavers.ie

Kultursaat (Association of Central European Biodynamic Plant Breeders)
www.kultursaat.org

Open Pollinated Seeds
www.open-pollinated-seeds.org.uk

Soil Association
www.soilassociation.org

The Millennium Seed Bank
www.kew.org

Zukunftsstiftung Landwirtschaft (Futures Association Agriculture)
www.zukunftsstiftung-landwirtschaft.de

Note

At the time of writing all the varieties cited in this book were available commercially in the United States and in the United Kingdom and Europe. Some may require a little detective work to track down but should be located via the Internet without too much searching. Seed savers and seed libraries hold many wonderful old varieties that cannot be bought commercially, so if you enjoy growing heirloom plants, do consider joining these organizations.

BIBLIOGRAPHY

Beeton's Dictionary of Everyday Gardening, James Askew & Son, 1910.

Beeton's Gardening Book, Ward, Lock & Co., 1882.

Bremness, Lesley, *The Complete Book of Herbs*, Dorling Kindersley, 1988.

Bridgeman, Thomas, *The Young Gardener's Assistant*, Thornburn & Co., 1847.

Campbell, Susan, *Charleston Kedding–A History of Kitchen Gardening*, Ebury, 1996.

Cheal, J., *Practical Fruit Growing*, George Beel & Sons, 1893.

Culpeper, Nicholas, *Complete Herbal and English Physician*, J Gleave & Son, 1826.

Freeman, Ella M., *A Home Vegetable Garden*, Macmilliam, 1922.

Gear, Alan, and Stickland, Sue, *Heritage Vegetables*, Gaia Books, 1998.

Gerard, John, *Gerard's Herbal*, Bracken Books, 1985.

Griggs, Geoffrey, *The Englishman's Flora*, Helicon, 1975.

Guillet, Dominique, *The Seeds of Kokopelli*, Association Kokopelli, 2002.

Hedrick, U. P., *The Small Fruits of New York*, Albany, 1925.

Hogg, Robert, *The Fruit Manual*, Langford Press, 1884.

Jabs, Carolyn, *The Heirloom Gardeners*, Sierra Club Books, 1984.

Jeffrey, Josie, *The Mix and Match Guide to Companion Planting*, Leaping Hare Press, 2014.

Jeffery, Josie, *Seedswap*, Leaping Hare Press, 2012.

Organ, John, *Rare Vegetables for Garden and Table*, Faber, 1960.

Roach, F. A., *Cultivated Fruits of Britain*, Basil Blackwell, 1985.

Roberts, Harry, and Wythes, George, *The Book of Rarer Vegetables*, John Lane, 1907.

Roberts, Jonathan, *Cabbages and Kings*, Harper Collins, 2001.

Shewell-Cooper, W. E., *The ABC of Fruit Growing*, English Universities Press, 1954.

Smee, Alfred, *My Garden*, Bell & Daldy, 1872.

Stocks, Christopher, *Forgotten Fruits*, Random House, 2008.

Sudell, Richard, *The New Illustrated Gardening Encyclopaedia*, Odhams Press, 1950.

Suttons Spring Catalogue and Amateurs Guide for 1857.

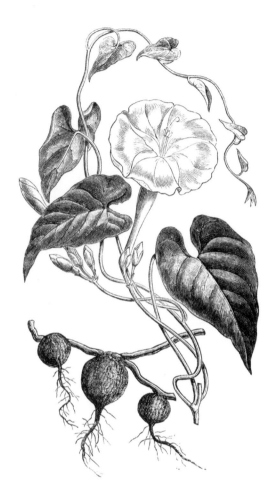

Vilmorin-Andrieux, M. M., *The Vegetable Garden*, John Murray, 1885.

Watson, William, *The Gardener's Assistant*, Gresham Publishing, 1936.

Weathers, John (ed.), *Commercial Gardening*, Gresham Publishing, 1913.

Weaver, William Woys, *Heirloom Vegetable Gardening*, Henry Holt & Co., 1997.

White, Gilbert, *The Natural History of Selborne*, George Routledge & Sons, 1789.

Whitehead, George E., *Garden Herbs*, A & C Black, 1944.

Wilson, Anne (ed.), *The Country House Kitchen 1600–1950*, Sutton Publishing, 1998.

Yepse, Roger, *A Celebration of Heirloom Vegetables*, Artisan, 1998.

INDEX

INDEX

ACKNOWLEDGMENTS

Mr. Etty begs to acknowledge the kind assistance of the following in helping to bring this vade mecum to its fruition: Lorraine Harrison, esteemed wordsmith, D. Gambell for his keen legal mind, N. Farley for his mastery of the Babbage difference machine, D. Warner for his hard work & due diligence and, most especially, to Mrs. Jane Warner, his longtime companion & muse. He desires also to dedicate this tome to the memory of Mrs. J. Warner (nee Etty) & Mr. P. Warner and to the brightest of futures for Joseph Peter Thomas & Samuel Victor Philip.

The publisher would like to thank the following individuals and organizations for their kind permission to reproduce the images in this book. Every effort has been made to acknowledge the images, however we apologize if there are any unintentional omissions and would be grateful if notified of any corrections that should be incorporated in future reprints or editions of this book.

Page 196: Library of Congress, Washington, DC

Page 197T: Alamy/LH Images.

Page 197B: Bridgeman Art Library.